"THE PROLOGUE WAS SO POWERFUL, I was afraid the story would lose altitude. But from there it took flight and never stopped soaring."

–David Ryback, Ph.D.,
author of Dreams That Come True

ADVANCE PRAISE FOR TAKING STOCK

"MICHAEL, I WANT YOU TO GET THIS BOOK IN PRINT *SOON* so I can give it as a gift to many people including my father, and my girlfriend who just lost her husband at the age of 39 to a courageous but heartbreaking battle with lymphoma and a brother to leukemia 20 years ago . . . "
> – *Nanci Hersh*
> *a childhood friend of the author (written in a letter)*

{NORWOOD} HAS CODIFIED HIS PHILOSOPHY of spirituality and investing in . . . *Taking Stock.*"
> – *THE WALL STREET JOURNAL*

"THE HUMAN SPIRIT SHINES THROUGH giving gentle instruction on how we might handle similar circumstances. Eloquent . . . Fascinating . . . "
> – *Al Frank*
> *author of* Al Franks' New Prudent Speculator

"A WONDERFUL PORTRAYAL of a universal, eternal search for meaning as one man attempts to find peace with God in the midst of life's greatest challenge."
> – *Rev. Betty C. Castellani*
> *Director of the Charles B. Eberhart Cancer Center*

"READS LIKE AN EPIC POEM that inspires us all to discover the possibilities and magic in life. Through this beautiful spiritual journey reminiscent of *Zen & The Art Of Motorcycle Maintenance*, a young man finds the wisest investments in life are the ones that come from giving and receiving of the sacred heart."
> – *Dr. Martin Finkelstein, D.C.*
> *author of* A Life of Wellness *& television*
> *host of* To Your Health

EVENTUALLY WITH EACH OF US, the thought of dying brings the thought that when the funeral is over, except for the fleeting memories of family and friends, any evidence that we ever existed will be gone. I believe it is the desire of all humanity to leave something behind, something worthwhile, something that will tell the world, "Hey, I was here. I lived, I loved, I suceeded, and I failed, but also I learned something. Something that I would like to give you. It is my last gift."

Michael Norwood is a wonderful, wonderful writer and we need to keep our eye on him. Here he has accomplished what most writers would find impossible. *Taking Stock* is not only the story of a young man's search for life's meaning and his struggle to become his own person, it is a sensitive and often brilliant tribute of a loving son to his dying father. A rare tribute that allows his father to indeed present his last gift to the world."

> -- *Sara Flanigan*
> *Recipient of numerous awards, prizes and nominations for her two novels,* Sudie *and* Alice, *and for her made-for-television movies.*

This book has been written in tribute
to the workers of
HOSPICE:

And any person who has put
their heart and soul into the care of another,
raising themselves up to touch the face of angels.

Above all, for
MOM:

Recipient of wings, who survived the greatest storms,
but who yet sails through life at full mast.

THE 9 INSIGHTS OF THE WEALTHY SOUL

TAKING STOCK

by
Dr. Michael R. Norwood

Global Publishing

Grateful acknowledgement for permission to reproduce the following material:

Excerpt from **JONATHAN LIVINGSTON SEAGULL** by Richard Bach. Copyright ©1970 by Richard D. Bach and Leslie Parrish-Bach. Reprinted with the permission of Simon & Schuster.

ORDINARY MIRACLES, by Alan & Marilyn Bergman and Marvin Hamlisch, Copyright ©1994 Threesome Music Co., Famous Music Corporation, Red Bullet Music. All Rights Reserved. Used by permission of WARNER BROS. PUBLICATIONS U.S. INC., Miami, FL. 33014

Excerpt from **STANDARD & POOR'S** April 5, 1991 STOCK REPORT ON DSC COMMUNICA-TIONS. Reprinted by permission of Standard & Poor's, a division of The McGraw-Hill Companies.

Multiple excerpts from **VALUE LINE**: Copyright ©1997 By Value Line Publishing, Inc.. Reprinted by Permission. All Rights Reserved.

"Electric Man" Cover Photograph: © 1997 by Michael R. Norwood
Cover Illustration and Design: Mark Herron
Cover Text Design: Shashi Sonnad
Text Design: Shashi Sonnad & Beth VanDyke
Editor: Colleen Goidel

Publisher's Cataloging-in-Publication
(Provided by Quality Books, Inc.)

Norwood, Michael R.
    Taking stock : a soul's journey through life, death, & the world
of investment / by Michael R. Norwood ; editor Colleen Goidel ;
illustrator Mark Herron. -- 1st ed.
    p. cm.
    Preassigned LCCN: 97-93697
    ISBN: 0-911649-02-8

    1. Fathers and sons. 2. Parents--Death. 3. Norwood, Michael R.
--Family. I. Title.

HQ755.86.N67A3 1998   306.874'2
                                  QB197-40738

ISBN: 0-911649-02-8
SAN: 2 9 9 - 3 6 2 7

Prologue

*T*hey were at once the most beautiful and the most difficult words I'd ever heard spoken. My mother and I stood by the doorway, helpless spectators when we heard them.

Henri had entered the room just a short while ago. She had stood still — almost as still as my father's unmoving body — remaining that way for what seemed like minutes.

My mother and I glanced at one another, curiosity penetrating our distress. And though it didn't lift the darkness of that distress, the curiosity was a light. Tiny and distant, it was the same light just on the other side of all great pain, if we just knew how to step through.

The curiosity persisted. What was the nurse doing in her stillness? It seemed she was "sensing," I thought. But sensing what? Was it the presence — or lack of presence — of a spirit somewhere between its earthly and its celestial home? Later, when asked, she would say she had been looking for respiratory signs. But at that moment, her silence appeared more a merging; she momentarily one with her patient.

My mother had told me the hospice nurse was special. I had been flying from Atlanta to my parents' Florida home every weekend the last four months, every other weekend for another four months before that. It was a trying time both physically and emotionally, trying to build my new practice, attending my own patients, then on the phone with my mother and father every day and actually back in Florida every weekend. But compared to what my parents were bearing, it was a small load for someone young and healthy.

Nevertheless, a tremendous burden had been lifted when Henri had begun making her weekly visits. Her straightforward ability to look death in the eye, to smile and talk about it honestly and compassionately to my parents, had an immediate effect on both of them. It is a skill doctors generally lack, the point when all their medical advances and knowledge become useless, the point when most of them start concentrating on other patients.

This was the first time I had met Henri. She always came on Tuesday. I was there this Tuesday because I had not returned to Atlanta the last weekend knowing that my father was "close enough" to where I could no longer leave him or my mother even for a short four- or five-day period.

Our introduction was brief. A whispered hello and a shaking of hands in our foyer. My mother apprised her of the situation and she went straight to my father's room.

It was then that Henri stood there. I glanced at my mother, as frozen as the nurse. What could I do for her? What do you say to someone who is losing her partner of more than 40 years?

Henri finally moved, kneeling beside the bed. The metallic bars, the electric crank, the medicine table were all too familiar. A small wave of horror had passed through me when I arrived home Saturday. It was nearing two decades since another hospital bed had been brought to our home to claim dominion over the bedroom I grew up in, a frightening dragon image whose presence had incinerated the innocence of my childhood. I had forced myself to throw off the emotion, reminding myself that the previous ordeal had been the single most important experience in determining my values and path in life.

My father's body remained still, but suddenly, as if sensing Henri's nearness, he awoke, lungs gasping, eyes fluttering. He looked around, bewildered, frightened. Beside me I felt my mother's emotion, felt helpless to comfort her . . . or to aid him.

"It's okay, John," the nurse smiled, taking his hand. "It's just me, Henri."

He focused on her, on the soothing voice. "Henri?"

"It's me. I'm right here." And then she said it. Words that were so straightforward, so to the point. Words that were gentle as prayer but which took the courage — no, the guidance — of Grace. Words that at once shocked but which transcended the greatest comfort, the highest kindness.

"You almost went last night, didn't you?" she said.

My father nodded, then began crying. It was only the second time I had ever seen him cry. He, former international businessman, former boxing coach, former military pilot and commander who imparted nothing but strength to his division of quivering, diarrhea-stricken young men on their way across the Atlantic to their first — and for many their final — combat mission during World War II. Crying uncontrollably.

Henri's eyes brimmed behind her glasses, but the smile remained. My mother's body wracked silently beside me. I bit my lower lip, tears just a blink away, but not coming until a long time later, as I write this.

Every night for nearly the last half year my father had gone to sleep with the prayer that this would be his last night. That he would be put out of his pain, out of the misery of seeing his once proud 180-pound body slowly wither to half its original weight.

But last night was different. It came after a day when none of the medication had provided relief. Even tranquilizers wouldn't put him out. Finally, past midnight, he took four more — double the maximum dose — and fell into a deep, troubled slumber.

The spare room where I was staying was adjacent to my bedroom, our temporary hospital ward. I had gently led my mother into her room down the hall, insisting she close the door to get a good night's rest.

"But what if he goes tonight?" she protested, expressing the agony and unknowing she had gone to sleep with every night the last half year.

"Mom, you need to rest. I don't want to lose . . . I don't want you to collapse." I had stopped myself just in time. "I don't want to lose you, too," were the words I had almost said.

It happens to many caregivers; after months — sometimes years, as in my mother's case — of tending to a terminally ill spouse, the caregivers themselves have a stroke or nervous breakdown. I knew my mother was already in the first stages of adrenal exhaustion. Afraid to leave my father's side, she would still have to run out to buy something two, three times a day in the Florida heat, trying to cater to the every whim of a dying man.

Night brought no relief, only compounded the problem. Until last week when they brought the hospital bed, she lay sleepless in the same bed with my father, aware of his every movement, his every breath, not knowing if it would be his last.

"I don't know if I feel right about this," she said, resisting my efforts to close her door.

"Mom, you haven't slept properly for over six months."

"But you don't sleep either when you're so close to him with your door open."

"Don't worry, I sleep. Besides, I'm younger than you."

"But what if you don't hear him if he wakes?"

"I hear his every movement, Mom."

"Then you're not sleeping."

"I do," I sighed. "I just sleep with one eye half open."

"Why don't you let me switch off with you in a few hours?" she persisted.

"Because your body is already exhausted." I touched her shoulder. "Mom, we have no way of knowing. Dad may not go for weeks . . . maybe months more."

"Oh, don't say that," she whispered. We had already gotten past the point of feeling guilty about praying for the end of his misery. Only those who haven't experienced the horrors of a prolonged terminal illness can moralize about such thoughts.

I kissed her on the cheek, guiding her into the room. "Everything will be okay, Mom. Go to bed." With that gentle command, I shut the door behind her. I had no fear she would wake up. Despite her reluctance, once she lay down, exhaustion would quickly claim her until morning.

In complete darkness I navigated my way to the end of the hall. I stood outside my father's room, attuned to every movement within. Though I could have entered without a creak, I remained outside. In the morning, after my first night home, my father told me he had "felt" I was in the room with him throughout the night.

"I woke you?" I asked, horrified to have disturbed him.

"No," he shook his head. "No. It was just a sense of you. As if you were constantly there."

In fact, I had checked on him countless times throughout the night, sleeping a half-sleep, attuned to the slightest movement from his room, to every barely perceptible creak from his bed each time he shifted weight. Only in this way could I be sure to wake up if he did. Though the nurses didn't understand how he could still walk, he refused to call us when he had to use the bathroom, his fierce pride providing a strength that long ago should have left him. And in the darkness, half asleep, his stumbling gait could result in a fall. Thus my vigil.

"You have a very reassuring presence," Dad had told me that first morning. Reflecting on those words, I began to understand how when someone is just a thread away from crossing over, things like a feeling, a presence or a sense of something become more of a reality than anything we've grown accustomed to perceiving our entire lives through our five senses.

But now, my fourth night home, outside his door, I wanted nothing to interrupt his sleep, even something as ethereal as "a presence." Besides, standing still in the darkness, head cocked to the side, some neurological circuit to a sixth sense of my own was opened to replace my lack of sight. This, added to the sounds coming from within the room — the slow, stertorous breathing, the bed's tiny metallic creaks — provided near complete information as to my father's state.

Once sure of his comfort, I back-stepped from the complete darkness of the hallway, moving in degrees like in a tai chi exercise, one foot behind the other, into the moonlit obscurity of the spare room. Inch by inch I closed the door, sliding it across my fingers in the last degrees of its arc so as not to make any noise as it settled into the jamb.

Only then I turned on the lights, slowly letting out my breath and moving to where a two-inch thick piece of foam covered by a sheet lay on the floor — my makeshift bed brought with me from Atlanta this last weekend.

Too wired to sleep, I glanced at the clock. 12:30. I picked up a thick book laying beside me on the floor. Herman Wouk's *The Caine Mutiny* had been my bedtime companion for the last eight months of weekends spent at my parents. Better than a powerful sedative, I needed only pick up the 1951 classic to find transport away from the heaviness of my immediate world. It took a few minutes, but by the second or third page I felt whisked aboard the rusting battleship Caine, living out the harrowing story of Ensign Willie Keith as he and the crew faced the perils of World War II under the insufferable leadership of Lieutenant Commander Philip Francis Queeg.

Hearing the '40s dialogue, reading how Keith would entertain the crew on the piano with then-hits *If You Knew what the Gnu Knew* and *Begin the Beguine*, another sensation would overcome me. It was the feeling of excitement for the heyday of my father's time, the excitement of youth and the freshness of looking forward to the future.

In the last years, coming home on the weekends and going with my father to the golf course, I was continually struck by something mundane: My father and his buddies — all in their 60s and 70s — were indeed once young men. Products of a generation, they bore traits and a dialogue distinct from my own, but carried the unmistakable insignia of youth like that which I bore from my generation four decades after my father's.

It was a revelation, like growing up and realizing "The Ice Cream Man" and "The Garbage Man" and "The Milk Man" were individuals with an entire spectrum of life outside the childlike perception of them as embodiments of the daytime hats they wore.

And perhaps for that reason, *The Caine Mutiny,* more than any other book I could have picked up at the time, provided a release for me. I would at once be removed from my immediate circumstances, but with no guilt. Somehow, as opposed to feeling I was abandoning my father, this story was a medium through which I was in fact getting to know him better.

Suddenly, a creak. I dropped the book and leapt to my feet. In one motion I turned off the lights, opened the door and was in my father's room. I can't describe how I perceived it through the door, or how I distinguished it from the other tiny sounds of a house at night, but I knew instantaneously this sound was different. I can only describe it as the same sixth sense of a mother who suddenly breaks from a conversation to bolt out the door to a child who has fallen from a swing. On recollection, the person who'd been talking with her can always recall some tiny sound, but the translation of that into a call for help seems possible only through the filter of maternal instinct.

"Are you OK, Dad?" I asked in the darkness, already knowing he was not.

His hand was groping on the nightstand, knocking over the bottle of valium he was trying to return.

"Dad, I'm here," I repeated, lightly touching his arm.

"Huh? Michael?"

"Yes. It's me, Dad."

He flopped back, grimacing, still trying to upright the bottle. I gently took it from his grasp and replaced it for him. I tried to keep my voice calm. "Dad, are you OK?"

"Not so good," he clenched his teeth. Then summoning that awful strength of his, he took hold of my offered hand and anchored himself back to the present. "Son, I want you to listen to me."

My stomach knotted and I wished I could somehow save him from saying what I sensed was coming.

"Take care of your mother," he said.

I looked over at the bottle of pills, not knowing how many he had taken. I blocked the awful thought out, knowing it was unimportant, it being his decision at this time when he was so close anyway. I squeezed his hand. "You know I will, Dad."

"I know, son." He took in a breath, floated off for a second, then pulled himself back. "Grieve for me one or two days then get on with your lives, understand?"

"We will, Dad," I nodded, fighting the natural instinct to deny what he was saying. I blinked away the mistiness in my eyes. "We'll miss you, Dad."

He was silent for a long moment. Just when I thought he had floated off and I should leave the room so as not to disturb the peace of what might be his final sleep, he whispered, "I wish I could have left you some money, son . . . wish there would have been more where your mother wouldn't be needing everything of what there is."

I shook my head, wishing he somehow could have let go . . . at this moment at least . . . such mundane concerns. "No one could have left a son more, Dad."

He was silent. I said, "You've prepared us in every way, done everything a father could possibly do." In fact, he had spent the last six months showing my mother and me *everything:* from teaching her such simple things as paying bills to showing me how to spray the house for bugs and the degree to which I should maintain the plant beds so they wouldn't be overtaken by the lawn. In his perfectionistic fashion, Dad showed us all the little things we would eventually have learned easily on our own, but which would have overwhelmed us if we had to learn them all at once. Though at times he could drive us crazy with his impatience and intensity over these little things, we never had any doubt that it was his way — his final way — of showing us his love.

In as many words I told him this, let him know I knew it. Then I said, "And as for money, you've left me more than any father could have left a son. You've left me a legacy. You taught me your system."

Though his humbleness kept him silent, I could tell I was touching something deep in him, something that calmed the struggle. His voice was hoarse. "You learned well, son."

"I had the best teacher." I didn't know where the words were coming from, only knew I was saying the right things. Over the last months, I had prayed to God — something I was relearning how to do — to give me the words when the time came. Now He appeared to be answering.

"I didn't think . . ." It was taking all Dad's energy to speak. "I didn't think you'd ever take to the stock market."

After two years of training me and fighting a disease, fighting an inexorable clock, fighting his own perfectionism — after two years of fighting his impatience with a son's dull-headedness for anything financial — he said it: "I'm proud of you, son."

For a moment I didn't know what to say. For me it had been two years of confronting the greatest differences between us, all my college years' frustration relived; he then pushing me to stay in the secure path of a healthcare career education, me continuing to veer off, writing stories when other students were up all night studying, me going to Hollywood to peddle television and movie scripts while my peers were off on summer vacation.

And now, one and a half decades later, having been successful in healthcare — having even grown to love it — finally having achieved a balance between it and my writing career, here was Dad, pushing me to add one more thing — a *financial* thing — to the precarious teeter-totter of happiness I had achieved. He even went so far as to write a 3,000-word article entitled *THE 9 INSIGHTS OF THE WEALTHY SOUL* outlining everything he wanted me to learn just to make sure I had something tangible with which I could follow through.

It seemed to be an ancestral struggle between us, unfinished issues of our forebears that had been passed down to us, through his DNA to mine, as tangible as the blue eyes we both possessed along with all the males on his side of the family. But something had gone askew in my gene mix, some mercurial imprint that had skipped over me or perhaps was nullified by the chromosomal pool of my mother's family. Somewhere in there the love of creativity had been implanted, and whatever legacy of a business mind that existed was constantly overshadowed by my preference for art and literature, for indulging in all that was beautiful and intangible.

It was the source of all the great tension between us — my father the pragmatist, me the idealist — a high-tension-wire relationship always on the verge of snapping saved only by an underlying span of love.

Then two years ago the time came when, out of this love for him, out of the necessity of securing my mother's future, I had given in. And now, after countless weekend lessons, after years of allowing myself to be pulled into his world leaving little time for mine, after years of confronting the greatest differences between us . . . he was proud of me.

I didn't know what to say. His words described all that love that was between us . . . and all those differences.

How did one phrase contain so much? I realize now that the pride I felt in hearing it — and he in saying it — was the bridge that had all along connected us.

"Thanks, Dad," I finally whispered.

He was silent so I added: "And listen, I want you to know, in every way possible you're leaving mom and me secure. Jeez, with *THE 9 INSIGHTS OF THE WEALTHY SOUL* as a guide, how can I go wrong? A school kid could follow your system."

Through a haze of pain and drugs, he had summoned every bit of his remaining strength to type out this outline for me approximately a month earlier, not letting anyone enter the room for hours at a time over the course of a week to interrupt the fevered pitch of this last outpouring of love, strength and knowledge. And though one can actually see the pain of his struggle etched in each keystroke of the original paper — the multiple typos attesting to the degree to which his normal perfectionism was compromised — the genius of his thinking still shines through with supreme clarity.

"Anyway," I continued, "if you consider the 40, 50 years I have ahead of me, along with the lives of your future grandchildren and their children, your system will eventually bring the family more than any inheritance you could have left. What's that favorite expression of yours?"

He weakly smiled. I waited, then repeated it for him. "Give me fish, I have fish for a day. Teach me to fish, I have fish for a lifetime." He nodded, drifting off.

"I love you, dad." I kissed his forehead, gently placing his hand back on his abdomen. "Rest now."

Eyes closed, he nodded again, barely perceptibly this time.

In the dark, I backed out of his room. I stood by the doorway several minutes, unsure of myself, unsure about leaving him. I finally returned to the spare room, sat on the foam, *The Caine Mutiny* at my side, staring at nothing for a long time.

How does one act after speaking what may be last words to one's father?

*T*he sun woke me, as it always does. For a few moments I lay still, enjoying the peace of early morning. I listened to the birdsong, enjoying the serenade. Through the closed window I could even hear the slight slap of surf a block away. I slowly focused my attention to the noises in our house. Complete silence.

I bolted upright, suddenly back in the drama I had left less than four hours earlier. I listened carefully and instantaneously knew two things:

My mother was still asleep — highly unusual, she normally waking at 5:30 every morning; but maybe not unusual now knowing the depth of her exhaustion.

And from the adjacent room, where my father slept, also complete silence.

I was on my feet and into his room within seconds. His body was unmoving, unbreathing. A sense of disbelief took hold of me. After two years of illness and the last five months of going to bed, not knowing if it would be his last night — he praying it would be so, to be spared further agony — was this finally it?

I stared and stared for what seemed liked minutes. The full-time nurses that came the following days would tell me it was, in fact, about 45 seconds between his breaths. They would say it was phenomenal that anyone could survive in such a suspended state for as long as my father had; even more phenomenal that each morning for weeks ahead he would wake up from this state. And most amazing of all, that he would wake up and with what little life force he had left, watch the Financial News Network, call up Fidelity's Touch Tone Trader to check on the stocks — both the ones we owned and the ones he *still yet* had the presence of mind to consider buying — and counsel me further in taking over as family financial manager once he was finally gone.

But this morning, this first occurrence of such long periods between breaths, this day after I thought I had said goodbye for the last time the night before, the sudden wheeze that emitted from his lungs caught me by surprise.

And several hours later, waking with the same gasp, it caught him equally by surprise to suddenly arise and find himself still alive, his hand being taken by the hospice nurse; his wife and son standing in the doorway, silent, helpless spectators.

And then the question, the beautiful, bewildering transformation of a lifetime's worth of fears and ponderings about mankind's greatest mystery into a single statement that materialized one man's near-death into a sudden acknowledged reality.

"You almost went last night, didn't you?"

And finally, the incredible, uncontrollable tears from my father, those from the nurse and my mother, and the silent ones . . . those yet still partially locked within me.

Henri, the nurse, at last smiled. "Where's Kevorkian when you need him?"

"Give him my regards," my father answered, amazing me . . . amazing us all . . . with his clarity.

And from there, the almost script-like precision of repartee between nurse and patient, the humor, the strength and honesty of an experienced flight-controller guiding a heroic pilot in from stormy clouds for his final landing.

"You brought your magic wand again," my father smiled, exhausted but comforted at the end of their communion.

"Right beside my stethoscope." She patted his hand, rising to let him rest.

With a glance behind us, my mother and I followed the nurse from the room to let my father return to his quiet journey.

It was many years since I'd had to face the journey of another loved one. Now, through fire, with my father, those deepest lessons I had learned were being rekindled again.

And it is only because those lessons lay at the most central core of all that I became, and that that journey was one I — that *we all* — will one day have to face with our parents, possibly with other loved ones, and with our own lives, that I sift through the pain and try to crystallize what I have learned.

Part 1

THE GIFT OF STOCKS & BONDS
from a Departing Loved One

I have a gift for you!
You who have been giving
all your gifts to me.
I who have nothing
to give in return
other than a receiving vessel
into which you pour
in my final days
all your heart
and a piece of your soul.

I who leave you
neither goods nor acclaim
for the chunk of life
you have invested with me.

YES, INDEED I DO,
HAVE A GIFT FOR YOU!

It is stock
In your bond of love
In your investment in
unconditionality
In your gentle rising
while taking my hand
as I lead you
to the realm of angels —
your genuine home.

The stock that I leave you
dear son, dear daughter,
is this secret account
you will be drawing upon
the rest of your days . . .
Until we meet again
at the point I let go
of your selfless hand . . .
to discover a home
in a most wealthy land!

Chapter 1

Five months earlier . . .

"Michael!" the urgent voice of my mother bolted through the telephone, electrifying me. Was this finally it — the emergency for which we had been preparing ourselves for months; the single event for which no amount of preparation ever is quite enough?

I tried to keep my voice unaffected. "What's happened, Mom?"

"Michael, your father's a genius!"

I sighed, runaway currents of adrenaline dissipating. "I know he's a genius, Mom. Why's he a genius now?"

"*The Wall Street Journal* just came out with their year-end report. Do you know what he did?"

"What did he do, Ma?"

"Your father picked the number-one performing stock for last year!"

"He did?"

"He did! From all those thousands of stocks!"

"You mean out of *all* of them? All the stocks on the New York, American and Over the Counter exchanges included?"

"All those," she beamed. Though a mature woman, my mother retained a certain childlike quality, as if just waiting to find a lollipop behind everyone's back. I could see her prancing as she chimed, "I bet you can't guess which stock."

I didn't hesitate. "DSC Communications."

She gasped. "How did you know?" There wasn't the slightest disappointment in her voice; she had expected me to guess right.

"A little birdie, Ma," I grinned.

Though it had taken a genius to buy the then-maligned stock when my father did, it didn't take much of one to now surmise that it was the year's number-one performer. And though my father's 40 to 50 percent average per-year return on the 8 to 12 stocks he maintained in his portfolio would have made him the envy of almost any Wall Street broker, DSC by far was the stellar performer. From the time my father bought the communications stock and sold it nine months later, it went on to double . . . triple . . . *quadruple* in value. Then, even to my father's amazement, it went on to *quintuple*. And then, within three years it soared to more than *28 times* its original value!

A low of $4.50 per share to its later high of $126. No, it hadn't taken a genius to answer my mother's question regarding the year's best performer.

"Is Dad there?" I asked. I wanted to congratulate him, knowing how much it meant to him.

"He's just coming out of the shower." Her voice turned to a whisper. "It's unbelievable. He was like a crazy man today — out in the hot sun, clipping all the hedges, fixing the fence, mowing the lawn — the whole hullabaloo. I was really scared. No man in his 70s should be working at that pace. Never mind someone with what he's got."

When my father got on the line, his voice, as usual, was like the calm oceanic depths of the Florida Atlantic next to which my parents lived. "Hi, son," he said.

"Hi, Dad. Heard you were out tearing up the neighborhood today."

"Yeah," he chuckled. "I was hoping I'd have a heart attack."

My mood abruptly keeled. This wasn't the first time he had mentioned his desire for a quick, sudden death rather than the slow, painful one he was having. And like a sailboat in the wake of an oil tanker, my mother and I still lagged several months behind my father's gradual, calm acceptance of what was inevitable.

Dad quickly covered. "I guess your Mom also told you about DSC."

"Yeah," I brightened. "Number one."

"I could kick myself for selling it when I did. If I had held on a little longer, we could have made a fortune. Your mom would have been sitting pretty."

"Hey, you bought it when no one else did. That was the real trick. Everyone else is just now hopping on the bandwagon. As you say, all the juice is already squeezed out of it. And Mom'll be fine."

"Um." His voice echoed unexpressed depths of largely uncharted territory. Continental plates shifted there and roiling submariner currents flowed — a direct contrast to the surface-dancing mountain stream bubbling of my mother's forever youth.

"Hey, you made a *triple*," I said, enjoying the way the lingo rolled off my tongue. Little more than a year ago a *triple* to me had been something I enjoyed seeing the Atlanta Braves make. That was all before Dad's urgent lessons began. I added, "And you made that triple in less than nine months!"

"Actually," he said, somewhat assuaged, "it quadrupled before I sold it. But don't let that make you think we can do that every time. DSC is an exception. If most investors earn 10 to 15 percent a year, they're happy. And so should you be."

"Yeah, Dad, but with your system you're averaging between 40 to 50 percent."

My father was naturally conservative and disliked me to get caught up in the instant-money fever that was the downfall of many investors. But after a lifetime of financial struggle and the nearly unfulfilled destiny of a young boy's genius — and especially with all he was going through now — reflections of his recent success, I knew, provided a comfort that was like bathing in the Florida Atlantic's gentle, tepid waves.

"We may be doing better than most people," he cautioned, "but I don't want this success — especially with DSC — to make you start thinking short-term." His voice became professorial. "What's the golden rule?"

"Buy when no one else wants a stock, and think long-term." The constantly grilled lesson was mimed, me a well-trained parrot of my father's genius.

"And what's long-term?"

"Three to five years."

"And how do you know when a stock is at its low?"

"You don't. But you see when it's taken a sudden drop to half or one-third its price from the last year, then invest half of what you want to invest. If it drops another 10 percent, invest some more."

"Do you invest in just any stock that's dramatically fallen?"

"No. Only those which are safe and have excellent appreciation potential based on all the other criteria."

"Which is?"

"Increasing earnings, high sales figures, low price-to-earnings ratio, possible new product development and good management. To name just a few," I quickly added.

Even through the phone line I could feel my father's satisfaction. I glowed.

Chapter 2

The news of cancer hits like a truck, I remembered reading. And despite more than a decade in the health field, that was exactly how it felt.

I received the news via the same medium I had heard the news about my father's triumphant stock selection — through the phone line.

Since age 18 when I left my parents' Sunrise Key home to begin my first year of college out of state, a large part of our relationship was carried out in this manner. It's probably no wonder my father liked telecommunications stocks such as DSC and MCI; the number of emotions we've shared through those fiber optic networks had made us worthy of owning part of the companies.

Those lines have been a sort of family cradle; placental nerves and blood vessels through which we've been mutually nourished and cherished with each thought, and shared triumph and hardship of our separate lives.

I had just returned to Atlanta after spending four days with my parents in Florida. "Michael, why are you even bothering coming down?" my mother had argued before the trip. "Your father will be in the hospital only a few days. It's a waste of your money."

"Your mom's right," Dad said. "It's a simple operation, removing a stomach polyp. They don't even have to open me up — just insert an instrument down my throat and pluck it out. Like removing a bad tooth."

"Delta's having a special," I fibbed. (Well, maybe not — I hadn't yet checked with Delta, so maybe there was a special). "Besides," I continued,

"I haven't been down to see you for a few months. It'll give me a chance to relax."

So I went, the trip and the surgery indeed turning out to be uneventful. My father was back on the golf course before I left. I returned to Atlanta with the comfortable feeling of banality.

Two days later I received some news. Unrelated but extraordinary news. A health and environmental feature I had proposed to a highly respected magazine had been accepted. Using my text and photographs, the publication would later turn it into my first cover story.

Whenever something good happens to me I try not to tell anyone at first, to enjoy the untouched emotion by myself. I usually manage this feat approximately five minutes into my next encounter.

Thus I decided to resist my initial temptation to immediately call my parents. Summoning vast stores of willpower even I didn't know I possessed, I didn't phone until 15 minutes later.

Calm and cool, I told myself as the line rang. First act normal, then perhaps give a couple of oblique clues, then bowl them over with the news!

"Hello?"

"Mom!" I said just a bit too quickly.

"Oh, hello, Michael."

The dimmed musicality of my mother's vivaciousness didn't register. I plodded onward. "Mom, is Dad there?"

"No, he just left."

"Darn!"

"Is everything all right, Michael?"

"Yeah. Fine! I'll tell you about it later."

"OK."

"Mom, *Atlanta Magazine* bought my article!"

"Oh, they did? Congratulations."

"Thanks!" I glowed, only slightly perturbed for having let the news out so prematurely, more perturbed with the first inkling of something wrong. "I'll be getting $2000!" I tried once more.

"That's wonderful, honey."

Something wasn't right. I thought a second, my excitement waning. "Mom, you didn't say 'I was thinking about you.' "

"What?"

"Every time I call, you answer, 'Hello Michael, isn't that funny, I was just thinking about you.' " I mimicked her easily but without humor.

"Michael, I . . ."

"Yes?"

"I don't know how to tell you this." She paused. "And I hate to tell you it now, after all your good news . . ."

Things began to slow. As if from a distance, I heard myself say, "What is it, Mom?"

Her voice contained a forced lightness, part of the family strength which unfortunately had been cultivated to unnatural degrees from years of sickness leading up to a past loss. "Well, Michael . . ." She hesitated again. ". . . they did the biopsy on the polyp they removed from your father's stomach . . ."

Time froze with those words — or more correctly, became a looking glass through which I suddenly stepped. And from the other side I witnessed myself receive word about something that it seemed I long ago knew.

What I'm describing is so hard to explain. How in an instant, the information was already understood, processed and . . . and accepted . . . before my mother had the next words out.

". . . and well, honey, they found the polyp was cancerous."

It indeed was a feeling of being hit by a truck, but it was a truck that I somehow had already seen barreling inexorably forward. As if whatever invisible strand that connected me to the present was suddenly reined in and the entire unseen web of the future was revealed. As if the words suddenly focused me in on that awareness and thus there was no cause for denial or refusing to let go of a past that could no longer be.

It had happened to me before, upon receiving the news of the war-related death of my best friend from Israel. The knowing, the accepting. The sadness.

It happened to me again. A day after my father's comment, "I was hoping I'd have a heart attack," another close friend, Chap — a doctor and writer like me — was found dead in his clinic. From a heart attack.

Perhaps it's the faculty of a writer, that feeling of not knowing where the words come from; the sensation, once complete, that the novel was written even before pen touched paper. Through some elemental prestigitation of time, all the pieces fall together, making a book, a chapter of our lives.

But in these circumstances, making unhappy sense.

With Chap, with my Israeli friend.

And now with my dad.

THE 9 INSIGHTS OF THE WEALTHY SOUL
by
John Norwood

INSIGHT
(Insight 1)

Just as diamonds are very rare and are created in the depths, so too are the very exceptional buying opportunities in stocks. These "gems" appear to the few discerning when they are least popular and are a pariah to the overwhelming majority.

For one or more reason they have fallen to the depths, but to the insightful *(those who are prepared to do the heavy digging), the road up is long and very fruitful.*

If the digging (research) shows the potential for a strong recovery, the likelihood of doubling or tripling and possibly more lies ahead.

Caution: my method is replete with refutations and inconsistencies. Why then does this system have any merit?

Who said it was going to be easy!

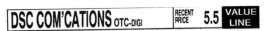

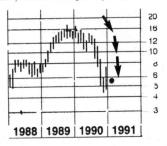

Chapter 3

"Aghh!" I exclaimed. "I'm never going to get this."

"You're already getting it," my father said. "Be easier on yourself."

"I don't have your facility for numbers. My mind thinks with words and images. Not figures."

It was a basic difference between my father and me. He was left-brained, analytical; I was right-brained, creative. It was easy for me to see the genius of his stock-picking system, to see the beauty and simplicity of the whole. But something in me refused to retain the parts, as if there were no right angles in my brain into which the sharp-edged details could fit, only slopes and parabolas.

"Go ahead, just try reading it again," my father encouraged.

Remembering the promise I had made to myself — to take his lessons without complaint — I took a deep breath, and stared once more at the places my father had carefully outlined in yellow on the *Standard and Poors* report:

Earnings for 1991 are tentatively projected at $0.70 a share, versus the $0.47 reported for 1990 . . . DSC said nonrecurring charges needed to write-down assets of a minority-owned joint venture and for estimated restructuring costs reduced 1990's fourth quarter net income by $6.3 million ($0.15 a share).

"Do you see it?" my father asked. "What's so important in those statements?"

I concentrated, forcing myself to read it a third time. Somehow the numbers wouldn't focus, kaleidoscope pieces that kept revolving, refusing to click into a steady place. Whereas I could read a passage by Shakespeare over and over, gaining more appreciation and insight with each repetition, or endlessly study the intricacies of the body's symphony of physiology, I couldn't get past the first 10 words of a financial report.

"Read the first line out loud," my father instructed.

I sighed. " *'Earnings for 1991 are tentatively projected at $0.70 a share . . .'*"

"Stop," he said. "Now, tell me what that means."

"They expect to earn $0.70 a share. Is that what you mean? That's easy."

"Exactly," he smiled. "Now read the second part of the line."

I looked at him. He nodded for me to do it.

" *'. . . versus the $0.47 reported for 1990.'* "

"What does that mean?" he asked.

"That means that . . . that the earnings for last year, 1990, were 47 cents a share — much lower than the 70 cents-per-share earnings they're expecting for this year."

Dad smiled again. "Now read the last line."

" *'DSC said nonrecurring charges needed to writedown assets of a minority-owned joint venture and for estimated restructuring costs reduced 1990 fourth quarter net income by $6.3 million ($0.15 a share).'* Oh, jeez," I said from the corner of my mouth, the financial report suddenly gibberish again.

"Hold on," my father said to calm my frustration. "You're a writer. Skip all the details. Just tell me the key word in that sentence."

I read it again silently. " 'Nonrecurring'?"

"Great. Now put it all together, and what does it all mean?"

"DSC expects their earnings to be much higher in 1991 than in 1990 because they won't have to pay any more restructuring — whatever that means — costs." I exhaled. "Darn!"

He gleamed triumphantly. "Now, using that ability of writers to see beyond surface appearances — using your *insight* — do you see why I'm so interested in buying it?"

"Because the price is at a two-year low," I said, my enthusiasm mounting, "and they're supposed to do much better this year than last, so . . .'"

"So, you tell me."

"So there's most likely only one way the stock price will go?" Dad smiled. "Up."

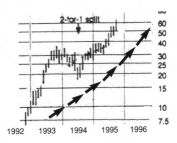

DSC COM'CATIONS OTC-DIGI

RECENT PRICE **63**   VALUE LINE

DSC PRICE RISE:

11/91	2 1/4 (after 2-for-1 price split••)
09/95	**63**

•• A price split occurs when a stock price has greatly increased and the company wants to keep the share price low to make it more attractive to potential investors. Thus, with the 2-for-1 split of DSC, if an investor owned 1 share at 126 *before* the split, the investor would own 2 shares at 63 *after* the split.

Chapter 4

I had long resisted my father's efforts to teach me about stocks, but with his diagnosis of cancer, two things happened. The first was he decided to get back into the market after three years away from it. This would herald his second major comeback after twice in his life being wiped out financially. The first time was from a circumstance beyond his control.

Some of my earliest memories are from when I was four or five years old, pre-dawn in the back seat of a car during icy northern winters. How many times did we take this trip from our Edison, New Jersey, home, where I spent my early youth, to the steaming runways of Newark Airport? Every few weeks it seemed my mother would be hustling our tiny family into the car to pick my father up or see him off on a trip to the Orient. After years of tremendous work and expense, he was just beginning to establish himself as a force in the custom trade market, importing products he designed and manufactured abroad then sold wholesale back in the states.

The woven hanging plant basket, the water-filled Christmas scene handshaker that filled with snow when you shook it, the tiny flower-filled plastic Italian Gondola model — my father was the originator, designer and producer of all these items, which my mother and I still see on the shelves of major department stores to this day. Dad would import the first products to the states, trying to sell as many as quickly as possible before much larger, more powerful competitors copied the idea and flooded the market. It was frustrating and exhilarating for him all at the same time, his creative genius and inexhaustible energy always trying to stay one step ahead of the market.

Hong Kong, Macao, Taiwan: these were my father's destinations where he was wined and dined royally by the most powerful Asian families as they sought his production orders. The combination of his creativity, business savvy, good looks and caring manner made him a rising star in the Asian business world. My parents, both Depression children, thought they were going to be millionaires.

Then it all ended. The trips across the world, the fantastic travel stories I grew up hearing, the excitement and the dreams. *Poof.* Gone, just like some boyhood fantasy. I was perhaps 10 at the time and never completely comprehended what happened until one day, nearly a decade and a half later, when I was speaking to my mother's childhood friend Rita.

I was in my 20s and complaining to her that any time I did something out of the ordinary — such as going off to Hollywood when I was still in chiropractic school to try selling television scripts I'd written or, as I was then doing, selling my first practice to fulfill a dream to live overseas — my father would blow up at me. Though I hadn't lived at home since the age of 18 and always ended up following my own instincts, I nevertheless was affected by the continual tension between my father and me.

Even more, though I hated to admit it, was the almost preternatural hold my father had on me; how he, like no one else, could get me to doubt my own instincts as if by some ancestral shock wave he sent racing through my genes.

"I don't understand it," I told Rita, my voice edgy with long-suppressed anger. "It's like I've got this schizophrenic image of my father. I remember him when I was a kid being a great risk-taker himself, this dynamic man who was always traveling off to the Orient developing his import/export business, developing new products, having exotic adventures sounding straight out of a James Clavell novel."

"I know," Rita said.

"He used to love talking about it . . . about incredible feasts with Chinese businessmen, about volunteering for service in World War II, about going through fighter pilot training, about being an officer in charge of 200 men in Germany . . ." I fought for control, unable to stem the long-held dam of wrath-tinged frustration. "I just can't mesh those images with the picture of him now, so security conscious, so ultra-conservative, always furious at me whenever I diverge slightly from the mainstream . . ."

"Yes?" Rita encouraged.

" . . . I skipped my senior year of high school, exempted a year of college, received a doctor's degree when I was 21, and went straight into running my own practice — all without ever taking a vacation. I mean, don't I deserve to be a kid for a little while? Dammit, don't I deserve a break?"

She sighed. "Yes, sweetheart. You do. And you do know your father is really very proud of you."

"Well, why does he act that way then," my voice raised even higher, "as if I don't know how to run my own life? For crying out loud . . . am I crazy or am I right? Isn't he different than how he was when I was younger?"

"You are right. He is different." She paused. "It's what happened with Janie."

My hardlined thoughts suddenly blurred. "Janie?"

"Six years of sickness, six years of medical bills and operations. But that was only the financial toll."

"Oh, God," I whispered, anger held for years suddenly vaporized. How could I never have made the connection? My brow had broken out with a thin film of sweat. Without realizing it, I was punching my thigh, so ashamed of myself for not seeing the obvious, for not having understood earlier; for all my self-centered babbling.

The ordeal had begun when Janie was 12. I was only 10. I was never told until near the end, after six years of illness and multiple operations and radiation treatments, that my sister had terminal brain cancer.

"It was difficult on you," Rita finally responded gently to the silence. "When it all ended, you were only 16 — old enough to understand what was happening but not old enough, perhaps, to comprehend everything."

I shook my head.

"The emotional toll cost your father much more than all the bills. Your sister was just 18 when she finally died."

I didn't want my parents' friend to continue. I already knew what she was going to say.

"Yes, your father did change. He is very security-minded now. Very. Probably too much so with you. But until you have children yourself, you'll never understand what it means for a parent to lose a child . . ." Her final words seared deep inside me.

"It took all the fire out of him."

Chapter 5

"Here's one place that hasn't changed," I smiled to the young Vietnamese man as we entered the restaurant doors of the Southern barbecue pit, the wooden plank floor squeaking beneath us as soft country-western music mixed with pungent smells of roast pork and fresh cole slaw to delight the senses. It was six weeks after the day my father had received the chilling diagnosis.

Behind the rims of the same style glasses he'd worn when we first met as students 15 years earlier, my friend's eyes glowed. "It looks just the same," he gently nodded, the emotion of his nostalgia touching me. Material things held little allure to Antoine, but to memories he had great attachment.

"Look who's still here," I pointed to a middle-aged woman who was chattering away with a family in animated Southern dialect as she rang up their bill.

Again my friend's eyes dilated, a tiny smile lighting his face. He moved slowly to the woman as her customer went out the door, waiting patiently but with barely disguised emotion as she finished placing the cash in the register.

My friend's lower lip trembled with latent laughter and love, a flash of the same image I still have of him from our school days. Just as the owner was looking up, he said, "Do you remember me?" I saw the woman squint, her first reaction that of surprise, seeing a young Asian in a place normally populated by local country folk. Her eyes suddenly blinked.

"Why landsakes *alive!* It's Antoine Ky!"

I couldn't help enjoying my friend's pleasure as the owner took his hand and held it in hers. She asked him about Mrs. Ky and a half-dozen other questions. I stood back, knowing she wouldn't remember who I was. I had not been a frequent customer like my friend.

When we were finally seated, Antoine said, "Thank you for bringing me here, Mikey." He used the affectionate name he had always called me since we met in chiropractic school when I was just 18 and he was 27. I was the youngest student in the college then. Antoine had been the only person with whom I hadn't felt the age disparity. More than a decade and half later, despite our nine-year age difference and the 500 miles that separate us, he is still my best friend.

A waitress pranced up to the table. With a huge smile reflecting pure peaches and magnolias, she said, "Hi, ya'll! What'll it be for yuh today?"

I let Antoine do the ordering. In Atlanta for a weekend seminar from his practice in New Orleans, he had requested I take him to this restaurant in rural Smyrna, Georgia, a favorite of his when we were students at Life Chiropractic College 12 years earlier. Neither of us ate much meat, particularly pork. But Antoine loved the ambience of Deep South hospitality — the wood-pit burning stoves and the lives and accents that hadn't yet been sterilized by the tremendous growth Atlanta had undergone since we first came to the city.

Once the order was taken, the waitress country-two-stepped away, hips jiggling and Clairol-blonde hairdo bobbing above her. After a moment, I turned to my friend who noticed my admiring approval of the receding figure.

"Mikey is a man now?" he managed to softly ask, despite that his belly was pumping with barely contained laughter.

"Shut up, Antoine," I replied affectionately, slightly blushing. "Mikey's been a man for a long time now."

My friend's tender humor burst out of him in wave after wave of huge belly laughs. Though I had long ago gotten used to the unexpected gusto of his laughter, it nevertheless always managed to touch something in me; that someone so quiet and so deep could also contain such explosive joy.

The status of my virginity had been a subject I had confided in Antoine alone when we were in school, he having always been a quiet master at pushing my buttons in a way that not only had made me laugh at myself, but gently made me grow. "Is Mikey a man yet?" had been one of his favorite buttons to push back then.

I looked at my friend now and smiled mischeviously. "Antoine has been much more of a man than Mikey has these last years. Four little girls . . . that took a lot of work!"

Now it was Antoine's turn to blush. "So many changes since we were students," he shook his head. "How could it be so long ago already?"

I also shook my head, unable to imagine how fast the time had passed.

"But more changes for you than for most of us, Mikey."

"Yep," I nodded. "Here I am in my fourth practice already, having lived in five different countries while everyone else has settled down in a nice town, with a nice car, a huge home and 1.5 children. I guess that's the price of not having sowed my wild oats like everyone else before I graduated."

My friend looked at me softly. "But not just simply changes of location, Mikey. Many changes of life for you also." He touched my arm. "How is your daddy?"

My senses abruptly rocked. I took in a deep breath. Maybe it was because he had been through so much himself, having been separated from his parents when he was just seven years old, a refugee from the war in Vietnam, first in Japan, then in France, later having been close to death for two years from a medication overdose when he was in his teens. But Antoine, more than anyone else I knew, always managed to touch me in the deepest places.

I took another breath and began telling him all that had taken place since the day of my father's diagnosis.

Chapter 6

For weeks after I learned of my father's diagnosis, I was numb. Deeply buried memories of pain, of cries in the night, of helplessness during my sister's cancer reawakened from long dormancy. So many years later I was still confused as to what I would do when I eventually married. Though I loved children, the idea of having any of my own frightened me. So many things could go wrong — mongolism, blindness . . . cancer.

. . . Death.

Despite knowing that my sister's passing was the most important experience of my life in shaping me — how strong it had made me, in that all other travails that came along in life were somehow lightened by comparison — for many years after my sister's passing, I was certain I would one day get a vasectomy. This was the only way I could ensure that I would never again have to sacrifice a chunk of my life to all the turmoil and heart-rending helplessness that are the daily bread of the caregiver.

I, as of yet, have not gone for the procedure. But the fear-borne impulse is still with me.

My father's diagnosis also put my mother in shock. She had all the same memories I did but compounded exponentially, for there is no greater loss than that of a parent who must watch powerlessly as his or her child slowly dies. To have lived through such a period, to have recovered from the brutal emotional and physical trauma, then to have the barely healed wound suddenly ripped open again with the prospect of losing her partner of 40 years in the same manner, paralyzed her.

Only Dad, recipient of the diagnosis, seemed calm. Like a rugged sea piling that stays firmly anchored as the boats moored to it are tossed and shattered by a tempest, he appeared totally collected after the initial tidal-wave shock.

"I never thought I would live through World War II," he told me. "I'm in the beginning of my 70s, so I figure I've been given 50 more years than I ever bargained for."

I stared at him in wonder, suddenly seeing all the attributes that had qualified him for pilot training those 50 years earlier in the army.

"What about the surgery, Dad?" I tentatively asked, unsure of him; of my own emotions as well. "Mom said the doctor wants to do it immediately. She said you told the doctor you needed a few days to decide." Despite my effort to sound calm, I couldn't keep a tremor out of my voice.

He gently smiled. "I'm still deciding, son."

I nodded, not knowing what else to say, unable to read him but able to imagine the wild swinging scales of emotions weighing on his mind. On one hand he was facing *death*, his own *end*, the fear of the blackness and void many of us carry in deep subterranean emotional vaults, as if by locking them away we can forget their existence:

> *When thoughts of the last bitter hour come*
> *like a blight over thy spirit,*
> *And sad images of the stern agony, and shroud, and pall,*
> *make thee to shudder and grow sick at heart . . . ** *

And my father had to face this *now*, not in the young man's way of contemplating some distant future for which he finds solace by the very difficulty of associating it with the fervor and passion of being in the heart of life.

On the other hand I knew Dad was thinking of my sister, weighing our past experience of medicine's effectiveness in being able to do anything consequential for her illness . . . and the price she had to pay for us putting our faith in that society. That price was branded forever in my family's heart.

I cleared my throat, said what I had to say despite that I wasn't sure if I could hide the cracking in my voice. "I'll support you whichever way you go, Dad."

He looked deep into my eyes and I felt compelled to embrace him; this, despite that our love usually wasn't expressed through physical ges-

Thanatopsis, by William Cullen Bryant

ture.

He grasped my shoulder and said, "Thank you, son."

Chapter 7

"Here ya go, boys!" the waitress bobbed up to the table with steaming plates of barbecue chicken, baked beans and Southern-style hush puppies, interrupting a long silence that had befallen my Vietnamese friend and me. I had just finished recounting the events that had taken place with my father in the six weeks since his diagnosis.

The waitress plunked a bottle of homemade hot sauce down on the table, saying: "This'll put some hair on yo' chests!" She flashed us one last impish grin then pirouetted away.

We managed to smile after her. But when we turned back to each other, our grimness returned.

"Your daddy is so *strong*," Antoine whispered, shaking his head. "I don't know if I could be so strong."

I toyed listlessly with the barbecue. "I don't know if I could either, Antoine."

My friend perceived my emotion, grasped me by the forearm. "But *you are*, Mikey. *You are.*" Shaking the arm, he gently smiled. "You are your father's son."

I nodded. Somehow Antoine always was able to elicit from me the feelings I had difficulty showing others . . . even myself sometimes. But also, always stirring in me some strength, and so much the deeper for its acknowledgement of the weakness.

"Sometimes bravery, Antoine, is just a coverup for fear." I blankly poked at the food, thinking of my father. "The deepest," I added, my previously carefully contained emotions now feeling like a physical weight I couldn't lift.

My friend removed his hand. "Tell me what your daddy decided," he whispered.

Chapter 8

Despite the doctor's urgent pressing, my father had had the presence of mind to take several weeks before announcing his decision. And if his answer had amazed us — despite our understanding what led to that decision — it stunned his doctors.

"I'm not going to have the surgery," he announced.

My mother and I were open-mouthed. "Is that what you've decided? Is that your final decision?" we asked in disbelief.

"I'm feeling great now," he explained. "Even if the surgery is successful, I'll never be able to eat normally again with part of my stomach gone. And I may have years of chemotherapy to face." Unspoken were the memories of my sister's death. During her six-year battle with cancer, the three of us witnessed the ravages that artificial prolongation of life can wreak.

"I'll trade a few good years for twice as many bad ones," was my father's concluding argument. He had waited until after dinner to tell us. With those words he rose, saying, "I'm going into the garage."

I was left at the table with my mother. I could see the horror in her eyes, the horror that would have been there had he decided upon surgery, as well. But then, at least, we would have had the comfort of conventionality supporting us.

I pushed away from the table. "Let me speak to him," I tried to reassure her, physically aching that there was no way to do so. Maybe it was from the years spent as a child, trying to fight the unseen enemy that was terrorizing my sister; but I have a reflex to this day that is so protective of women, at such times I feel an actual force inside me that would *kill* if I could visibly see what was threatening my loved one.

"There's got to be a different way," I had whispered over and over again throughout the years of surgery and radiation my sister had received, watching her progressively get weaker, sicker, losing her hair while other girls her age were getting bat-mitzvahed, celebrating their sweet-16ths, preparing for graduation prom . . .

But back then we knew no other way. It was less than a year after Janie finally died when I first heard about the holistic field. My mother and I had stopped to have our posture checked at a health booth set up in a mall by two chiropractors. I didn't know what a chiropractor was at that time. However, when I went home and read their pamphlets, I was immediately captivated.

The literature described how the nervous system controlled the body, and how if there was interference in the nervous system via a pinched nerve, potentially anything could go wrong: ulcers, migraines, even possibly *cancer?* But most importantly, it talked about how chiropractors fixed these areas of interference by correcting misaligned vertebra affecting the nervous system's control.

This makes such perfect sense! I remember thinking. If only we had known about such a thing during Janie's illness . . .

Two years later, after passing a battery of specialized state and national tests that allowed me to skip my senior year of high school and one of the two years of undergraduate college courses then required, I was in chiropractic school.**

To this day I still don't have the answer for cancer, but after so many years studying everything from chiropractic to acupuncture to herbal, homeopathic, ayurvedic and mind/body medicine, I know the power of these gentle procedures and often wish I could take back time to that hopeless period of my sister's illness.

With the numbing emergence of cancer in my family again, at least now I had the experience of thousands of patients behind me. So when I went into the garage to speak to my father, despite my shock at his decision, I didn't necessarily feel that refusing surgery spelled death.

There are other ways, I reassured myself. *So many other ways.*

When I entered the garage, Dad was wiping mud off a six-iron. "Hey, son," he said to me. "Gotta keep these beauties clean."

"Yeah," I nodded, momentarily at a loss for words as I watched him baby the club. *Thank God for golf,* was all I could think.

**Today, a four-year Bachelor of Science degree is required to get into most chiropractic schools.

His rediscovery of the sport had been a blessing for him. When I was in chiropractic school, I had used the last few hundred dollars I had earned from a night job to buy him a membership at the Pelican Bay Golf Course in Sunrise Key. He made me ask for my money back, angered that I had spent it "needlessly." More than a decade later, still striving to recover financially from the toll the years my sister's medical bills had exacted on the family savings, he rejoined the club. The joy and release it provided from his intense preoccupation changed my father's life. Especially now, finding that his time was being cut short by cancer. It was the one anchor, the one blessing he still had left.

"Yep." He continued to fondly wipe the mud off the six-iron in our garage, "These beauties you bought me are allowing me to drive 30 yards further. No one can figure out what the sudden change is in John Norwood."

I took his lead. "Thirty yards, huh?"

"Thirty yards. I'm feeling so good, I almost think the doctors made a mistake with their diagnosis." He looked up at me, his eyes somehow belieing his confidence, his expression begging me to concur.

"That's not why you're refusing the surgery, is it Dad?"

He shook his head, sighing. "No, son. It's not." He pulled another club from the golf bag. "I want to go out like a candle, burning — as the saying goes — brightly to the end. If my time is limited, I don't want my last years to be with half my stomach missing, unable to ever eat a full meal again, unable to play golf, pumped full of chemotherapy . . ."

I shook my head, speechless for a moment. I touched his arm. "I don't want that for you either, Dad," I whispered.

Neither of us could speak, the unspoken memory of my sister's final year hanging in the silence. I summoned all my strength, "Dad, why don't you let me start you on a holistic program?"

"Son . . ." he started to say.

"We can start with some gentle homeopathic remedies. They'll help reduce your stomach's bacterial count, which is often a precursor for cancer formation."

"Michael, I . . ."

"I'll put you on a mild detoxification diet and get you some of the latest books on mind/body healing."

"Michael . . ." he tried again.

"I can even get you an appointment with Deepak Chopra, you know, the endocrinologist who just wrote a bestselling book on the mind's effect on healing cancer. I've met him personally through seminars . . ."

"Michael!" my father suddenly barked. But as soon as he saw he had gotten my shocked attention, his eyes softened. "Listen, son, I don't want to do *anything*. Do you understand? *Nothing*. Not surgery, not drugs, not vitamins." He sighed. "I just want to work on securing your mother's future and live life to the fullest in whatever time I've got left. I need my mind to be at its clearest if I want to leave your mom with at least some financial security. And drugs will just screw that up."

"But the procedures I'm recommending *won't*," I desperately countered.

He shook his head, sorrowful . . . alone . . . not expecting me to understand. He tried one last time: "Your books and your remedies are all fine, but they'll just keep my mind on it. I simply don't want to die captive to this disease."

I was too stunned to answer. Of every possibility, I could never have imagined this being his response. But I did understand. That was the horror.

I did.

Chapter 9

Ever since the conversation more than a decade ago with my mother's friend Rita, I had slowly learned to be more understanding of my father; to try to see his behavior through his eyes, not mine.

However, despite my father's overbearing protest back then concerning my travel plans, I went overseas anyway. But with greater understanding of his position.

My original plans to stay abroad for half a year turned into three years. During that period I danced flamenco until wee hours of the morning in Spain, crossed desert mountains on camel with ancient Bedouin tribes in the Egyptian Sinai, and shared love, life and wine with a teacher from Switzerland, a chicken farmer from Nigeria and a recently released political prisoner from then-communist Rumania. I also learned three foreign languages, discovered what it was like to feel at home on two continents, and felt the pride of running my own clinic on one of them. Most of all, I experienced the wonder of fulfilling a childhood dream.

It would have been very easy for me to stay abroad. Somehow, the riptide of goal achievement that had roared through me in America, buffeting every cell in my body since I was a teenager, was replaced by the solid beachhead of another orientation. Friends and family seemed to form the bedrock of life overseas, not "the job."

Paradoxically, this more than anything compelled me to return to the United States when I would have been perfectly content to stay abroad. There, having absorbed these values, I was nevertheless as far away from realizing them as the 9,000 miles that separated me from my family. More than ever, I realized how important I was to my parents — and how important they were to me.

So I returned to the United States and discovered my parents in a situation that gladdened my heart; but which, after being wiped out by the medical bills from my sister's illness, would ultimately lead to the second devastating financial crash in my father's life.

*A*fter a year and a half of Europe's 18th century architecture, an equal amount of time in the biblical atmosphere of the Middle East, and stretches in the remote desert sands of Northern Africa, I was awed by the modernity of Orlando's International Airport. The airport's tramline from gate to port and the giant Disney World figurines floating from the ceiling left me opened-mouthed, feeling dreamlike after years on the other side of the Atlantic. Though I had grown up in America, my arrival was more *deja vu,* as if recalling something from another lifetime.

My shock was replaced by pleasure in seeing my parents, and the brand-new Nissan Maxima in which they came to pick me up. As we drove the 70 miles back to Sunrise Key and I listened to their update on all that had gone on in my absence, a slow realization began to dawn on me.

In the time I was gone, my parents had become, hmm . . . *well-to-do.* After all they had been through with my sister's death and the years of struggle afterward to regain an emotional and financial foothold, material success — something I had previously never given much value to — suddenly seemed a blessing worthy of highest thanksgiving.

"Your father's done very well for us," my mother said, as if reading my thoughts.

"Um, I see," I said, patting the suede seat, suddenly feeling as if I should be wearing something nicer than the faded jeans and T-shirt that had been my garb for nearly three years now. "In the market?" I queried.

"That's right," my father nodded. "And the savings you told me was OK to invest for you a year ago?"

"Yes?"

"Well, you've got almost double now."

"Dad . . . what can I say? Huh! Thanks."

"Just don't spend it all in one place."

"Actually," I laughed, "I will. On opening a new clinic."

"That's acceptable," he smiled. And for the first time I could remember, I wasn't bothered by him telling me what was right or wrong for me to do with my life.

*F*our months later, after an extended trip out West to decide the state in which I wanted to practice, I chose, of all places, Atlanta, Georgia. Though I loved mountains and for that reason had wanted to practice in Colorado or New Mexico, the closeness of Atlanta to my parents' home in Florida — and my familiarity with Atlanta after having gone to school there many years earlier — factored into my decision to settle there.

Once I found an office, I sought a bank loan. Whatever interest I would have to pay was going to be much less than the amount I was earning with the money my father had invested in stocks for me. But to my amazement, despite a perfect credit history and two successful past practices, I was refused by three banks!

When Dad heard the news, he said, "Forget the banks, son. Let me give you the loan."

"Are you sure, Dad?" I was bewildered.

"Of course I'm sure," he scoffed.

And what a wonderful feeling it was to accept this money from him! I had contributed to what my parents had given me toward my chiropractic education with savings from jobs as a teenager, taking out student loans and working part-time while in school. Though my parents had been willing to give me their every last cent for my education, I never wanted to be a burden on them after all they'd been through with my sister. The success and financial stability my father had achieved from his import/export business had been shattered by the overwhelming medical expenses during my sister's illness; Dad was nearing retirement age when I entered chiropractic school, and they would need all their savings.

But now, to suddenly see that money was no longer a problem? To sense that my parents finally had the security they deserved after years of such tremendous distress? To see that my father had actually become a "man of means"?

"Don't even pay me back," he told me.

"Are you kidding?" I laughed. "If I accept the money, that's out of the question. You'll have everything back within two years."

Despite my rejection of his offer to not pay him back, what I was feeling most of all was my father's pride in being able to help his son.

*T*hen it happened. I was six months into my new practice, just beginning to see things start to work out. My parents drove the eight hours from Sunrise Key to visit me. I'll never forget the day. How ironic and how painful it was that fate chose it to occur when we were all together.

The date was October 19, 1987. Monday. What later would be called *Black Monday.* Dad had suspected the market was due for a major correction (a drop) for quite some time. Stock prices were higher than ever before, stock dividends were near an all-time low, and Price-Earning ratios were in the ozone — all meaningless things to me, but clear smoke signals to my father of something ominous to come. It was a particularly dangerous time for my father's portfolio because he had made most of his money through options, something I still don't understand because my father refused to teach these to me — his way of making sure I'd stay clear of them. What I do understand, however, is that with options, if you're sharp — and lucky — you can win big-time, as my father had. But like any gamble, there is also the possibility of losing.

For six months, sensing the danger, my father heeded his instincts and took appropriate precautions. He maintained all his winning *Call Options* (betting each stock would go up) but took out a *Put Option* on the S&P 500. (The S&P 500 is a compilation of 500 widely held stocks.) Taking a *Put Option* on it was like betting that the entire market — including my father's individual stocks — was going to fall.

This was like putting a lot of money down on three favorite horses to win, while putting less money down — but for much higher odds — on the same horses to lose. If all your horses place in the top three, you win — but less than you would have because you also placed a bet they would lose. If your horses lose you still win, because of the higher odds they wouldn't.

The problem occurs after nine races when you see that the odds have been correct every time. Suddenly you find yourself tired of continually paying out part of your winnings for betting both ways. Thus, on the 10th race, you throw caution to the wind and bet only on the favorites.

Like bets on horse races, options are only good for one *race,* or one period of time (typically for a one- to nine-month period). Afterwards, the option/bet must be placed again or it expires.

So after six months of paying these high "insurance premiums" yet continuing to watch the market soar, my father, like many investors, got tired of seeing the fantastic profits from his call-options being lessened. Thus, at the end of July 1987, he stopped renewing his "insurance policy" put-options on the S&P 500 and joined the jubilant mood of the country in joyous money-making.

Then came that October Monday. The day my parents drove up to Atlanta to visit me. The weather in Atlanta had been beautiful, autumn's hand painting the city like Monet's palette on fire with reds, yellows and purples.

But by late afternoon a chill wind blew in. It was time for the leaves to fall, the season to change. And it would change overnight.

None of us had the slightest inkling of what was transpiring that day. By the time we turned on the television that evening, the greatest damage was already done. Today, flipping through stock charts, one's eye is immediately caught by the sickening straight-line plunge, 508 points instantly lopped off the Dow Jones Industrial Average morning high of 2,246. In that single day, many stocks fell anywhere from three-quarter to half their value.

And in an instant, all those wonderful sensations I had experienced — seeing my parents finally secure, feeling the wonder of accepting my father's money to start me in practice, thanking God that after all the years of hardship, my parents were finally on firm ground — in one split second, all these things were destroyed.

"Don't sell, don't sell!" I beseeched my father. "The market will come back! It *always* comes back!" I was repeating his words, and he knew it because he had said them so often. And even though history would prove this right (within a year and a half, the market would hit a new all-time high), because of my ignorance, I couldn't at that time understand the untenable position my father was in.

"You're right, son," he weakly smiled, proud of me even through his pain. "But I've got to pull out anyway."

What I didn't understand then was how options expire in a limited time, how if my father didn't pull out immediately he could lose *everything*. How there was *no time* to wait for the market to turn back around.

All I could feel was this terrible heaviness in my chest, this sense of helplessness, of devastation. But beyond this, what I remember most from that eve of seeing a life's savings reduced to almost nothing, was how my parents behaved.

There was no crying, no yelling, no tearing out of hair. Despite the tremendous emotion I knew they were experiencing, all I remember is the calm, painful resignation deep in their eyes.

It would have been much easier seeing a more outward display. But what would finally cut deepest into me was a realization: that after losing a child, perhaps this wasn't so bad.

As if to confirm my thoughts, my father looked up at me. His face etched in pain — similar to the physical pain I would see him in many years later — he said: "Son, despite how difficult this is, you should remember that there is no grief so terrible, nothing so overwhelming that you can't live through it until a brighter day."

I have thought often of those words, thought of them in the weeks ahead when the television news talked of how during the Great Depression some people jumped off of buildings and others put bullets through their heads for the same reason my parents now might have.

Dad didn't want me to forget this lesson, wanted this experience to be something I'd take through life with me. To further his point, he said the words that he would later put on paper, words that seemed the hallmark of his life. Words and a lesson he managed to pull from deep inside, transcending through his pain from that core of love; all so that his loss might be my gain.

"Whoever said life was going to be easy?" he said.

| MCI COM'CATIONS OTC-MCIC | RECENT PRICE | 19 | VALUE LINE |

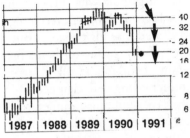

Chapter 10

TIMING
(Insight 2)

*N*othing I say can be set in concrete, the reason being that each stock is unique and must be judged on its own merits. *THE ONLY CONSTANT IS TO BUY WHEN THE STOCK IS NEAR OR AT ITS LOW FOR THE PAST YEAR OR TWO AND THINK LONG-TERM!!*

Dad was at his low after Black Monday. Older than my mother, his main concern had always been that she would not have a financial struggle once he was gone. After finally having achieved his goal — then see it just disappear — he was suddenly left knowing that in another five to seven years, after simply paying the mortgage and other bills, there would be nothing left.

In his early 70s, comebacks were difficult. But that was exactly what he proceeded to do.

For a long time he made no move. Just watched and studied, watched and studied, forever watching the Financial News Network, forever studying what he had done right, but coldly, analytically dissecting where he'd gone wrong. The puzzle was how to make back what he had lost, but . . . how to do it *safely* this time. Like constructing a giant jigsaw in some back room of the house, he pieced the answers together over three years, his plans known only to him.

"You're not thinking of getting back into the market?" my mother and I asked him over and over during that time, sensing something brewing beneath the poker exterior.

"Nah," he shrugged us off. "I just enjoy watching the numbers."

"John, I don't want to gamble what little we have left," my mother would warn, deathly frightened of losing everything.

"I said don't worry," he'd lose his patience. But each day he'd give us more and more to worry about, sitting for hours by the television, scrutinizing the stock programs, combing *The Wall Street Journal*, underlining, cutting out, taking notes, playing with figures.

Then on November 16, 1990, his timing less than a month after the ignominious third-year anniversary of Black Monday, my father made his move. Like DSC Communications (which he wouldn't invest in until 18 months later), MCI was another telecommunications stock. He broke the news about this first stock purchase to me when I came home for a visit a week later.

"Why did you do it, Dad?" I asked him, unable to conceal my fury.

"Son . . ."

"*How* could you do it?" I berated him. "You know how scared Mom is."

"If you just let me ex . . ."

"I really can't believe you did it! I really can't. I mean, what were you *thinking*?"

"Son . . ." he started again, but before I'd let him get a word in, it slipped out of me.

"*Haven't you lost enough already?*"

There was a stunned silence, then a sharp intake of breath. "That's exactly why I have invested," he spit, eyes flashing, his face suddenly, dangerously changed.

I knew too late what I had done, knew that more than anything else he hated to be confronted on financial decisions. I had crossed the line onto his turf and had done so violently, activating some primitive brain chemistry, a fight-or-flight reflex that most men seem to have but for which he had a hair trigger.

I kept silent, the moment dangerous, the only thing to do, to wait.

His features finally softened. "Listen, son," he sighed, not noticing the color return to my own face. "Your mother and I don't have much left and I'm too old to go back to work with hope of earning anything. This is the only chance I have to bring us back some measure of security."

"But Dad, the risk . . ."

"I know. Don't you think I've thought about it? Don't you think I've *agonized* over it? Why do you think I've waited three years before investing again?" I was silent, my disapproval already spoken. "Let me show you something, son. I want you to see what I've invested in."

"Dad, you know I don't have any mind for that sort of thing."

"If you have mind enough to tell me not to invest, you should have mind enough to at least have some idea what it is you're telling me not to do." He was not a person with whom you could argue. So as not to provoke him further, and wanting to give him at least some recognition for the tremendous decision I knew it was for him to re-enter the market, I nodded.

As he flipped through a thick stack of notes, he said, "Most people look at the stock market as a gamble. And I admit, the way I was playing before with options was exactly that. But it doesn't have to be that way."

"How can you avoid it?" I asked, trying to keep the doubt from my voice.

"Well, let me ask you this." He was comfortable now, back on his turf. "What is the one investment almost everyone wants to make because of the great security it implies?"

I thought, then shook my head.

"Think!"

"Their home?"

"Right! Now let me ask you something else. Why do people consider real estate to be so much safer than stocks?"

"That's obvious. Because real estate constantly rises in value."

"Constantly?"

"Well," I hesitated. "I guess it has its ups and downs, too. But over the course of 10 or 20 years, the length of time most people buy a home for, there's generally a good increase in value, isn't there?"

"That's right," he smiled. "About 4 to 8 percent a year." He waited for me to ask my next question.

"Well, that makes it a much safer investment, doesn't it?

"Does it?"

"Well, yeah." I stomped, not seeing what he was getting at, feeling uncomfortable with his deftness.

"How much do you think the stock market rises per year?"

I thought a minute, realizing I couldn't even guess. "No idea."

"For the last half-century, stocks have risen an average of 12 percent a year, and over the last decade it's been 18 percent a year, which obviously is much better than real estate."

"18 percent?" I couldn't help being impressed. "But why then are stocks considered so risky?"

"You tell me."

I thought a minute. "I don't know."

"Take your time."

I thought some more. "Is it because of the length of time people usually invest in stocks compared to land or a home?"

"Exactly," he beamed, inexplicably proud of me. "Exactly the mistake most people make with stocks, and exactly the mistake I made playing options."

My head was swimming, trying to keep up. "What mistake was that?"

"Playing short-term. Gambling."

"Wait a second. Are you saying the stock market doesn't have to be a gamble?"

"Not if you think long-term. Playing long-term, the market can actually be safer than real estate."

"C'mon, Dad," I scoffed. "Safer? Even you can't believe that."

"Safer," he confirmed. "Let me give you an example why. Those same stocks I was forced to sell because I was playing options, do you know how much they've increased from their high right before Black Monday's crash?"

I shook my head.

"60 percent. That's 60 percent in roughly three to four years, or about 15 to 20 percent a year . . . and that's after they fell on average to 50 percent to 60 percent their original value!"

"Umm." I was, of course, thinking about the profit someone could have made if they'd had the foresight and timing to invest when the stocks were at that 50 to 60 percent value rate (was that a possible *160 percent* profit they would have now made?) But I wasn't about to concede any points to my father.

"Uh-huh. So, they went up," I said. "15 to 20 percent a year?" Even that sounded pretty good. "But I still don't see what makes them safer. Stocks still seem much riskier to me."

"Well, how many houses can I afford to invest in with the money we have now? Only one — the one we live in — maybe one more if I really want to go out on a limb, right?"

"Yeah . . ."

"Whereas how many stocks could someone invest in even if they had, say, only five or ten thousand dollars?"

"I don't know."

"As many as they'd like, depending on how much or how little they'd want to invest, right?"

"Uh-huh."

"So what does this mean as far as risk is concerned?"

"It's being spread out," I nodded, still dubious, deciding I wasn't going to let him catch me up in his logic or excitement.

He sighed, sensing my resolve. "Son, I know that no matter what I say, the fact that we lost so much money can't be erased. But I've spent three years figuring out everything I did wrong."

"Dad, the whole world can't be mistaken. Despite everything you say, the consensus is that the stock market is extremely risky."

"It's considered being risky because everyone thinks of stocks in the short term, quick gains and losses. Have you ever heard of anyone trying to make a profit in real estate after just three to six months from the time of purchase?"

"No," I conceded.

"Well, that's exactly what most people try to do in the stock market. Just look at the advice from almost every stock analyst." He showed me a half-dozen of the latest reports from the country's largest investment firms. "Their recommendations are all for the three-to six-month period ahead. You see? Who would think of making a real estate investment for that amount of time?"

"Hmm."

"In my book, that is pretty risky. Yet that's how the majority of people invest." He let it sink in. "Now, I'm sure you're also aware that there is a quiet minority of people who have made fortunes in the stock market and have done so relatively safely. They've made their money by riding out the Black Mondays and by not putting themselves in a position where they have to withdraw during the bad times. *TIMING - IS - EVERYTHING!* What land investor sells his property for a loss when property values decline? None. They buy low and sell high, and do so usually over the course of years, even decades. The same idea works in the stock market, but for some reason very few people play that way."

I rubbed my chin. "Maybe it's because in the market stocks are always given an exact dollar value, so you always know how much you've gained or lost. In real estate you never know the exact value of your property until you've sold it."

"Exactly." My father smiled. "Because people see their losses in exact numbers during the bad times, they become more emotional and more likely to pull out. That, or they put themselves in positions — like I did with options — where they *have* to pull out. The key is to *not - do - any-thing* that upsets your *TIMING!*"

I let his concept sink in before asking: "But what about how people always say you can make fortunes in real estate because you have so much leverage? Darn, you can buy a $100,000 home for as little as 10 to 20 thousand dollars down. You can't do that in stocks, can you?"

"Well, you can, but not with as much leverage. If you have, for instance, $20,000 to invest, you can open up what's called a margin account, where your broker will lend you an additional $20,000. But remember, when you borrow money, whether in real estate or stocks, you're greatly increasing your risk. Why do you think there are so many home foreclosures?"

"Umm." I thought a minute. "You know Dad, everything you say makes perfect sense. But I don't see how you can want to risk what little you have left in the market."

"You're right, son. Any investment has its risks. And I'm actually glad you are so conservative because it will someday save you from making many of the mistakes I made. But with all the fail-safe measures I've developed, I've removed a tremendous amount of the risk. Besides, if I *don't* do something, we won't have any money left in another six or seven years anyway. And I don't want to leave your mother in that postion when I'm no longer around."

I sighed, not knowing how to respond.

"Dad, you don't ever have to worry," I finally said, wanting desperately to relieve him of such lack of security, but which in truth I had no way of relieving. "My practice is doing well now. I would never let you or Mom be wanting."

"That's kind of you, son, but you don't make enough for all of us, and you need to save your money for your own family some day." He shook his head. "Son, this is something I've got to do. And not just for our financial stake . . ."

He left the words hanging, not wanting to say the words I knew he was feeling; unspoken emotion that cut deeper into me than anything. The knowledge of how important it was to him — to all men — that he was *"a provider."*

Thank God he's healthy, I thought to myself. Most men wouldn't dream of making a comeback in their 70s.

As if to break the seriousness of the emotions he knew he had evoked, he brought the conversation back to a more material level. "Michael, there's one last thing I haven't mentioned which I'm doing now to make our investments even safer. It's something only the really elite winners do."

"What's that?"

"I'm investing in stocks that have already dropped to their lows — meaning a high percentage of investors have withdrawn from them."

All my fears soared again. "God, now that *really* sounds risky," I blurted. After all he had done to get me to see his point of view, to convince me what he was doing carried minimal risk, I couldn't believe he now could be so foolhardy. *What was he thinking?*

"Does it really sound risky?" he asked. "Just think about it. If these stocks are already at a low, if a Black Monday does come, they don't have far to fall. Just think what a fortune probably a few people made right after Black Monday, the few that *had the timing* to invest in stocks everyone else had pulled out of when the stocks fell to 50 percent to 60 percent of their value of a few days before. In the three years since, these people at least doubled — maybe even *tripled* — their money."

160 percent. Wasn't that what I had figured before? "I don't know, Dad . . ."

"Know what, son?" His tone was not at all challenging. It was as if he was wanting me to express my doubts now. As if to show me . . . to let me *see* they were invalid.

"I don't know. If there's not a Black Monday, why else would these stocks drop so drastically unless they're near bankruptcy?"

"Excellent question!" he beamed. "You are dead-on correct. Many companies that have fallen to their lows *are* near bankruptcy. But, there are a select few — if you know what to look for and know how to confirm they are indeed a strong company — that have fallen only because the far majority of investors in the stock market are thinking short-term and thus are over-reacting to some temporary bad news. It's almost like looking for stocks that are going through a transient Black Monday; a situation that has great significance to you as an investor but little to the company from a standpoint of its strength and long-term stability."

"I'm not following," I said impatiently, my ignorance of the market combining with all the worries I had for him losing everything rendering rational thought useless.

"Let me show you what I just invested in," he smiled. "The reasons I bought it exemplify everything I'm telling you about timing. Here, take a look at this."

He handed me a stock report from *Value Line* and said, "This is MCI, the long distance phone carrier."

"Yeah?"

"Look at the very last line on the graph. Tell me what has happened to the price of the stock."

"It looks like it's dropped pretty dramatically."

"Now look at the graph lines for 1987. What do you see?"

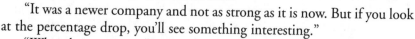

"It looks like it took a similar drop," I nodded.

"That was during Black Monday, right?"

"Uh-huh. But it was even lower then."

"It was a newer company and not as strong as it is now. But if you look at the percentage drop, you'll see something interesting."

"What do you mean?"

"Well, read me the high and the low stock price for 1987." He pointed to where these figures were listed.

"A high of 12 and a low of 5 when it dropped."

"That's about a 60 percent drop, right?"

"Uh-huh."

"So what's the high and the low this year, in 1990?" he pointed again.

"High of 44, low of 18."

"That's approximately a 60 percent fall also," he said, doing the mathematics for me. "Isn't it?"

"Yeah?"

"So in a sense, conditions with this single stock resemble another Black Monday, don't they?"

"Yeah," I nodded, "But how can you be so sure it's going to go up?"

"Well, if you're interested, another time I'll show you how all the financial figures indicate it's a very strong, growing company. But the main thing to understand now is why it's taken such a tremendous drop in just a few weeks' time."

He showed me an article in *The Wall Street Journal* that explained how MCI was taking a major one-time loss as a result of overhauling its computer systems. This expense was reflected in a dramatically lower quarterly earnings report, the health of which determines whether most investors buy or sell.

"It's a classic overreaction of the market, which is largely comprised of short-term investors," my father explained. "But look at the figures near the upper left-hand corner of the *Value Line* report where it shows MCI's three-to five-year projections."

"Where it says '1993-95 Projections'? "

"That's right. What percent increase are the analysts expecting?"

"It says a low of 165 percent and a high of 295 percent. Hmm."

"So what does it say would be the annual return using those figures?"

"28 percent to 41 percent a year."

"And that's over five years, not three or four in which case the yearly return would be somewhere between 45 to 100 percent a year, right?"

"Umm."

He continued on for quite some time, but I had already reached my saturation point. His logic seemed infallible, but it couldn't erase the sensation deep in my gut that he was going to lose every last penny he and my mother had left.

$\mathcal{T}$he risk my father was taking seemed inexplicable to me, for I wasn't born with a single strand of the gambling chromosome he seemed to me to have in such abundance. But what I would do soon after — or what I would give him permission to do for me, I should say — was perhaps even more inexplicable.

This act was steeped in my desire to no longer challenge my father. I wanted to support him and give him the respect and recognition he was due — not because he would follow through with his investment plans no matter what I thought, but simply because of the fierce pride and love I felt for him, knowing that after all he went through, he still had a fire left in him.

It was on this basis — to show my confidence in him, despite that deep inside I knew he was going to lose all my money, as well — that I asked him to invest my savings along with his.

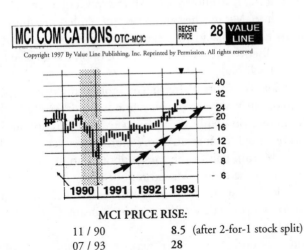

MCI PRICE RISE:

11 / 90	8.5 (after 2-for-1 stock split)
07 / 93	28

Chapter 11

On the surface, our small family fit the mold of perfect *Happy Days* characters — especially my father who, in the eyes of my friends, was always someone quiet, tranquil and wise. But his waters ran deep . . . as did the fault line of our relationship. Forty years my senior, he exerted constant force trying to manipulate my life to the way he saw most fit. With my own stubbornness of character, I could easily provoke a violence in his nature that lay carefully hidden just beneath his calm surface. Like some unearthly creature, it would strike with the speed of a serpent and the fury of a Great White. My mother and I became skilled mariners, able to tiptoe across my father's placid seas, gauging every ripple our footsteps would create lest we discover we were treading not upon the Galilee that day, but the waters of Loch Ness.

When I was 16, shortly after having gotten my driver's permit, I was turning into our driveway on my bicycle as my mother was backing her car out of the house. Suddenly there was a tremendous splintering noise. I watched in horrified fascination as my mother's fender proceeded to shear off the entire bottom half of the garage door jamb.

Once clear of the threshold, she got out of the car, face ashen, hand to mouth. She looked at the door, then turned to me. For a moment, we stood transfixed, eyes wide and breathless. "Oh my God," she said. "Your father will kill me."

I could only nod. My mother began to nod with me. And suddenly, within those movements a tiny bubble began to rise. It emanated from a trait I inherited from her, one which *did* fit the *Happy Days* caricature. And now, within our nodding horrification, it was surfacing, this wholesome sense of the absurd manifested as just the slightest hint of grins. They played off one another, expanded, and suddenly, uncontrollably, my mother and I were doubled up in helpless laughter.

I was laughing so hard my stomach hurt. My mother emitted such wails, a neighbor would have sworn she was being beaten. It felt, in fact, as if there was some unseen audience, as if Allen Funt would suddenly pop out from behind the bushes to tell us his *Candid Camera* crew had rigged the entire event. Splinters were everywhere, the side of the garage was ripped off and we were hysterical.

"Oh, gosh," my mom finally said, wiping away tears of laughter. "What are we going to do?"

I coughed, spitting up phlegm. "I don't know. I'll say I did it."

"What good will that do? He'll kill *you*."

"Oh. Right." And suddenly we were doubled up again. We calmed down quicker this time, the desperateness of the situation coming into focus. I said, "Well, let me take the blame anyway. I've got more of an excuse. I just learned to drive."

"No, honey, I can't let you do that. Besides, you know your father. He'll rant and rave, but he never does anything else."

She was right, of course. My father's eyes would bulge, the hair on his neck would bristle into a beastly auric mane and his stance would become frighteningly aggressive with every indication that he was out of control. But at the last moment there was something that always stopped him, some invisible force that would freeze his balled fists and enable him to stalk away without violence, the forest floor shaken only by his tremendous roar.

Despite our laughter, that roar was something we learned well not to elicit. It came from some deep hollow in him, some uncontrollable force. Though it established him as King of Beasts, it bespoke another story — one that was hidden even to him, and one which would surface only years later to reveal itself as a jagged stiletto point that was slowly hemorrhaging his heart.

Despite his placid exterior, despite that he had always been reasonably healthy beforehand, near him one could always feel something brewing beneath the surface, some great unexpressed emotion. If I analyzed why there was a part of me that hadn't been surprised when I first heard he was diagnosed with stomach cancer — as if on some deep level one could have seen it coming, as if it somehow made sense — it was because of this. Beyond my love for my father, I often felt my own stomach churning around him.

"Emotion that's not expressed on the outside may one day explode on the inside," was what a nurse told us years later. Whatever it was and wherever it came from, because of the way it sometimes erupted — particularly when things went slightly askew — that anger was something my mother and I would do anything to avoid.

"Listen," I suddenly brightened as I stood with her before the devastated garage door siding. "I've got an idea. How much time do we have before Dad gets home from work?"

My mother looked at her watch. "An hour and a half, maybe two." Desperation was in her eyes again. "My gosh, what can I do? I've got to leave. I'm already late for my dental appointment."

"Go," I said, hustling her into her car. "Just let me take care of it."

"Michael, what are you going to *do*?"

"Don't worry. By the time you get home, he'll never know anything happened."

She glanced at her watch, then at me, then at her watch. "Oh, gosh. I hope you know what you're doing!"

I waved her away. As she drove off, she lowered her window and yelled out, "If he gets home before I do, tell him *I* did it."

"Don't worry!" I yelled back.

Once she was out of sight, I walked to the destruction that lay at the side of the garage, suddenly not feeling nearly as confident as I had made myself appear. Examining the shattered construction, I saw that there were several large splinters of wood on the ground. The main board, however, was still intact on the jamb. A ray of hope returned.

Though cracked with the broken half angled 40 degrees, if I could flatten the board down . . . yes . . . very gingerly, without breaking that tenuous connection . . . Yes! . . . I could surely piece together everything else . . . There!

The next two hours I spent sawing, nailing, spackling, sandpapering and painting, all the while feeling the pressure of the clock upon me.

At dinner that evening, my mother couldn't keep from flashing me continual, surreptitious grins. I timed my winks back when my father would look down to fork his next mouthful.

What a glorious sensation it was, this triumph over potential disaster. And Dad never the wiser!

It wasn't until that weekend I discovered otherwise. After spending two hours clipping the hedges, I entered the garage, my shirt plastered with sweat and my arms freckled with leaf bits and pollen. To my shock I found my father standing there, tapping the nearly invisible line where I had repaired the sheared-off garage door jamb.

"You do good work," he intoned.

I was suddenly breathless. "Thanks."

I waited for him to speak, his silence almost worse than the dreaded fury. *How could he know?*

"I'm not talking about the hedges." His eyes were narrowed into slits.

"I know."

He tapped the wood again, then turned on the ball of his foot. "Nice job."

Dumbfounded, I watched him enter the house. Had he not turned to close the door behind him, I would have never seen it. But, to my further amazement, I saw he had just the tiniest hint of a smile.

It wasn't until years later that I had the guts to ask him. It turned out he just happened to have been passing our home in his car with an important real estate client at the moment my mother had sent the wall tumbling down. Unable to stop or interrupt his meeting, he had been forced to contain his anger.

*T*hat was one time we managed to get off easy. But it wasn't always like that. The fury of his adrenaline surges seemed to come from somewhere beyond his control. Confronting that fury was like facing a lion's charge. All that's left is to close your eyes and brace for the inevitable. But at the last possible moment, right as you're expecting impact, suddenly everything turns quiet. You open your eyes and there is the King of Beasts, inches from you, chest heaving, fangs bared. Then with one last roar, he's gone.

This was a scene played out many times throughout my late teens. And as perverse as it may seem, it contained within it the reason for my most profound respect — and love — for my father.

Pulling himself out of that state took a Herculean effort. Many other men who continually get to that point eventually finish the act, enacting the violence. I can't recall a single incident of my father ever laying a hand on me. I assume it was that powerful, powerful mind of his which would snatch him back from the throes of the terrible demon memory I now know was lurking inside him. As if at the last possible moment, just as the primitive, mammalian brain was going into overload, a synapse with the higher consciousness suddenly fired, revealing the holy spark of the true man.

Nowadays, when I listen to patients who have shunned their parents because of similar conflicts unrelated to sexual or physical abuse, a part of me relates, knowing that it's not right for parents to manipulate children in any way. But the deepest part of me feels a profound sorrow for these clients, for no parent is perfect and we all have our histories. Speaking to these patients, I have the feeling of a mutinous crew who has traveled across a great sea, sometimes wondrous, sometimes stormy. Once brought to the long-sought shores of their adulthood, instead of anchoring and caring for the faulty but reliable vessel that brought them the great distance, they cut its towline. At once the vessel is set adrift, but they are now left alone on some distant land which they thought was a great continent but one day discover is just a deserted island.

I'm grateful I never fell into this trap. I thank God that at the critical point in my life when I had been on the verge of doing something similar, I met . . . well . . . an *angel.*

I had just moved to the west coast Florida town of New Port Richey, where I began working with a doctor who would turn his practice over to me in six months. It should have been a time of unparalleled excitement for me — after years of schooling, I was finally entering the professional world with a wonderful opportunity to have my own practice. Instead, however, it was a season of great anguish.

I came to New Port Richey after a half-year of post-graduate studies in Iowa. While there, I met Patty. I was 21, and she was my first love. With Patty, the winter cornfields of the Midwest became a fertile dreamland where I would live out the verdant fantasies of every young man.

What I remember most were the innocent nights. How snow-covered meadows stretched into planes of suspended time. The sound of our midnight laughter pushing one another on ice-covered swings; how with each dizzying ascension the moon seemed to pull from the night sky and kiss us in turn on the cheek. How the shadowy footprints we'd leave crunched behind us would seem part of a past of not knowing each other that could never catch up to us again.

But catch up, it would: first, when I finished my studies and had to leave Iowa. Then, six months later, when instead of receiving the letter that would confirm our plans of Patty coming to Florida to visit me, I received the phone call informing me she had become engaged to another man.

Relating the story now, I smile at how easily those old sensations are rekindled and how time can heal even the most mortal wounds. But back then all I could feel was an exquisite, blinding pain. For weeks I walked around dazed, going through the motions with patients at my new clinic, coming home and aimlessly wandering the streets of Tarpon Springs.

This Gulf Coast town was a fantastic cultural icon, home to thousands of Greeks who maintained their ancestral integrity as if unaffected by the Disney World invasion of tourists and the look-alike retirement communities sprouting up all around. With a thriving sponge-diving industry, wondrous nightclubs featuring belly dancing beauties, and restaurants, such as Pappas, built aboard ancient Greek trawlers, Tarpon Springs stood alone amidst its sterile neighbors. Though I could have lived closer to my practice in New Port Richey, there was no choice regarding where I'd settle after my first visit to this quaint little live-in postcard.

But after Patty's phone call, the cobblestone streets became a maze through which I paraded my confusion. So much filled my mind, I saw only ghosts of the outer world, my eyes movie screens upon which I couldn't turn off the constant projection of my furrowed internal terrain. I was the youngest chiropractor in the nation at 21, about to take over my first practice, and already brimming with the secret knowledge that I wouldn't last in it more than a few years. I loved Tarpon Springs but I felt choked by the traffic of Highway 41, smothered by the lack of people my own age, and tormented by the realization of my greatest fear.

Though I had loved studying the body, I was never able to see myself entering into practice. I had the unfettered spirit of a poet and the heart of an artist, and the idea of working in the closed environment of an office eight to ten hours a day gave me palpitations. All along in school I imagined I would be saved by becoming established as a writer in Hollywood, called by Twentieth Century Fox at the last moment to say they were buying one of my movie or television scripts. For the short time I spent in Hollywood on my three-week summer breaks, I had been *so successful* in acquiring agents, managers, editors and actors who had fervently promoted me beyond all expectation. Unfortunately, in that very limited time, I hadn't sold any of my scripts. But fate had something else in store for me, as I can only see now: wonderment and fulfillment in the health field that I wouldn't begin to touch or understand until more than a decade later.

The only thing that salvaged me from my tortured thoughts about entering practice had been Patty. With her for the last year, the idea of becoming a doctor, having my own office, owning a nice car and a white picket-fenced home suddenly seemed the highest and noblest of goals. When my American Dream came crashing down, however, the illusion that I could ever be happy in practice came tumbling along with it.

*I*t was a Saturday when I met Kostos — the angel. And as these things go, I have only faint recollection of how I began talking to the ridiculous looking pot-bellied stranger, nevermind telling him my deepest troubles, which I had never confided to anyone.

I remember aimlessly walking in my depression around the cobblestone pathway of one of Tarpon Springs' many lakes, oblivious to the gentle breeze wafting off the January waters and unaware of the elements of fate gathering at that moment to provide me with lessons that would last a lifetime. I faintly remember a sudden swish by my ear, being lashed in the cheek by the half-brained backswing of a fisherman's pole and then untangling myself from nylon loops of 20-pound test line. And from that, perhaps I can piece together what happened next.

"Yo ho there, younga man." The gravelly-voiced stranger turned to me in slow arthritic motion. "You a gotta watch where a you're walking. You a got my line all tangled up a now!"

I ran my fingers across my cheek, checking for blood. Cursing out the man never occurred to me; somehow the sting of his rod had felt good, a cosmic force of sorts that jolted me back to full consciousness for the first time in weeks.

I stood and gawked at the riotous-looking stranger. Quite unconsciously, despite myself, a smile formed on my lips. He was dressed in a white bathing suit, oblivious to the 50-degree temperature. The skin on his arms and face was dark and wrinkled, accustomed, it seemed, to harsher forces in his lifetime. His belly hung far over the nearly lewd level of the top of his bathing suit, appearing like the ballooned pouch of a gluttonous pelican filled with more mullet and water than it could ever swallow.

If I couldn't tell the man was Greek by his accent, the Mediterranean face gave him away instantly. Stubbled with graying whiskers, the skin there and on his shoulders and belly was ornamented with dozens of moles that bespoke a lifetime of exposure to relentless sun. The exotic purple prescription sunglasses that hung cockeyed on a beak nose were totally incongruous with the otherwise earthy appearance of the man.

But most outstanding in the comic demeanor was his emblemed captain's cap. It at once finished the cartoon image, yet at the same time hinted at another soul. A soul of someone who had, at some point in his life, wielded power.

Though I remember the second part of my encounter with him as if it were seared in the folds of my cerebral cortex, I can't recall what happened in the interim. I must have just stood there, watching him fish for some time, as if it were the most natural thing in the world to be slapped in the face by a stranger's fishing rod. And I'm sure it seemed the most natural thing in the world when, after a while, this complete stranger said:

"Heya, you got some a problem, young man. C'mon, you can tell it to a Kostos. Nobody understands a problems like a Kostos. I was a millionaire three a times in my lifetime, lost it every time on a woman and a gambling. And I'm a now the poorest, a most wretched 70-year-old former casino owner you a ever met . . . and duh most god-damna happy one-a, too!" With a vicious cast of his line, which I managed this time to duck under with split-second timing, he proclaimed: "There ain't a god-damna ting you can't a tell to Kostos!"

And so I told him . . . about Patty, about my broken heart, about my life, about it all. Just as if it was the most ordinary thing in the world that this stranger should ask.

And just as naturally he said the words that lifted my burden as if it never had been there.

"Boyo, yousa 21 a years old, yousa duh most young a doctor I ever met. Yousa just startin' dis here wonderful life, gotta everyting goin' for ya wit looks anda everyting, and look at duh dammed a mess you gotta going on in datta head." Somehow, instead of insulting me, his words made me see, really made me see myself.

"Boyo," he continued, "You should a write datta younga lady duh biggest tank-you letta like nobody ever has. She's a done you duh biggest a favor anybody ever coulda. Boyo, at your age, wit what you a gotta goin' for ya, you a gotta be a crazy tinkin' about hookin' yourself up wit just one a girl. You shoulda be goin' out wit a *million* girls!"

Anyone else could have said the same thing. Others *had*. But somehow, coming from this man at this particular point in time, the words resonated with near biblical meaning.

But he wasn't done with me yet.

"Somethin' else is a botherin' you, boyo," he said. "You can tell a me. C'mon kid, nowa's duh time. Boy, get dis goddammed ting off your chest. Yousa 21 years a old and Kostos can see it's a been dere almost as long as you a have!"

How did he know? How had this man, this crusty old fisherman who never met me before in his life, read into the deepest, most holy part of me as if my heart were an Essene scroll and he a scribe knowing exactly where to unfurl it to my most shrouded secrets?

So I told him. I told him about wanting to be a writer. Told him about thinking that I'd never enter practice. Told him, most of all, about the extreme tension between me and my father, how I couldn't do anything without my father wanting me to do something else, how every conversation between us the last few years had turned into a shouting match.

"You wanna be a writer?" he asked, his eyes almost popping out. I meekly nodded. "Boy, what you a got to write about? You only 21 a years old. You a gonna spend your life a writin' about udder people's lives? Dats duh saddest ting I ever heard."

My eyes must have betrayed my hurt, for he affectionately grabbed the nape of my neck with surprisingly strong, calloused fingers, shaking me to my roots. "Listen, kid. I can see you gotta heart a gold. Datsa why all deese tings are a boddering you. You a got duh heart and duh soul of a writer, dat I can see fer sure-a, too." He puffed up his chest. "So does a Kostos for datta matter. Only ting, Kostos don't know how to write." The air was blown out with a wistful sigh. "But you . . ." His voice rose. "You got an oppertunity to have it all. To help people, to earn a good a livin', to make your parents proud — and at duh same a time, to have all duh hard and duh wonderful experiences of duh world so you got sometin' ta write about, instead of about someone else's life. You undastanda me?"

I nodded, something deep inside stirred.

"Now about your father." His voice suddenly became stern. "Boyo, let me tell you a sometin'. Your parents? *Dey'se - duh - mosta - important - ting - in - duh - world - to-a - you.* Do you *hear* me?"

I nodded, not daring to speak.

"I a got a son. Dat boy calls a me from Callyforni *three times a week!* You hear, *three!* He a don't, he knows I come out a dere and I box his a ears! And you know a why?" I shook my head. "Of course you don't, because nobody ever told ya. No kid a knows. But ya know what?"

I shook my head.

"Every damned a parent knows. Because I gave birth to datta boy, datsa why, and for no udder reason. I gave a datta boy life, and whaddever dere may be between us, I lova dat boy like a nuttin' else in dis world."

I felt weak.

"And you know whatta else, kid? Your daddy feels a duh same way 'bout you. Datsa why he's always tryin' a tell you what to do. Undastand?"

I nodded, not comprehending why I, who never shed a tear, suddenly was afraid to blink.

"Now, let me ask you a sometin' else. You a gotta brothers and a sisters?"

I shook my head no.

"Damn! Dat's even worse."

"Well, I had a sister," I said. "But she died of cancer five years ago."

Kostos slapped his forehead, almost falling over backwards into the lake. "*God-a-damn!* Datsa duh *worsest.* You can't get no *worse* dan dat!"

"I know," I whispered.

"Boyo, you gotta any idea how *important* you are to your parents? You even *begin* to know how much dey lova you, how much dey worry about a you?"

I shook my head.

"Dere ain't a second dat goes a by in any single day dere notta tinkin' about you. And you know sometin' else? Wit all dat hard time yousa cryin' about dat your daddy gives a you, dere's only one ting dat he really wants from a you."

He stared at me. I whispered: "What's that?"

"Respect. Dat's all. Respect. Just datta you listen to him. Listen to duh advice he's a gotta give from all his years of experience, goin' tru all dem hard a times. Just like I demand from my a son."

I was speechless. The fisherman gave me a few seconds to let it sink in. "You a understand datta, boy?"

"Yeah," I said, but suddenly feeling some of my old rebelliousness rising. "But what do I do when he wants me to do something I don't want to do?"

"You say, 'Yes, Dad, yes, sir, yes Dad.' "

"And?"

"And den, providin' dat you'va decided not to take summa his advice . . . you go out and do exactly as you was a wantin' to do."

The reply dumbfounded me. For a moment I was speechless.

"But won't he be mad at me for not following what he said?"

"He won't have duh chance if you don't tell him until after yousa gone ahead and done whatever it was you a wanted. Right?"

His psychology was boggling. It defied all logic . . . but somehow it made perfect sense.

"Listen," he put his coarse arm around my shoulders. "Your dad don't wanna you doin' exactly like he a says. No more den I wanna my son to. He won't have nuttin' to be a proud of datta way. Your dad just a wants you to *hear him out,* fer cryin' out loud."

Those words I did hear. And they spelled a changing point in my life. For sure, I'd have many more fights with my father over the years, but none so vehement or so prolonged that I would let them create any shadow of a doubt that I still loved and respected him. I realized that my father, like Kostos, was from the old school. There was nothing I could do to change him, change his need to advise me; yes, even to boss me. But Kostos was right — however tarnished, however obscure the message after passing through the filter of my father's pysche, everything he said came from his deepest core of love.

So even though we'd still fight — almost as if by biological principle — I'd always end up swallowing my pride and calling a few hours later to tell Dad I was sorry. To tell him I was taking into consideration what he said. To simply say "thank you."

And it wasn't until now, now that I no longer have someone to consult with, someone to . . . yes . . . even *fight with* to iron out my own thought processes, that I realize how much I did indeed value my father's opinion. For why else did he always get to me if I really wasn't seeking his approval? And how I now wish I had him here, if only to bounce an occasional idea off him.

After my encounter with the Greek, whenever I wanted to do something I knew would meet my father's harsh disapproval, I did as the fisherman advised — not tell my father until after the deed was done. This was how I sold that first practice after owning it less than a year and a half.

Though I was making more money than most 21-year-olds could imagine, I was completely unhappy — with the town, with the style of practice, with my entire life. And looking back, I thank God for my decisiveness, otherwise I would now be a very rich but totally miserable young man probably with a drinking or drug problem. Though it would take years, I would eventually find my niche in the health field, one that would bring me unimagined fulfillment — and incredible happiness to my father for seeing me so fulfilled.

But when I decided to put that first practice up for sale, I knew the fisherman was right. I couldn't tell Dad. So I waited until after it was sold. And to my amazement, when I did tell him, though he was stunned — *shocked* — he accepted it. What else could he do at that point?

Strangely, I never again ran into the fisherman, try as I might to later find him around the lake casting his murderous line. But like some odd, brown, oversized angel, he served a divine purpose in my life just when it was needed most.

I now realize that our times of greatest strife may often become our moments of greatest revelation. Such was what I learned with Kostos, what I learned from what happened with my father after Black Monday and, on a more material level, what I learned after watching what happened with the stocks, such as MCI, that my father picked when they, too, were at their lows.

And since that day of meeting the crusty old fisherman, there always has been a prayer of thanks in my heart that he was sent my way.

And for my father who, though less than perfect, nevertheless perfectly loved me.

70

| NEC CORP. (ADR) OTC-NIPNY | RECENT PRICE | 26 | VALUE LINE |

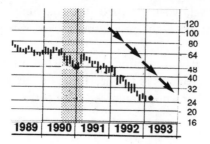

Chapter 12

PATIENCE
(Insight 3)

You should decide to make a buy only after researching your stock thoroughly in the public library with The Wall Street Journal, Value Line, Analyst Watch, Security Research Company *graphs,* Standard & Poors Stock Guide, S&P Reports, *etc. Then buy only 1/2 to 1/3 the maximum quantity you'd like to own. If the stock drops another 10 or 20 percent, buy additional shares. If your first order turns out to be not at or near the low sought, you can average down by this method thereby assuring you that your purchases bring you out closer to the actual low. Remember, if you liked it at, say, $40 per share, you are certain to like it better at $36!*

"Research, research, research," Dad exhorted me. *"Timing, timing, timing.* And *patience, patience, patience.* Never *ever* buy a stock on a hot tip or a whim. This is the way many individual investors buy . . . and the way they get burned."

Though this lesson about patience concerned stocks, it was a lesson he had reiterated to me many times previously regarding business. Years earlier, when I was still in my 20s, after I returned from overseas ready to resume practice in the U.S., my father had told me over and over again, *"An inch is a cinch, a mile takes a while."* Despite that my initial reaction to any of his preachings often made me act like I hadn't heard what he said, *an inch is a cinch* became my watchword during the initial difficult year when I opened my downtown Atlanta practice. And when I finally acquiesced to let Dad teach me about the stock market years after that, it wasn't surprising that one of his first lessons was about patience.

"Do you know how long I followed DSC Communications before buying it?" he asked me.

"How long?" I queried.

"Nine months." He handed me a fistful of newspaper clippings from *The Wall Street Journal.* "Here's everything I read about it during that time which assured me I was getting into something worthwhile." He pulled out the *Value Line* report from when he first became interested in the stock.

"What date does that have on it?"

"October 19, 1990," I read.

"And what price was the stock at on that date?"

"Seven."

"Right; it fell from a high of 17 the previous year. Now here is our buy sheet from Fidelity Brokerage. What date did we purchase it on?"

"July 14, 1991."

"For what price?"

"4.5."

"So I first saw it at about 7 when I began to *think* it might be an excellent buy, it having fallen from 17. But I didn't get the stock until nine months later when, after great research, I *knew* that it *was* an excellent buy . . . and, to boot, it had fallen an additional 30 percent to 4.5." He looked me in the eye. "So what does that tell you?"

"It pays to be patient."

"Exactly. Especially when you consider that I just sold DSC when it hit 18, which means I quadrupled our initial investment. If I had bought the stock when it was at 7, I would have made only 2.5 times our investment — not bad, but not nearly as good or as safe, because I didn't know the stock so well then, which is my main point."

I looked past my father at two blue jays playing a game of tag above our hedges. It was a hard time to try to absorb all this information about stocks. I was so busy getting my new practice under way, I had to force myself to concentrate on learning something so far outside my field of interest like the stock market. Especially now, having sold my downtown practice several years earlier to get away from the more structurally oriented manipulation-type cases. Suddenly in this new practice, I was able to apply everything I had begun studying when I was in practice overseas. Clinical kinesiology, homeopathy, herbology and acupuncture consumed my thoughts as I tried to add more and more to my knowledge base to deal with the types of serious illnesses I was beginning to see. Finally, more than a decade since graduating from chiropractic school, after leaving three practices because of dissatisfaction and boredom, I was qualified to do work that absolutely captivated me.

I was, nevertheless, surprised how easily the concept of doubling, tripling, *quadrupling* a stock investment could capture my attention. But beyond this, beyond my distaste for dealing with so many numbers and so much *business,* something else was running through my mind as my father talked. It was a persistent thought that continued to disturb even the excitement my father managed to create.

"Now look at this stock, son," he was telling me. "NEC Corporation. Big Japanese enterprise. Recognize it?"

"Yeah, umm . . . I think so."

"They make semiconductors for computers. One of the largest producers in the world . . ."

I was only half hearing him. My mind kept going back to another conversation. A conversation with his doctor. A secret conversation.

"Their stock has been sliding for a number of years now," Dad was saying. "Along with all the Japanese stocks. It's at about 45 now, but it was up above 90 just a few years ago. I suspect it's got a ways more to fall . . ."

Fall? Was that what he was saying? That's what it felt like, pretending at this normal conversation. *Falling . . .*

"In another few months, I'm almost willing to bet you NEC will hit below 30. And I'm going to buy some of it then, because the Japanese economy will sooner or later turn around."

I was falling. He was falling. Me, for my pretended interest in what he was talking about; for my occupation during the week with my practice when I barely had time to even think about Dad's illness and what the doctor had told me. And my father; he, for so easily blocking out what was going on inside him. Cancer. *Falling.*

"What if NEC falls lower than you suspect?" I heard myself ask him. "Or what if it takes the Japanese economy longer to turn around than you suspect?"

"Excellent point!" my father smiled, so pleased with me. "When it hits 30, I'll invest perhaps one-third what I really want to invest. If it goes down another 10 to 20 percent, I'll invest another third, and so on. Truth is, you never know when a stock hits bottom. I was just lucky with DSC. But it was *well-informed* luck. Don't forget that. With NEC, my research leads me to believe that in a few months it and the Japanese economy will be near bottom. In any case, it's a giant company. It most certainly will rebound sooner or later."

Does everything rebound? I wanted to ask. *Can you insure that? Do you know that with certainty?*

Dammit, I suddenly said to myself. *Stop it! Just listen to him. Don't think about it. Forget what the doctor said . . .*

"Are you listening to me, son?"

I jerked. "Yeah, Dad. Sure. Sounds like you may be onto another winner."

He was looking at me closely, sensing my distractedness but unable to make anything of it. He decided to let it go. "Just remember. Research, timing and patience. Those are the keys. But the main watchword for you, son, is *patience.* Don't ever forget that."

"Patience," I nodded. Patience. *I've got to have more. Like him.*

Despite his urgency to secure a future for my mom, despite that he *knew* this would take time; despite that on some level he must have felt the clock ticking against him . . . so much faster than he could possibly know . . . how patient he indeed was!

"I will remember that, Dad," I said.

And to myself I vowed, *I will.*

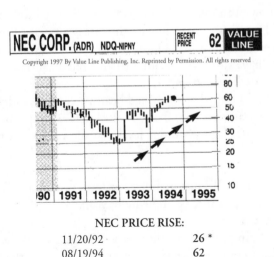

| NEC CORP. (ADR) NDQ-NIPNY | RECENT PRICE | 62 | VALUE LINE |

NEC PRICE RISE:

11/20/92	26 *
08/19/94	62

* The discussion in this chapter took place in 1990 before NEC hit 26, when it was still priced in the 40s.

Chapter 13

"Is he in denial, Mikey?" my Vietnamese friend asked, our plates only half touched after over two hours in the southern barbecue restaurant.

"I don't know, Antoine," I shook my head. "He's so hard to figure out. On one hand he seems to have looked the disease straight in the eye and faced it down with his decision. On the other hand, now having made the decision not to have surgery, he hardly lets me talk to him about it."

"Have you tried?" my friend asked.

"It's difficult." I poked at the baked beans, feeling an indefinable hollowness. "All he wants to talk about is stocks. He's desperate for me to learn what he knows. I guess on one level that shows he's not in complete denial."

"How's that, Mikey?"

"He keeps saying, 'If I just had three or four more years, I'd have your mom sitting pretty. Just three or four more years . . .' "

"What does that mean?"

"Well, he's doing so well in the stock market, I think he's probably tripled their money in just a few years. The problem is that they started off with so little money. But the way he's going, in another three or four years he and my mother will never have to worry about depending on their paltry Social Security checks to live on." I was unconscious of my fork slipping from my fingers. "It's just not fair, Antoine."

My friend eyed me with concern. "What's not?"

"After a lifetime of work, of paying so much money to the government, at this point in his life my father shouldn't have to worry about how they're going to survive."

Antoine shook his head, more to himself than to me. He then touched my arm, looked me gently in the eye. "Is it just that, Mikey?"

This was getting difficult. I shook my head, sighed. "What's unfair is that after such a hard lifetime, my father should come up with this whole system now . . . right at the end . . . right before he may have a chance to see himself enjoy the fruits of all his work, his genius . . ." My vocal cords felt constricted. "That at this point, he should still have so much to worry about. And that I . . ."

"Yes?"

I tried to swallow the lump in my throat. "That I, of all people, being so disinterested in anything related to finances, to stocks — so turned off by it — that I should be the one who will eventually profit most from his work."

My friend's hand stayed on my forearm, allowed me to experience my guilt. He then persisted. "But Mikey . . . you still haven't said why you don't think he's entirely in denial?"

In his compassionate but spiritually tenacious way, Antoine kept bringing me . . . *closer.* Dangerously closer. I shifted uncomfortably. "Because that's why he's so desperate for me to learn his system . . . so I can take over . . . finish securing my mom's future. Why else does he keep saying, 'If I just had three or four more years . . .'?"

My former classmate was silent, his feelings mirroring my own only as someone very close to you can do. He finally looked me in the eye. "Mikey, why does he keep saying that?" He paused. "And why did you say *'right at the end'* before? That it was unfair your daddy should come up with this whole system *'right at the end'*?"

I shook my head, words not coming.

"I thought you said your daddy's still playing golf, still so healthy looking?" My friend squeezed my arm. "You said you had a private conversation with your father's doctor. *What did he tell you?*"

There it was. With unerring instinct, my friend had honed in, had arrived at the source of my greatest anguish, the arrow that pierced the heart.

"What did he tell you?" Antoine repeated when I didn't answer. "Mikey, what are you keeping locked inside?"

I couldn't look him in the eye, just shook my head, eyes cast down, afraid to blink. "I don't know if I've done the right thing, Antoine," I finally whispered, the table, my plate, a blur.

"I don't know if I've made a big mistake."

Chapter 14

he doctor's call had come when I returned to Florida two weeks after my father's announcement not to have the surgery. I had made a flight reservation for this return as soon as I had arrived back in Atlanta. Despite the financial pressure I was under starting my new practice, I totally ignored this consideration, knowing my parents needed all the support I could give them.

In the weeks in Atlanta before returning to Florida, amidst my 14-hour work days, I attempted to collect my haywire thoughts regarding my father's illness and his decision. Being in the health field was helpful in the process. Despite the upheaval of emotions that occur when cancer strikes a loved one, when you deal with illness as a career, there is at least the part of yourself to turn to that is accustomed to being the objective insider. But even that takes you only so far.

It was usually late at night, as I lay in bed, when all the distractions of the day would disappear, that that which never left the back of my mind throughout the exigencies of the day would come unbidden to my thoughts.

Did he make the right decision not to have surgery? Is he in denial? I would lie there thinking. *Does he have the emotional strength to follow through with his decision? How strong a grip does the cancer already have on him . . . ?*

And just as prominent were thoughts of my mother: *How is she react-*

ing? How can she sleep at night knowing the clock may be ticking for the man she is lying next to? What is it like facing the possible loss of a partner of 40 years? Does she have the strength? And: *Does she have the strength to be a caregiver for the second time in her life?*

Will, God, she have to be?

Therein lay a deep trauma for me . . . a trauma, but at the same time another advantage I had in collecting myself; chilling and warming at the same time.

Having been through so many years of the same illness with my sister when I was younger, forgotten reflexes were already awakening, helping me cope, objectify, figure out what I needed to do to continue with my life despite the fact that a large portion of my time . . . my soul . . . was now required to serve the needs of my loved ones.

I had weathered my sister's death well, with minimal scars, with, in fact, a heightened spirituality. This was her gift to me. How much easier that experience made it for me to deal with the rest of life's problems, how no deep stresses seemed to stick to me, how all the other traumas of life paled compared to what I had seen my sister go through, my parents endure, myself face, just 17 years earlier.

But despite the strength the experience with my sister's illness and death had given me, I realized it also had changed me forever . . . and in one ominous way. Beyond my love of children, I have, as mentioned, struggled with the idea of having any of my own.

And therein lies my issue, the one major one I have yet to this day to resolve, to overcome. The issue of *fear* . . . *fear* of having to go through the same experience again . . . the pain, the heartrending helplessness of being a caregiver, of having your life turned upside down as you watch someone you love slowly die.

It is a fear we all have, but this fear was greater in me than in most people. I knew what it meant, had spent my childhood experiencing it, and knew that I never wanted to go through it again.

And now, not with children of my own, but with my father, that one great fear was being realized.

*W*hen the doctor's call came, Dad was outside inspecting my latest hedge-clipping work. I had just finished taking a shower, readying for dinner, when my mother came running into the room. "Michael, it's your father's oncologist!" She was breathless, her eyes those of a startled doe. "He wants to speak to you. *Alone.*"

"To me?" I creased my brow.

"That's what he said. He was very urgent. Quickly! Pick up the phone."

My pulse began to race, some warning signal triggered inside. Purely on instinct I waved my mother away, saying: "All right, let me speak to him. I'll join you and Dad for dinner as soon as I'm done."

My mother gave me a frightened look. I nodded to her, then proceeded to the bedroom, closing the door behind me.

I went to pick up the receiver, but my hand suddenly froze. I hadn't the slightest idea what the doctor wanted to talk to me about, but I abruptly experienced a . . . premonition? No, perhaps an *awareness?* Or some *feeling* . . . something sensory, rather than intellectual. Another *deja vu?* Try as I might, I couldn't identify the sensation.

I finally picked up the receiver. "Hello?"

"Dr. Norwood, this is Dr. Roberts. I understand you're in the health field." The voice was clipped, down to business, Northern.

"Yes?"

"Of course you know about your father's diagnosis with cancer. Do you know the specific diagnosis, though?"

"No," I replied. "Not yet." In fact, I had asked my parents to get me the full medical report but it hadn't arrived yet. But I didn't say this, feeling somewhat lightheaded, in a strange space as I talked to the specialist, but something so familiar about this space. My chest ached with tension but my voice was calm, as if one part of me was somehow watching the other part talk.

"Let me fill you in then," the doctor said. "I think it's important that you know the full picture. Especially considering your father's decision." On another occasion I would have enjoyed the doctor's New York accent, the same intonations resonant in a distant part of me from growing up in that region, like chords of some childhood song.

But now I found no comfort in the voice. Somehow it grated me. Maybe it was how rushed he sounded, maybe it was the underlying tension in his voice covered up by the mathematical coldness — as if by being very scientific, human emotion could be surgically excised.

"Go ahead," I said, my own voice no longer sounding even, my emotions not as unfathomable as his.

"Your father has adenocarcinoma of the lesser curvature of the stomach," he pronounced as if addressing a pathology class, not the son of the man he was referring to. "Adenocarcinoma, or cytologically malignant gastric glands."

My mind reeled. Somehow, putting a specific name to the cancer gave it frightening proportions. During the silence in which he left me hanging, I tried to gather my scrambled faculties. I knew the classification of the cancer, could almost visualize its entry in *Boyd's Pathology*. I forced myself to slow my thinking, tried to control my reaction, waited to hear what the doctor had to say.

"Yes?" I entreated.

"This type and this location of adenocarcinoma is highly malignant. Your father has to get the surgery." Then just before he said his next words, it came to me; where that sense of *deja vu* I was experiencing was coming from.

It was the same sense that I had felt when my mother initally told me that my father had cancer, when I found out Avishy, my Israeli friend, had been killed; when I was informed that Chap, my chiropractor/writer friend, had died of a sudden heart attack. That same sense of time slowing down, of other-worldliness . . . of somehow already having known.

And then the pronouncement for which I had no warning:

"Without the surgery, your father has no more than 6 to 12 weeks left to live."

A physical paralysis enveloped me. As long as there had been just the ethereal sense of what the doctor was going to say, I had managed to maintain the detached state. But the actual pronouncement — the precise *time* verdict — brought me crashing down, like a daydream that's ended by a head-on with a locomotive.

I was too stunned to reply. It was too much to take in, as if some internal circuit board had been overloaded, wires snapping, chips melting.

The original pronouncement of cancer had been one thing. With my father looking and acting so healthy, death — though suddenly brought frighteningly into consciousness — still was hard to relate to the vibrant image.

However, being told Dad had a maximum of 12 weeks — *less than 90 days* — just wouldn't register. *How could it be? How could it be?*

Did the doctor know who he was talking about? The former pilot, the former boxing instructor, the impregnable image that still existed in the memory of a young boy's mind; the often iron-hard unyielding but loving man who that young boy — now a grown man — still loved? Did the doctor have any idea that this was who he was talking about?

But the numbers — *6 to 12 weeks* — created a reality that allowed for no other possibility; they didn't cause the long-held image of indestructibility to fall apart, but rather to atomize. There was no matching the two, nothing to bridge the breathing image of life with that of certain impending death.

When some semblance of reality started coming back to me, I heard myself whisper, "Does my father have any knowledge of . . ." I couldn't say the numbers. ". . . of the time span?"

For the first time I heard the slightest hesitation in the oncologist's voice, the first sign of his own difficulty coping in his trying specialty. "I don't think so. I . . . don't think I told him." He quickly added, "I didn't think he was going to refuse the surgery."

But just the small hint of humanity was enough for me to regain a foothold; as if the doctor's science was dangerous sliding pebbles leading me to a cliff, his humanness the one solid rock that kept me from tumbling over.

"There's no chance of a spontaneous remission?" I reached.

"No such thing," the doctor blandly stated, back to the cold-science self again.

"But he's not exhibiting a single symptom," I managed to argue.

"Are you going to wait until he does?" He paused, expertly gauging the effect of his words on me. "Listen, if he doesn't have the surgery, your father is going to *die*. And he's going to die in a lot of *pain*. More pain than you can imagine. Stomach cancer is one of the most painful forms of cancer there is."

I collected myself, waiting for the eye of my hurricane of emotions to allow me to regain footing again. My years in the holistic field, working with thousands of patients with numerous conditions that had been pronounced "incurable," reading similar accounts in books such as *Space, Time & Medicine* by Larry Dossey, M.D., and *Quantum Healing* by Deepak Chopra, M.D., abetted me in finding safe harbor.

"I would think he'd at least be exhibiting *something*," I managed to at last reply. "Did you know he's out playing golf every day?"

There was a stony silence, the winds and tidal surges of my internal tempest momentarily abated by the doctor's inability to answer. I waited, unsure, finally saying, "There's got to be some people who beat this thing. I'm sure there's not a 100 percent fatality rate. Every disease has its documented cases of spontaneous remissions."

"Never heard of such a thing," was the oncologist's final reply, leaving me to pick through the devastation of my emotions.

*F*or some time — it must have been several minutes — I just stood there, the uncradled phone receiver held limp in my hand. If Bell South's recorded message of *"If you would like to make a call, please hang up and dial again . . ."* hadn't started, I don't know how long I would have remained like that.

I unconsciously placed the receiver back on its cradle, thought finally coming.

For some reason my father hadn't been told the length of this "sentence"; had received the shock of the cancer verdict but had not been informed he was on "death row." I silently thanked God for that. Whatever angel acted as guardian of mind/body health had been present. The verdict of cancer had been enough then to absorb.

But now I faced the prospect of having to be the one to tell him. In a moment, I had to return to the family room where my parents were waiting for me to begin dinner. My mother would have told my father I was talking to his doctor. They would ask me what he said.

Damn! If I only had more time . . .

Think! I forced myself. *Think!* But what came was not thought but emotion. And emotion that went deep . . . so deep. Emotion which touched the most exquisitely sensitive nerves.

During the six years of my sister's illness, my parents had never told me her illness was fatal until several months before she died. And they never told my sister at all. Or so I thought. Until the surfacing in a yet-to-be future day of my father's long-buried memory of most unfathomable pain . . .

However, for just about the entire length of those difficult years, I participated in giving my sister all the hope and joy we believed a 12-, and finally 18-year-old girl should have. It wasn't until after her death that we found Elizabeth Kübler-Ross's landmark books on the care of the dying, which confirmed for us everything we had feared most in our elaborate charade: that my sister knew all along. That the dying always do. That the coming of death by terminal illness is as if scripted in our cells. That there's no denying it to the patient. And that — however slowly death comes — we all receive the subtle but clear Morse Code as if by preappointment between us and our creator.

But most of all, that long-term denial — usually more by the family than the patient — creates more subconscious stress than being open and allowing the person to come to terms with this calling of the soul. Dr. Kübler-Ross delineates these stages as Denial, Anger, Bargaining with

God, Depression and finally, Acceptance — all of which a patient should be allowed to pass through to finally reach peace. My family's experience with my sister told us that this truly would have been the best way, if we had just been able to surmount our own fears.

So where was my hesitation coming from?

Think, I commanded myself again. *Think!*

And then I knew. My father bore no signs of a dying man. And I knew all the signals, having witnessed without realizing what dying looks like for six years with my sister.

Now ... according to the doctor ... with my father ... 6 to 12 weeks? Did this seem correct? Something I could believe?

And then I understood my hesitation. It wasn't. It wasn't something I could believe. And more importantly — it wasn't something I thought my father would believe.

Whatever statistics the doctor was quoting — whatever scholastic, empirical or experiential data he was relying upon — it didn't match my own perception.

But was I right to assume this would be my father's perception? *Was I, myself, in denial?* The question would haunt me over the next days, the next weeks, the next months. But until there was some sign, some indication that I . . . that he . . . was denying a *reality,* how could I add this to the burden he was already carrying?

He already knows he has cancer, I thought. He knows it's fatal and he's steeled with decision about not having the operation. *Would telling him this 45- to 90- day judgment change his mind?*

This was the other question that would haunt me. Looking deep, so deep into my father's pscyhe, examining the way he had already reacted, all I could hear was what he had repeated over and over:

"I never thought I would live through World War II. I've already been given 50 more years than I ever bargained for."

And: *"I'll trade a few good years for twice as many bad ones . . ."*

But *years?* I thought. What if he knew it was just *months?* Maybe . . . *weeks?*

The thought gave me chills. But suddenly it was very clear to me. *Very* clear.

No, I decided. It wouldn't make a difference to him. It wouldn't change his mind about the surgery. And it wouldn't make him believe death was any closer than as far away as it already appeared to him.

But it *would* upset him, *would* possibly turn off his immune capability and *would* distract him from the path he's chosen — of continuing to live his life normally without buckling under the shadow of C A N C E R.

And suddenly my thoughts cleared. *No, I'm not going to tell him,* I decided. Shaking my head, I sighed, wiping the mistiness from my eyes. *I'm not.*

*W*hen I returned to the kitchen, despite trying to make her voice sound even, my mother couldn't hide her anxiety. "What did the doctor want to talk to you about, honey?" she asked. My father just served himself salad, not missing a beat.

"He wanted to inform me of the specific diagnosis."

I watched my father fork up a tomato slice that had fallen on the table, looking only mildly interested in what I was relating. He poured himself salad dressing as I continued: "The doctor repeated that he wants you to have the surgery, Dad." I looked at him intently, trying to catch his eye, trying to gauge him. "He said not having it would be . . ." Suddenly I couldn't think straight, the indecision I thought I had surmounted rising again. ". . . would be . . . life threatening."

Dad screwed the top back on the bottle, shook his head. "I've already told you my decision, son. Nothing's going to change that." He passed the dressing to me. "Let's eat."

God's truth, I was ready to tell him at that moment, tell him it all; wanted to relieve myself of the responsibility of withholding from him "the verdict," the few months the doctor said was all he had left without the operation — the tremendous burden I knew I would carry the rest of my life if the doctor's prognosis turned true . . .

But the words just wouldn't come. Maybe it was the fact that he seemed so disinterested, his head lowered over his plate forking salad into his mouth, as if he had already dismissed what I had told him. Maybe it was some higher power that kept me from saying anything more, or the power of the decision I had reached while in the other room. Or maybe it simply was my own fear. But when I opened my mouth, nothing came out, as if I were some underwater guppy breathing bubbles.

But his bubble was not the one I was meant to burst that night.

*T*he bubble I did burst was my mother's, as fragile as it already was. And to this day I still feel the terrible weight of telling her all I had not told my father … mainly all that the doctor had told me. Was this my second mistake of that same night, even if opposite in nature of the possible mistake I made by not telling my father? She was fearful enough of all that was happening without this additional information, which only served to tighten the stranglehold that the news of C A N C E R already had on her.

But mothers can read minds, and when she approached me after dinner, I knew there was no hiding from her. She had answered the phone when the doctor called, knew he wouldn't want to be speaking to me for just any reason. So I told her about the 6 to 12 weeks, saw whatever light left in her over the whole situation visibly flicker dead, felt a hollowness carve my insides out.

"He's wrong," I snarled, feeling the ghost of my father's wounded animal strike out at the unseen foe who at once had mortally wounded him and who now was leaving his pride enfeebled as well. "The doctor's just quoting statistics, computerized *numbers*. They don't bear any resemblance to the live man!"

My mother had visibly shrunk. "Michael, what do we do?"

I reached out and firmly grasped her shoulder, trying to transmit my rebellion to her, my *force de resistance;* anything to get her from collapsing under the weight I now so dearly regretted placing on her.

"Dad's had stomach problems forever," I spit, my jaw painfully tight. "This disease didn't develop overnight. It's been a slow process of years. Maybe even *decades*. Just because they happen to finally look in his stomach and find cancer now doesn't give them any gauge on how long it's already been there, or how much longer he has." My anger came through. "And giving him an opinion of 6 to 12 weeks certainly won't help him stay alive any longer."

She acquiesced, no fight left in her. I could only look helplessly upon her, my chest heaving, silently shaking my head.

The disease had already begun taking its victims.

Chapter 15

"Why, you boys have hardly touched yo' food!" the young waitress said, prancing up to me and my Vietnamese friend in the Southern-style restaurant. She put her wrists backward on her waist in good-natured indignation. "Y'all been here gettin' on three hours already and you haven't tried not even *one* of those deelicious hush puppies! Now either somethin's wrong with our cookin' or somethin's wrong with yo' appetites, and I know nothin's wrong with our cookin'!"

Gifts from God come in strange packages, and the smile this for-a-moment angel brought forth from our solemnity was a tremendous help just then, right as I finished telling my friend all that had transpired in the last weeks concerning my father.

"Now I'm going to give ya'll just another little while to do justice to those plates of yours, and if things are no different, why, you're going to force me to do somethin' I'm going to dearly regret."

Antoine raised his eyebrow in charmed alarm. "What's that?"

"Why, not charge you, of course!" And with that potent threat in the air, she spun on her heels and disappeared into the kitchen.

I picked up a piece of cold barbecue chicken and nodded to Antoine. "Looks like we better have some of this food." We smiled at each other and, despite our compromised appetites, began nibbling on the barbecue. We were silent for several minutes, our smiles slowly fading, both of us deep in thought. Then Antoine whispered, "How long is it now, Mikey?

Since you spoke to the doctor?"

I put my fork down. "Three weeks, Antoine."

His voice was hesitant. "Do you see any . . . signs?"

I had to smile, even though the irony saddened me. "Antoine, my father's still out playing golf every day." I shook my head. "I don't know what to think."

My friend gently looked me in the eye. "Mikey, can I tell you what I think?"

I nodded, eyes still cast down.

"I think you made the right decision."

I looked up, feeling the slightest light. Unbelieving.

"From what you've told me," my friend continued, "I think if you told him about the 6 to 12 weeks, it wouldn't have changed his mind about the surgery. But it would have depressed him, depressed his whole immune system. It might have even made the prognosis more of a likelihood."

"You think so?" I asked, incredulous that my friend agreed with me, unsure at first if he was saying it just to placate me.

"It may have proven to be a self-fulfilling prophecy, Mikey." His soft Vietnamese/French accented words conveyed all the wisdom and sincerity I had always known in him, a soul that knew no guile. "Just leave it as it is," he concluded quietly.

For several seconds I was speechless, just sat there blinking. I felt such gratitude, such thankfulness that he could so fluently mirror my own thoughts.

"But, Antoine," I finally managed, my voice turned to a whisper. "What if the doctor's *right*? What if his prognosis turns *true*?"

"It's out of your hands, Mikey."

"Antoine, what if it would have changed my father's mind? What if I'm responsible for him dy . . ."

My friend stopped me with his look. He stared me gently in the eye. "Mikey, it's time to turn it over to God."

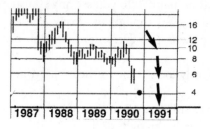

Chapter 16

SURRENDER

(Insight 4)

"*D*amn, damn, damn, damn, *damn!*" My father hit his fist on the table.

"What's wrong?" I sucked in my breath, trying to control my alarm.

He shook his head. "That's what I say every time I see what's happened to the price of this stock. Here, look." He handed me a *Value Line* report as I let out a hidden sigh of relief.

"Advanced Micro Devices," I read. "Wow, it looks like their stock has really jumped the last few months."

"Jumped?" my father squinted. "*Skyrocketed,* you mean. It was at a low of 4 right at the beginning of the year and now look where it's at. *Fifteen!* Almost a fourfold increase in five months' time!"

I whistled. "That *is* something. *Huh!* But what about it gets you so upset, Dad?"

"What about it gets me so *upset?* Because in December, I put an order in to my broker to buy it when it hit 4 1/4. It had been hovering just above there for about a month. *That's* why."

"You mean you didn't get it?"

He grimaced, shaking his head.

"But . . . *why not?*" I was appalled, suddenly feeling his loss of the missed opportunity. "I thought you said it went to a low of 4 at the beginning of the year?"

"It did. But a day before the stock dropped to 4, I cancelled the order."

My jaw dropped. "Why in the world did you do *that?*"

My father's smile was ironic. "Because hindsight, son, is always perfect, whereas foresight is often flawed." He shook his head with black-humored regret. "I had put the order in December 20. On January 3 it became obvious the Allied Forces were about to invade Kuwait. That was right at the end of President Bush's ultimatum to Saadam Hussein. I thought the stock market was going to take a dive as the reality and depression of the Gulf War set in. I figured I'd wait just a few more weeks and get the stock even lower."

"What happened?" I asked.

"The stock market soared! We won the war in seven days, and by the end of the month, Advanced Micro Devices had almost *doubled.*"

"Damn!" I said, hitting my fist on the table, and when I looked into my father's suddenly amused eyes, I began to laugh, realizing my reaction was the same as his.

"The lesson, son, is that no one knows it all. There are no certainties. You do all the research you can, then you take your best shot." He laughed at himself. "Just don't look back . . . but if you do, don't be too hard on yourself. No one has all the answers. Learn to *surrender.*" He suddenly was very serious. "No one can play God at this game."

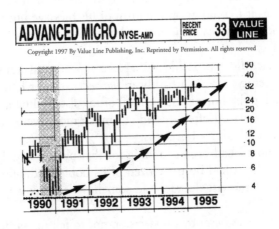

AMD PRICE RISE:

11/02/90	4
04/28/95	33

Chapter 17

*I*t was a question I asked myself over and over during that time: *Had I played God with my father's life?* Try as I might, I couldn't *surrender*. I couldn't do as Antoine had likewise counseled.

It's out of your hands, Mikey, he had said. *Turn it over to God.*

Yet the words did provide me comfort, did resonate in some deep part of me. It was as if I could grasp the form of his message but not the content; like looking at a beautiful postcard but not being able to experience the actual place.

Yet that place did exist inside me; a place of peace and comfort, of spirituality and serenity; a place I had been blessed to find when I was just a boy, experiencing the horror and turmoil of my sister's illness and eventual death. It was a place I often missed . . . much more even than the magical places where I had lived overseas.

For years now I had been searching for that place, knew I had grown up in it, knew that I had been a citizen of its noble land, and knew also, in the process of the last decade, had somehow lost my way back to it. Back home.

As much as I was beset by my decision not to tell my father the prognosis in the weeks that followed, I was equally tormented by the knowledge that I *was* being tormented; that I *couldn't* "turn it over to God"; that in the years since I had left Sunrise Key to go to college, in the time I had grown from a boy to a man, I had discovered many things, among them

. . . mortality. And in so doing, I had lost some special essence of my youth that had always been immortal.

Antoine was my sole connection back to that world. He still breathed the spirituality that had been the lifeblood of my adolescence, the resonance that had somehow brought him to me when I was still "in formation," still in need of a guide.

By the time I left chiropractic school, I had received more than just an education in osteology and neurology. Through Antoine and other souls I met like him, I matured in my understanding of my spirituality.

And then I somehow grew out of it.

I know it had something to do with entering the "real world" — with earning money, with the very materialism I had initially resisted in my father's efforts to teach me about the stock market.

But on another level I knew there was more to it than that, knew that the very nature of that surrender, that immortality, that spirituality, should be flexible enough to survive in the face of materialism. I also knew that my time overseas, as wonderful and "earthy" as it was, was ironically just as responsible for my losing that in my life which had been so precious — all that was intangible and ethereal; that place which was no farther away at any moment than a leap of faith and a spring of love.

The need I now had to re-find that place was almost a physical ache. Only there, I realized, would I ever find peace with all that was occurring with my father.

But how to find it, how to find it?

There was no airplane excursion back to that place, no Eurail pass, no Concorde service. The only ticket was through an inner journey, a journey of the soul; a journey, I had no way of realizing, I was in the process of embarking on through the hellfire of my father's demise.

Chapter 18

"*T*don't see how a few little altered cells can kill a man my size," my father said to me out of the blue one day during my then-weekly visits to Sunrise Key. He didn't understand why I was flying to their home every weekend, but for some reason he didn't protest. It was six weeks into the 6- to 12-week prognosis, the very beginning of the period in which the grim time bomb could detonate at any moment, the precipice give way, the roulette bullet fire from the sixth chamber.

"Those cells can't kill, Dad," I replied before I fully knew what I was saying. We were driving to my father's golf club to share a few hours playing a sport I secretly disliked. But that seemed unimportant now that I wanted all the interaction with him I could . . . While I could . . .

"They can't," I finished my thought. "Not if you keep up that attitude."

I was surprised at how easily the words came, as easily as my pretense at enjoying the golf lessons he was giving me. I was getting good at such pretense. And yet was it this that was keeping him alive? I surreptitiously glanced over at him. He didn't have the air of a man with only a few weeks left to live.

"Why do you say that?" my father asked.

"About the importance of keeping up your attitude? Because all my experience with patients, every book out there on the subject, relates how attitude is everything in fighting serious disease." I was surprised he was letting me talk about it. In the last weeks he had made little more than passing mention of the cancer and I had honored his wish not to fill his life with thoughts of it, even if the thoughts I wished to impart were ones I felt would help him fight it.

"Don't push ideas on him, Mikey," Antoine had gently counseled me. "Just have the intention of saying what there is to say, then wait for the opportunity. It will rise on its own."

And now I saw that my friend had been right. From the beginning of our relationship, Antoine had always counseled me similarly, against my inherent impatience, against pushing people before they were ready.

Amidst the graveness of our last discussion together at the restaurant, a sudden grin had come over Antoine following these words about patience. He asked, "Do you remember what happened with James Maserati?"

Despite myself, I too couldn't help smiling. James Maserati had been a student supervisor when we were in school. He, a fellow classmate, had gotten me suspended from clinic for a month for some minor infraction I had made of clinic rules. In truth, I was glad for the forced time off. I was in the middle of the first relationship of my life and was happy to have extra time to spend with my girlfriend.

Several days after receiving the suspension, Antoine was walking with me down a school corridor when coming suddenly from the opposite direction was James Maserati with a friend of his. The air suddenly filled with tension, like a seriocomic showdown in a TV western.

There were no tumbleweeds, but the scene contained all the drama — a face-off between the errant bandit (me) and the student sherriff who had brought him to justice. I could sense Antoine stiffening besides me, could see James wearing wrinkled shirt and tie, frantically averting his eyes behind thick black glasses, looking one second at the ground, the next at me, then at his equally tense friend, then at me, then to the ground again.

My gait didn't falter. I am tall and, though slim, I can be imposing. I could have just continued walking, just looked the other way, just let the moment pass into memory. But just as Antoine and I were coming upon the two, I moved into their path. In a single motion I reached down, took the student supervisor's perspiring hand in mine and with a huge, pleasant grin on my face, shook the limp hand enthusiastically up and down.

Without the slightest guile, I looked through the clinician's glasses into his stunned eyes and said, "Hey, James!" When I saw that I had his attention, I said, "Listen, no hard feelings, huh?" I gave him a few hardy claps on the shoulder, which somehow reverberated through him as if he were jello, smiled magnanimously, then nodded for Antoine, frozen in his tracks, to continue along.

When we were around a corner, Antoine stopped dead again, stared at me a moment with unbelieving eyes, then leaned over his knees as if he was going to throw up. Instead, he burst out with wave after wave of helpless laughter. I stood there, unable to contain my own grin but not 100 percent sure what I was grinning at. For my part, I hadn't thought twice of the incident.

"Mikey," my friend finally grasped my arm, trying to balance himself. "Mikey is very good at breaking ice!" Again, he was heaving with laughter.

By now, I had started laughing. "But, Antoine," I said between guffaws, "Did I do something wrong?"

He composed himself. "No Mikey. Nothing wrong. Just that maybe next time it will be easier — on the other person, at least —" he shook his head with a last grin — if you wait till the ice thaws just a little." His humor was all kindness as he looked me in the eye. "Then rather than crack ice, you can ride the wave."

I stood for several seconds, unaware that I continued nodding my head even once Antoine was silent. Then we walked on.

Many of the lessons I learned with Antoine were of a similar nature, through the medium of laughter and of such quality that I almost didn't realize the impact they had on me at the time. Like so much of what happened with my friend, his words concerning this particular event would reverberate somewhere in me for years afterward:

. . . *Wait till the ice thaws a little . . . then you can ride the wave . . .*

And now, in a much more serious circumstance, the seed that had been planted more than a decade earlier had borne fruit in the form of my patiently waiting for my father to open up concerning his illness.

"Attitude can mean everything, Dad," I said to him in the car. "When people receive the diagnosis of cancer, many become so depressed, they begin developing all the symptoms of the disease. It's as if their immune system collapses under the weight of the news." Keeping my eyes on the road, I looked at him through the corner of them. He looked fascinated. Encouraged, I continued. "You didn't collapse under the news. You've gone on living your life. Your attitude exhibits all the qualities Deepak Chopra and Bernie Siegel talk about in patients who get spontaneous remissions from cancer."

"Who are Deepak Chopra and Bernie Siegel?" he asked.

"Chopra is an endocrinologist and Siegel is an oncologist. Both were heads of hospital divisions that dealt primarily with cancer and both have written bestselling books about the role of the mind/body connection in the survival of cancer patients."

"Huh." He was quiet a moment. Then: "You used the term *spontaneous remission*. What do you mean by that exactly?"

I kept my voice even, trying not to exhibit any of the thrill I was experiencing that he was finally displaying such interest. The simple *knowledge* of this subject was the first tool for making the concept a reality. "A spontaneous remission means the cancer just suddenly disappears," I told him. "No trace of it left symptomatically, no trace via blood test, CAT scan, MRI or X-ray . . . nothing. *Poof*, it's just gone."

His voice contained wonder. "Does that happen very frequently?"

"No," I answered honestly. "Rarely. But with enough frequency to alert these doctors that there's something worth investigating there. And they found that although spontaneous remissions infrequently occur, it's just as uncommon to find patients who truly haven't let the news of cancer beat them psychologically. But most importantly, they discovered these two rarities usually coincide in the same patients."

"Meaning?"

"Meaning, patients who do have spontaneous remissions usually are the ones who aren't destroyed by the diagnosis."

My father looked deep in thought before responding. "Well, it's like I said, I don't see how a few tiny cells they had to use a microscope to find could kill a man my size."

I thought a moment, suddenly coming up with a visualization that could be very useful to activate his defense system. "Just think of those cancer cells as tiny grains of sand on the beach, Dad. Your body's immune system is like the ocean. Those few cells are nothing against the power of your internal sea. A few waves and they're washed away."

My father pondered this a moment, nodding his head. Then he said, "I don't see how they could kill me."

"They can't, Dad," I reiterated, his repeated remark perturbing me. "They can't. As long as the diagnosis didn't hit some deep level."

Was he grasping what I was saying? Was he truly confident or was he in denial? "Why don't you read some of these books I've been telling you about, Dad? There are many out there now. Not just by Chopra and Siegel, but by other specialists like Larry Dossey and Carl Simonton. If you start . . ."

"I told you, Michael," he interrupted me. "I don't want to think about it. I listen to what you say, but I don't want to focus my entire life around this problem. I'm going to die someday anyway; I'm just not going to die captive to this disease."

"OK, Dad," I acquiesced. "OK. I understand what you're saying."

And I did. In some way this was his manner of not succumbing to the disease. Maybe he was taking the most appropriate course for a spontaneous remission. Hadn't I always told patients that healing is under way when we are no longer focused on the part of ourselves that's in pain or functioning out of harmony with the other parts, that disease creates a focus of the mind on a bodily point instead of leaving it free to experience everything else in life? And that surrendering this focus was the first sign of recovery?

However, I had also learned it was first necessary for patients to acknowledge a problem before they could empower themselves physically and emotionally to rid themselves of it. Cancer *will kill* if undiagnosed. It *will kill* if unacknowledged. *Accept the diagnosis,* renknowned author Norman Cousins wrote, *but defy the verdict.*

All I had read, all I had seen documented, all I had experienced personally and with patients, led me to believe that *any* disease could potentially be reversed after acknowledging it and taking action . . . and only then perhaps attempting to put it aside and let God work His will.

"A diagnosis, then some positive step," I'd explain to patients, "whether it be a drug, surgery, an herb or an acupuncture needle, is just a means to jump-start our own self-healing mechanism so that the intelligence within us can bring all our parts back into harmony."

And this is what worried me most with my father.

"I just want to make sure, Dad," I said to him tentatively. "Are you sure you're not denying the problem? The troops first have to realize there's an enemy before they can pull up the drawbridge and get out their weapons." I smiled, at once trying to drive home my point but keep it light. I didn't succeed.

"Dammit, Michael," he became irritated. "How many times do I have to tell you? I know I have this friggin' disease, I just don't want to focus my life around it."

I left it at that, understanding the worst thing to do was provoke him. I flinched at having already done so. All the negative emotions — anger, fear, hopelessness — were shown to cause a release of enzymes that depleted serotonin and norepinephrine, depressing the nervous and immune systems. I was trying to empower him, to get his body to release its powerful endorphins and Interleukin-2s, the hormonal mobilizers of the immune system and natural cancer killers. If I could simply get him to read the books I had read on this subject it would help engender this state.

But what could I do?

I couldn't help wondering, was he really as mentally tough as he was trying to appear? Or was he in denial?

And then the question that was hitting hardest: With, according to his doctor, no more than six weeks now left for him to live, by not telling him, was *I* in denial as well?

*T*here was no finding peace for me in the terrible period that followed. And yet, during this time of great crisis, something began to open in me, some tiny bud.

In my quest to find why I couldn't embody Antoine's advice, in my search for what was preventing me from being able, as my friend advised, to *surrender*, to *"turn it over to God,"* I would look back to another time in my life, another long season filled with suffering and anguish and difficulty, to rediscover the answers I had then found . . . and now lost.

Unconsciously at first, then with increasing intent, I found myself slowly awakening long put-to-sleep memories. Of my youth. Of my sister.

Of my first experiences in the shadow of death.

Part 11

THE GIFT OF IMMORTALITY

I have a gift for you!
One that will last your whole life through.
It is especially for the very young;
Those who adults, in their taut paradigms,
fear may be traumatized
by witnessing so much of life
so very young.

But the very young
have no such paradigms
about the nature of death.
So in their innocence,
they sense my silent song
my onward journey
not having blocked ears
nor wounded vision
to the beauty of a soul's unfolding
before their very eyes.

Rather than just see the shell
where life once lived
they sense life
seeking a higher home.

And my gift for them —
and for you!
If you can but return to a child's eyes . . .
is that exposure prods the curiosity
of such a young mind
to search, to read, to become familiar
with all the beauteous mysteries and possibilities
that only love, birth and death contain . . .

That you may for the rest of your lives
not harbor within you
the greatest fear
the greatest angst of mankind.

For in your youth's experience
YOU - HAVE - CONQUERED - DEATH!
Having glimpsed now
a sweet potentiality . . .
The gift of IMMORTALITY!

Chapter 19

"*S*top! You're killing him!" I yelled at the faceless nurse, "You're killing him!" " I tried to move my legs, but they were frozen. "Stop it!" I yelled again, "Stop it!" But the disembodied hospital worker paid no attention to my tiny eight-year-old voice as she plunged the needle into my friend's arm that would spell his death.

"Nooo!" I screamed. "He'll die!" At that last moment Roger's eyes half-opened and through a haze, he looked at me beseechingly. My chest heaved along with his, my lungs tightened and my throat narrowed in sympathetic asthmatic constriction. "Don't do it," I gasped weakly again, saying the words my friend couldn't utter.

Then Roger's eyes slowly began to close. "No," I gasped. "Don't!" I pleaded with him. "Don't go, Roger, don't go!" But as with the nurse, my cries went unheeded and I was helpless as I saw the life and struggle leave my best friend's body.

"*No, no, no, no, no!*" I cried, my head tossing side to side, expressing the pain and impotency the rest of my immobilized body couldn't effectuate.

"Michael, wake up, wake up, son," a faraway voice was suddenly saying to me.

"No, no, they killed him, Superman, they killed him."

"Michael, you're having a bad dream," I felt the gentle shaking. "Wake up, son."

I wasn't sure where I was at the moment, the television hero's image having superimposed onto my dream, then my father's voice arising into that scene.

"Roger died, Dad," I trembled, feeling my father's arms around me. "They killed him," I still cried.

"Yes he did die, son," my father replied softly. "We can't change that."

"Why, Dad, why did they kill him?" I beseeched, feeling the horror of a nightmare suddenly acknowledged as being real life.

"They didn't mean to, son. Try to understand that. They were trying to save his life. Someone just made a mistake and gave him the wrong medication."

The tears that followed were softer, but no less expressive of my terror. Roger had been my best friend when he died — someone with whom I traded baseball cards, climbed trees and built forts. A year was a lifetime for an eight-year-old, and the nightmare was one that would lurk on the distant edge of my dreams for many more to come.

This was the image of death I carried throughout my youth, the only experience I had with "the abyss." And though after time, the nightmare memories of Roger's passing weren't registered on a conscious level, the fear, the horror, the pain — the exact emotions most people carry with themselves throughout life about dying — were the only emotions I had to associate with death.

Then, in my 16th year, my parents broke the news to me that my sister's illness of six years was going to take her, too. And on a clear winter day, it did.

Chapter 20

"*I* can't go." I shook my head, casting my eyes down.

My father clasped my shoulder. "I understand, son." His eyes conveyed a tenderness that I still remember. "But I do want you to think about it."

I nodded, hugged him, then my mother, then watched as they walked out the front door, dressed in solemn colors to drive to the funeral home where my sister lay at rest.

The last two days since the noon of my sister's death — the last two months since my sister had slipped into a coma — the last two years since we moved to Florida and Janie began her slow, final decline — suddenly had a surreal feeling to it. It was as if my parents and I had been out to sea for a very long time and had suddenly come to dry land. Our legs, having grown accustomed to constant uncertain pitching beneath us, were suddenly wobbly when we found ourselves on the steady ground of the future that lay before us — but without the one crew member who had weakened during our voyage and in her illness opened us to pouring every drop of our love into her care.

I had an etheric feeling as my parents walked out the door. Somehow it had something to do with the fact that they were so dressed up and I was wearing shorts and a T-shirt, the typical Florida dress I had worn the last two years during the vigil we had kept aboard our tossing nursing ship. I felt ultimately comfortable in this garb. I had taken immediately to it when we moved from New Jersey, where the majority of the year pants and a sweatshirt were necessary inside and a warm jacket outside.

But now, watching my parents leave, so formal, so carefully attired, I actually "felt" my casualness, "felt" my bare feet on the cool floor, "felt" the slight breeze of air through the fibers of my T-shirt. I was insisting on staying on the boat, guarding the deck of our past as my parents ventured forth on land to complete the formalities of the end of one journey and the beginning of another.

I couldn't articulate it then, why I couldn't go with them. Looking back, I know it had something to do with never having been to a funeral before.

And on some level, acknowledged more by my actions than by understanding, I couldn't let the first corpse I ever saw be . . . that of my sister.

Yet looking back now through the mist of the years that have passed since then, I know I had already seen her body.

I had been home only for an hour since I had left the hospital late in the morning the day of Janie's death. I had been pulling shifts with my parents, each of us relieving the other every five or six hours over the past eight weeks since my sister had slipped into a semi-coma, then into a coma. At 6 a.m. I had gently shaken my parents awake, the two of them having slept through the night beside my sister on cots the hospital had provided, at least one of them never letting go of her hand in our vigil to, on whatever level, let my sister know we were always with her.

Her time was near despite the artificial life support equipment being used against our will to sustain her battered life. She had been ready to peaceably leave her typhooned existence almost a month earlier. At that time, in 1975, there was no such thing as euthanasia or the "right to die." Karen Ann Quinlan was still a bubbly teenager who had yet a few more years of conscious life before becoming a national test case in her parents' desperate battle to get the courts to allow her to die after years of being artificially sustained in a coma.

And so our vigil. I do not remember much from that time. Yet I do remember certain things . . . about my sister's suffering. I do remember the last five hours . . . from the time I relieved my parents at six in the morning until they came back to relieve me at 11 . . . I do remember the clamminess holding my sister's hand.

I do remember being awakened an hour after leaving the hospital when my parents called to request that I return. That my sister had finally died.

And I do remember arriving in time to see the doctor enter, who, after checking the still body in front of us with his stethoscope, confirmed that the years of my sister's tribulation were finally over.

| FORD MOTOR NYSE-F | RECENT PRICE | 26 | VALUE LINE |

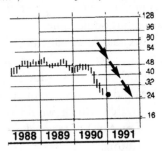

Chapter 21

GROUNDING

(Gift 5)

ook Value.
There are times when you will find a stock's book value at par or above the current price of a stock. If it is above or equal to the price of the stock, this is appealing, but certainly not always an absolute necessity if other factors considerably outweigh this indicator.

"Book value, in simplistic terms, is the dollar amount a company would be worth after it paid all its debts, liquidated all its assets and cashed in all its accounts receivables," my father was saying.

"Can you give me an example?" I requested, forever unsure of myself in grasping any of the new concepts he was teaching me about the stock market nearly two decades after my sister's death as he now faced the same disease that had taken his daughter.

"Sure," he nodded. "Take your clinic, for example. Say you decided to sell it today . . ." He suddenly froze midsentence.

I leaned toward him anxiously: "What's wrong?"

My father shook his head. "Given your history with your past practices — how little time you last in them — maybe I shouldn't be putting ideas into your head."

My sigh of relief was followed by laughter. Dad couldn't help grinning himself. "Well, am I right?"

"Yes you're right," I smiled. It felt good to be able to joke with him about this source of constant clashing between us over the years. "But now for the first time in practice, I'm doing exactly what I wanted for so long," I reassured him. "A completely holistic practice. So you've got nothing to worry about. Anyway, about book value?"

"Right. So, if you decided to . . . ahem . . . to . . ."

"To sell my practice . . . yes . . . we're just pretending, Dad. Go on."

"Yes," he continued, though eyeing me suspiciously. "Well, the book value of your practice would be the value of your equipment and supplies plus your accounts receivable, which would be any outstanding money owed you by patients. From this figure you'd subtract any outstanding balances you owed your creditors."

"OK. I think I get the idea. So relate this to buying stocks."

"Right. So when you pick a stock, the higher the book value is in relationship to the stock price, the safer the company is as an investment for you — the more *grounded* it is. For example, take a look at this report on Ford, a company I'm considering buying stock in now." He handed me a data sheet from *Value Line*, asking, "What does it say the book value is?"

I scanned the report. "It looks like $49.38 a share. Right?"

"Right. Let's just round that out to $50. Now, what is the most recent stock price per share?"

"$26?"

"Good. So write down a ratio of the two numbers: $50 book value per share to $26 stock price per share."

I followed his instructions, putting on paper $50/$26.

"So, that's approximately a 2-to-1 ratio, the book value being almost twice the value of the stock price, right?"

I stared at the numbers, the mathematical portion of my brain always functioning several hertz per second slower than his. "Uh, 2 to 1 . . . yeah, that looks right."

"So, let's say Ford went out of business today. Would the liquidated value of the company, the book value, be enough to pay off its shareholders?"

I answered hesitantly. "It looks like it."

"Yes, it would," he confirmed. "And by how much?"

"Two to one? Twice as much?"

"Excellent! The higher the book value per share is in relation to the stock price, the safer the investment is. The company is *worth* more, it has greater *stability*, it's on firmer *ground*. Make sense?"

"Perfect sense," I nodded, then thinly smiled. "At least while you're here to prompt me every step of the way."

"Of course," he agreed. "But the more you review the concept, the easier it'll become."

"I think I can see that."

"Good. Now back to Ford Motor Company having this 2-1 book value-to-share-price ratio. So if we ignored all our other criteria — which of course we never do — but if we did, could we say judging by book value alone that this was a financially secure company?"

"Yes."

"Right, very secure. In fact, as long as our other criteria give us a strong 'buy' signal, I usually consider even the reversed 1-2 ratio a safe margin to work with. Realistically, most companies don't have as high a book-value-to-share-price ratio as Ford does, so I'm somewhat flexible with this ratio — as long as it's not less than 1-2." He tapped the report. "But when you see a company that has as strong a financial foundation as Ford indicates — as strong *grounding* — and its stock has dropped so low with every sign it's going to rise, what does it tell you?"

I smiled, sure at least with this answer:

"Buy."

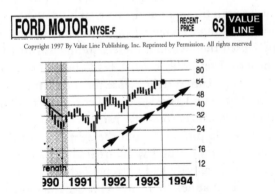

FORD MOTOR NYSE-F | RECENT PRICE 63 | VALUE LINE

FORD PRICE RISE:

12/21/90	26
12/17/93	63

Chapter 22

$\mathcal{E}$verything had seemed surrealistic during the two days following my sister's death. My mother's tears contained tremendous grief, but also the confusing emotion of the relief we all were feeling — relief for my sister, now finally at peace; and relief for ourselves, the weight of her suffering, pain and tortured nights finally over.

And there were my father's tears — something I had never seen before, he a pillar of strength throughout the years of his daughter's illness. But his tears carried something different than my mother's, something ominous. What I only sensed then without understanding was that he, of the three of us, was the most irreparably scarred. Had I been at the hospital to watch the tiny event that occurred right before the moment of my sister's death, perhaps I would have understood better. Perhaps I would have connected it to my father's own cancer so many years later. And perhaps I could have thus been able to help him more. But the existence of the few seconds of this occurrence was something I wouldn't find out about until it was too late, when his cancer already had a stronghold inside him. And it would reveal itself in the manner of many repressed memories: from out of nowhere and as a total surprise — to me, but most of all, to him.

Meanwhile, at that time following my sister's death, there was more surrealism. There was the confusion of my own feelings. What is a teenager supposed to feel?

My only basis for understanding death until that day was the horror I had experienced when my friend Roger died. But somehow that memory had little significance in preparing me for my sister's death.

Roger's passing had been sudden, a terrifying lightening bolt from a black sky that stunned all senses. One day I was trading baseball cards with my friend, the next he was gone.

With Janie, even though my parents had only told me in the last six months that the disease she had was cancer . . . that my sister was going to die . . . she had slowly been dying for six years. Though it had not been put into words, it was there to see.

The horror was in the memories of a fragile, uncomprehending child having brain surgery at 12 years of age, of having multiple radiation treatments over the ensuing years. Of the loss of her beautiful red hair from radiation treatments. Of its growing back, then the loss of it again. And then again.

Of Janie's trauma trying to keep up in school, of emotionally coping with the fact that she was so different from the other happy-go-lucky kids her age — on a surface level from the kerchief, and later the wig she had to wear to hide her thrice loss of hair; to the deepest level of her life experiences compared to the teenage girls around her who, as she moved from 12 to 13 and 14 into her 15th and 16th year, were busy primping themselves to attract boys in their gay pubescence while she had the same stirrings, yet spent her time praying no one would pull off her wig. And on the deepest level of all, during those first four years of her illness — certainly, even then — having the whispers of death in her soul.

And then there were her last two years. After Janie's third bout of radiation treatment. After my father's heart attack. After he knew he could no longer last with the pressure of the Northern rat race while coping with all that was happening to his daughter . . . when he moved the family to a peaceable seaside Florida town . . . when he was finally told there was nothing left to do to save his daughter . . .

The two years that followed. Janie's slow, tortuous final decline. Her slowly going crippled. Going blind. Being bedridden. Screams of excruciating pain in the middle of the night.

Me going to junior high school during the day. Pretending life was normal. Returning immediately in the afternoon to give my parents a break, a chance to walk on the nearby beach to recover whatever sanity was left for a mother and father who were slowly having their hearts ripped out. And the final six months. A nighttime nurse walking our hallways. The dragon metallic hospital bed that took over my room when it was one day turned into my sister's ward. And, at last, the final months of my sister's semi-coma then coma, in the hospital, her wracking, her clamminess, the memory of . . . yes . . . of *praying she would at last be taken ... praying she would at last be relieved from her misery.*

The mercy of God that she was now ready to die, had but a few hours more. And then the abrupt administration of the artificial life support . . . against our confused wills . . . against God's plan . . . to leave her for yet another month in a state no one should ever have to endure. That no family should ever have to watch befall a loved one . . .

So when to this day people still ask me how at 16 I wasn't destroyed when she died, when they say I must be *repressing* underlying fears of death, the first thing I ask them is if they themselves have ever been through a prolonged illness, a protracted death. And because I already know they have not — for only someone who has can understand how *death can be a blessing* — I no longer try to answer them. For anyone who has been through such an experience knows that the true horror is in *life* — what some people are chosen to endure until death — and not in death itself.

So from me there were no tears. Upon my sister's death there was only relief. Incredible relief . . . for my parents, for myself . . . but most of all, for my beloved sister. As well, I remember feeling no guilt for this relief, for it was relief of such tremendous proportion, there was no room for guilt — had anyone suspected me of such liberation.

There was grief, indeed. But grief over the tremendous pain I knew my parents were feeling and grief over the years of my sister's suffering. But grief over her death? That her misery was over? I had loved my sister and had tended to her, but I was overcome with another emotion at that time . . . a *sense* . . . of somehow knowing at that moment that wherever she was then had to be better than how she had lived for the last six years.

I didn't have the comfort then of realizing that this was the dawning in me of a spirituality; that the bud was readying to break surface, which it would the day of my sister's funeral. And that its blossoming would take place over the rest of my lifetime.

Chapter 24

Forty-five minutes after my parents left for the funeral parlor the telephone rang. When I answered it, my father's quiet voice came through the line. "How are you feeling, son?"

I swallowed. "I'm OK, Dad."

"Are you sure?"

"Yeah."

He was silent a moment, the strength of character that had seen him through the years of my sister's illness still resonating in his words. Like a mighty stone statue, he still breathed massive solidity. The fragile crystallization and fracturing of his underlying matrix from six years of having to go on with life, earning a living, supporting the family financially and emotionally despite being torn up inside over his dying child, had not yet clefted the surface. The only evidence of the hidden internal breakdown taking place had been the heart attack he suffered several years earlier, which he bounced back from out of sheer will power, knowing he couldn't afford to be sick with so much going on in the family.

But at that particular moment as he spoke to me on the phone from the funeral parlor, he was whole, inside and out, and as in so many other instances in my life when he slipped from his more rigid mode into unconditionality, I can look back and see how he was truly a vessel of some divinity.

"Son," he spoke with utmost gentleness, "I want you to think about coming here." Then he said: *"It will be good for you."*

The words left me speechless. *Where had they come from?* On the surface they made no sense whatsoever. How could seeing my sister's body *be good for me* ? And how could he say such a thing, knowing I had already clearly stated I didn't want to go?

Yet . . . yet there was something beyond the words. Something in the way he said them. Or perhaps something about the moment in which he said them. As if in the spontaneous flash when he first received the notion to find the funeral parlor phone and call me, he was guided to do so. As if some overseeing angel with implicit timing knew that this was the critical instant — despite my rejection — when I was open to change; change that not only would alter my life but that somehow seemed prerecorded in the evolution of my soul.

"Let me think about it," I heard myself answer him.

"Do that, son," he softly responded.

Looking back to what happened after I returned the receiver to its cradle, I have the eerie sense now of having been moved. I remember no hesitation, going to my closet and taking out my only suit — garb I normally studiously avoided. The last time I wore it was years earlier for my bar mitzvah in New Jersey. No hesitation in putting it on and no hesitation in getting in my mother's car and driving to the funeral home. As if whatever had moved my father to call was then moving me, as well.

*T*have no recollection of what happened when I arrived at the funeral home. No recollection of seeing my parents or anyone else, though they and others certainly were there. My only memory from that time is standing in front of my sister's casket and seeing her body.

And this I remember with crystalline clarity, for if each of us is given in our lifetime one great turning point, seemingly pre-determinined and upon which the rest of our lives pivot, this was mine. My total world view changed at that moment — not in some huge tidal wave crash, but rather in the manner of some kaleidoscope piece that suddenly clicks into place to reveal an entirely new vision of things.

A shell. This is a shell, the silent knowledge whispered in my every fiber. *This is not my sister. My sister has separated from her body and what I'm seeing now is her past home.*

I knew this with such startling certainty, it was not a statement but rather a state of being.

How can I describe this? How can I explain how at that moment, I suddenly understood that my sister had simply dropped her physical form to return to the essence of who she always was and always would be?

If I could just depict the complete understanding I had at that moment, if I could just relate this so others see what I saw, I know it would lift the fear and pain so many of us carry through our lives. Yet how does one share this knowledge, transmit this sense of love and peace I was so blessed to experience at that moment?

I only know the answer was contained in how *still* my sister's body was. Somehow I suddenly understood that, as sure as we know the wind exists by the grass it rustles and the leaves it blows, so too is the human soul for the time it inhabits the body. Just as we cannot *see* the wind, so we cannot *see* the soul except by the otherwise unmoving form it alone can animate.

In that pristine moment I suddenly understood that at some point the body — the physical vessel of the soul for the time of its temporal journey on this plane — wears out. And in the language my father would teach me many years later, like an ailing company whose assets might one day be used to pay back its creditors, so too the body eventually becomes a liability and thus must be returned to the Earth lender.

And finally, this soul — that which lives for eternity — is where we will find our true worth, our true essence. And like a company whose most priceless asset is the mind that conceived it in the first place, so too is the soul — the part of ourselves that no lender can ever recall except the Creator himself.

And therein, in this soul, is where we will find our true book value.

118

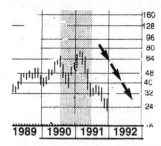

Chapter 25

BALANCE
(Insight 6)

*A*ssets versus Liabilities.
Is this ratio at least 2 to 1 current assets over current liabilities? If not, does the company have adequate financing to assure operating capital?

"Ideally, a company's current assets should be at least double their current liabilities," my father told me during one of our lessons.

"So how does this play with what you told me about the book value of a company needing to be at least half the value of a stock for you to consider the company sound?" I asked.

"You have to weigh all the factors collectively, but with most companies, that 2-to-1 ratio is a good general indication — along with a strong book value — that the company is on solid financial footing, that it is well *balanced.* Take, for instance, this computer company I just bought some shares in."

I took the *Value Line* report he handed me. "Compaq Computer," I read. "I know that company."

"It's a good one," my father nodded. "Their stock price has been battered this year because the dollar's been high, which has hurt their overseas sales. But the dollar will eventually go down and the personal computer market is a rapidly growing field with Compaq well placed to profit. And all Compaq's fundamentals are extremely strong. For instance, read me the assets-to-liabiities figures."

I scanned the page. "Is this it here?"

"Uh-huh."

"Let's see. It looks like their current assets are $1,806 million, versus current liabilities of $649 million.

"Good. So what ratio does that make?" my father asked.

"Umm, 1,806 over 649 . . . almost 3 to 1. Right?"

"Right. So without looking at the other criteria, does that sound well balanced?"

"Very well balanced." I hesitated. "Isn't it?"

"You got it." He smiled. "Figuratively and literally."

"What do you mean?"

"It means I just bought some Compaq stock for you, too."

COMPAQ COMPUTER NYSE-CPQ | RECENT PRICE **53** D | VALUE LINE

COMPAQ PRICE RISE:

12 / 91	3 (after multiple price splits)
07 / 97	53

Chapter 26

At the time of my sister's burial, my personal assets far outweighed my liabilities. I'm not referring to the finances of a 16-year-old boy, but rather the spiritual reserve I had built up from exposure to my sister's fight against death for so many years.

In life, as opposed to finances, the amount of money one has, ironically, may be more of a liability than an asset when facing the death of a loved one . . . or of oneself. People who have only pursued material gain their entire lives, foregoing a balanced development of the soul, frequently will find themselves emotionally bankrupt when it comes to coping with death. Thus they disappear when they are needed most by a friend or loved one; or, if they have a good heart, they get scarred by the emotionality of suddenly dealing in a world in which all their acumen and power provides little comfort in the kaleidoscope of mystery and intangibles that death makes one confront.

Comfortability with death — the most profoundly moving human experience — is a product of years — a lifetime's — slow development of a belief system. For some people that belief system is founded upon their religion; for others, by reading Far Eastern philosophy or such wonderful bestselling books as *Life After Life* by Dr. Raymond Moody or *Saved by the Light* by Dannion Brinkley.

Prior to starting this conscious exploration after my sister's death, my indoctrination came solely through the direct experience of *that sense* one develops during long exposure to pending death. And this is something I have great difficulty explaining, because *that sense* transcends the power of the mind the same way that we cannot "figure out" what happens to us when we die.

That sense is a product of the silence one feels around a dying person, the understanding that logic — the tool many of us use for understanding most everything else in our lives — suddenly has no role here. It has something to do with the feeling of helplessness; our powerlessness to *control* what is happening.

However, just one step beyond this state is *surrender.* Surrender of the highest, most spiritual order. Surrender in the sense of *grace,* of *blessing.* For isn't that what death ultimately is? The surrender of our bodies, the surrender of our minds to return to the grace of God? And in the case of someone watching a loved one die, surrender in the form of acceptance, of submission to God's will.

And therein is grace.

Beyond the horrible agony and emotional upheaval watching for six years — particularly the last two — as my cherished sister slowly died, I somehow felt this chord of grace struck inside me, felt it touched off by something going on deep inside my sister. Far beyond her pain and her confusion, which I felt in equal measure inside me, there was a *silence,* an *inwardness,* a *journey* her soul was readying to embark upon.

All these things I *sensed,* had no words for then as I attempt to provide words for now. Yet this core harmonic, lying in the base of us all, vibrated in me, resonated as if my sister was a C-tuning fork, and my soul one of the C-notes on the piano that reverberated when exposed to the same key.

Just as music may touch us in ways our minds can't comprehend, so too was I, without realizing, being moved by my sister's silent song.

So at her funeral — at that most difficult moment of watching her casket . . . her *body* . . . being lowered into the gound — rather than feel my world and emotions traumatically buried beneath the soil with her, I experienced another epiphany.

There was just the faintest sound above us at that time. It went unnoticed by the tense, softly crying crowd of my parents and relatives, their eyes cast hypnotically down at the lowering casket. But I heard the sound and my eyes were drawn upward.

High above us a passenger jet's silvery outline could just be seen as it wisped phantom-like through fluted clouds. I watched its slow-motion arc across the overhead sea until its pinpoint speck was breathed back into the halogen blue.

An almost imperceptible breeze tickled the hair on my wrists, whispered in my ears. And the tops of the watchful trees all around us swayed in subtle rhythms to the hymns of some eternal breath.

I felt that breath inside me at that moment, coursing through my lungs to my heart, permeating every cell and tissue with oxygenated life, then returning carbonated to the ethers through those very same lungs, to those very same trees, to that very same sky.

This is where I am. The silent knowledge coursed into me as if with those breaths. *Here, in the beat of your heart, on the wings of that wind, in the soul of that sky.*

As if from another space, I watched as my father pick up a handful of dirt, in the custom of our religion, and let it drop through his slackened fingers to provide the first covering of my sister's grave. With weighted step, my father moved aside to allow my mother, unspeakably moved, to do the same.

I am no longer there, the voice whisperd to me. *No longer in the shell that is man's body, that blessed but no longer useful vehicle. There I am no longer.*

And then it was my turn. My father placed his loving hand on my shoulder, as it had been there for my mother. I leaned down and took the cool earth in my palm to make sacrament of my sister's grave.

The soil slipped through my fingers . . . not in chunks . . . not in grains . . . but rather in molecules.

Here too am I. The secret message was left in my palm as if tucked in like a tiny note. *In the very same soil with which you cover my once-home, here too shall you find me.*

And as I tread away between my parents, I felt something turn me around for one last look as my sister was buried . . . and to receive one last message.

And the footprints I have left behind are but from the very same trail that still leads me onward . . .

Chapter 27

igh above the valley, bordered by an expanse of magnificent forest and rising into a broad-faced mountain with a snow-capped zenith, the spirit hovered.

Like rays of the sun covering everything, yet each beam focusing on a particular point, the spirit observed the entire paradise with all its being.

The valley was composed of a large lake whose crystal clearness reflected the verdant forest into which it blatantly cut. At the sight of such pristine beauty, the spirit dropped a single tear into the glassy water spreading concentric circles to each end of the lake, which rebounded back to the bosom of its formation.

A man appeared at the edge of the lake. He was already dressed in the garb of nature as he prepared to dive. As he hit the water, a school of fish assembled there did not dart away, but rather formed a circle into which the man gracefully plunged. When he broke the surface coming up, the fish began to swim with him in formation, all as one. Two snow-white swans joined nature's impromptu ballet, each taking up position on either side of the man. The man then stopped right in the middle of his stroke, brought his toes up perfectly straight and perpendicular to the water, and dived straight down. The two swans circled above while the fish dived with him; but before he ascended, half of them surfaced and swam in a circle like before while the two swans glided around them. Then like a dolphin, the man shot up the middle of the circle with the other fish on either side of him and landed on the outside of it.

One could almost hear music!

✑

The winter of my sister's death was followed by a spring of tremendous growth for me. Externally, no one could have told a difference. I returned to high school to the respectful hush of classmates who recognized me only as someone who had always been a quiet, pensive boy whom no one really knew. But somehow they had known about my sister's death, and some of them found the strength to whisper a few hesitant but much-appreciated words. Within a few days though, high school life returned to normal.

It was at home, in the silences of my bedroom, along the glades of my mind's whispering forests that buds were beginning to sprout, life was beginning to peek out from a soul's long hibernation. And from this winter stillness suddenly there was great motion; great migrations of knowledge from southern retreats.

How this worked, I cannot say. Like the miracle of birth, I don't know what mechanism can take two cells, turn them into one, then turn them into *life*. But somehow I know this same design was behind what happened to me that spring.

My entire life I had loved to read. But somehow, instead of the mysteries and spy novels I had always devoured, I suddenly found within my hands books of an entirely different genre. I cannot say how I came upon these books, but it was as if some internal radar had changed to pick up on these new frequencies, as if some elemental force was bringing to me — or me to — books of a kind I had never perceived of before.

The first was Richard Bach's *Jonathan Livingston Seagull.* How this book touched me, how the description of an ordinary seagull's evolution of flight and soul so mirrored the thoughts that had been fomenting within my own core, and how it gave shape to a reality I was only beginning to understand, I cannot describe. Though I read the entire book the first time in one ardent sitting, captivated from the first words onward, I would spend months — years — slowly rereading it, mining the rich ore of every word, swilling a solitary sentence, a single paragraph, around in my mind for days as an impassioned connoisseur might savor a rare wine.

JONATHAN LIVINGSTON SEAGULL

It was morning, and the new sun sparkled gold across the ripples of a gentle sea.

A mile from shore a fishing boat chummed the water, and the word for Breakfast Flock flashed through the air, till a crowd of a thousand seagulls came to dodge and fight for bits of food. It was another busy day beginning.

But way off alone, out by himself beyond boat and shore, Jonathan Livingston Seagull was practicing . . .

Had it been the strange title that originally caused me to pull it from the bookstore shelf? And was it, as is often the case with me nowadays, the first words of the story that captivated me, causing me to snap it closed decisively, knowing this book I would buy? How was it that in just the first few sentences of the book, almost like a hologram, I was able to sense the author's entire message, the content of his soul, in how he chose to pull from the hundreds of thousands of words of the English language the few that would encrypt the essence of all he had to say?

Through the years, I would read *Jonathan Livingston Seagull* over and over again, not just in English, but in Spanish, French and in Hebrew, as a way to learn those languages through material that not only captivated my attention but yet still stirred my soul. Borne upon the wings of an author's golden words, I would use this book to structure both the form and the content of four languages in my inner being.

The second book that came to me contained a message that found its way to my heart in a more oblique way. I do remember where I first saw this book, though. *The Source* by James Michener had lain on my father's bookshelf for years. Why I was finally drawn to pull it off that spring, I cannot say. I do remember that the thickness of the book — 1,088 pages — daunted me. Yet it was that very thickness and not so much "a message" inside that would provide me with the nourishment I unknowingly sought during that spring of growth.

The Source, a 1965 fictional bestseller, centered around an archaelogical site in Israel upon which 15 layers of civilization was buried. For each layer the scientists dug through, James Michener would spin a fascinating tale of that period's life. Starting with prehistoric man, the book spanned 12,000 years of history, through the time of Abraham, the Babylonians, the Romans, the Greeks, the Crusaders, the Turks and the British Empire.

It was in that span that I was struck with the sensation — the seed —

I am trying so hard to describe. *The temporality of man.* How, as Shakespeare put it, all the world's a stage, and man is but here for one brief act. How, if a person lives 10, 20 or 120 years, in the grand scheme of things it is still just a flicker of time. And whether or not someone's life ends prematurely, as had my sister's, in another 70 years — a blink — his generation is gone anyway.

Rather than giving me a feeling of futility, this notion gave me indescribable fortitude. Had I not experienced with my sister what I had — that *sense of soul* — to which Richard Bach's *Jonathan Livingston Seagull* had given form, *The Source* might have had the opposite effect on me. But indeed, I felt ingrained with a certain omniscience as I journeyed through the book — almost like a spirit that was observing the vicissitudes of each successive generation, sympathetic to each life's plight but kindly above it all in its knowledge and state of grace.

Several miles away in a small savannah, the spirit viewed a lion as it rollinckingly loped after a lithe gazelle. The lion's supple muscles rippled as the high-leaping gazelle managed to keep him just out of reach. The lion was almost upon him when the gazelle made a sudden feint to the left then a sharp turn in the opposite direction. The unsuspecting lion in trying to recover from falling for the feint went sprawling on the ground. The gazelle heard the rustling of grass and brush as the lion tumbled over and over flattening out a path. It loped back to where the lion lay dazed from the fall, then proceeded to lick its face. The lion slowly came back to its senses and affectionately pawed the gazelle's head. He then jumped to his tawny feet and resumed their game of tag.

As with *The Source,* James Clavell's novel, *Shōgun,* about an English ship pilot's personal journey of growth in Japan during the 1600s, wasn't a directly spiritual book. But like *The Source,* it too was a long book, and in the three months it took me to savor, a shift occurred in my own consciousness. It was as if I lived along with John Blackthorne, and as the sea pilot gradually underwent his transition from looking at the Japanese as barbarians to inexorably being swept into their life, culture and philosophy, I was swept with him.

Karma is karma, neh? was the catchword of the book, the phrase repeated over and over again every time Blackthorne was overcome by the whirlwind of politics, emotion and death.

> *"Be Japanese . . . Put this incident away — that's all it is, one incident in ten thousand . . ."*
>
> *"You must not allow it to wreck your harmony . . ."*
>
> *"Karma is karma, neh?"*

So it was, night after night, going to sleep with this continual tutoring received by *Anjin-san,* Pilot Major John Blackthorne, that this concept became ingrained in my own being.

Over the years there has been a multitude of other books that enlivened this spiritual sense in me. As with *The Source* and *Shōgun,* the books frequently weren't direct philosophy. Though there are many fantastic self-help books I treasure (*When Bad Things Happen to Good People, The Road Less Travelled* and *Care of the Soul* — books whose titles alone awaken something), my own being responded then more to stories — metaphors such as *Jonathan Livinston Seagull, The Prophet,* and *Alice* by Sara Carter Flanigan. It's as if when I can break free from my mind — the do's and don'ts of "education" — when I can get swept up in the drama and poetry and life of real or created but nevertheless *living, breathing* characters, I have new breath pumped into me.

The hallmark of each book that opened something in me was that I always felt if I could just plum the entire message of that one story, if I could just continue the season of growth the book sowed in me, I would have a harvest that would feed me for years.

Starting with *Jonathan Livingston Seagull,* such was the effect those original books had on me. It was as if something germinated inside, opening up some vessel for stories I myself would soon compose . . .

The spirit ascended to the top of the snow-covered mountain where the crisp air sobered him from the intoxicating beauty and harmony. Melting snow formed glistening waterfalls which fell endlessly down the sheer pink and white

cliffs of scintillating granite into large pools that fed the lake.

On the other side of the mountain, opposite the lake, a panoramic ocean reached out to the horizon. The setting sun, a brilliant red ball of blazing fire, cast irridescent hues on the shimmering water. Waves gently rolled onto the fine white sand of the shore where the warm ocean breeze sprayed angelic spume into nothingness.

Almost invisible from the ground, a falcon soared overhead. Gliding in large circles, borne as one with the wind, he appeared as if he might fly into oblivion like the spume.

Suddenly, the spirit felt a tightening of its being. Anxiety enveloped him as he had a feeling of being sucked away. In place of the beautiful waterfalls, forests, and wildlife, another scene suddenly dominated his awareness; a scene he would have preferred to forget; a scene anyone would have preferred to forget. A body lay on a hospital bed covered with cold, clammy sweat and shaking spasmodically. Tubes, needles, and sensors pierced the useless body all over, connected to machines that took the place of the body's vital organs.

The spirit felt another tightening — this one worse than the first, and suddenly the spirit was no longer viewing the scene, now he "was" the body! He also was no longer the spirit, he was only the "body." A body entombed in a coma, only able to conceive of one thing — the misery it was in.

Pain, pain, oh pain! Oh MERCY! Why did they have to bring his body back to life when it already had experienced the sweet relief of death? His life was one thousand times worse than they imagined death to be!

Yes, the life sustaining device had worked. **

**Life in Heaven, Death in Hell,* ©1975, Michael R. Norwood

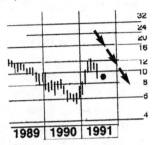

Chapter 28

GROWTH
(Insight 7)

*R*ising Revenues
Has the company enjoyed a growing volume of sales (revenues)?

"It's important to move forward," my father was saying. "Never backward. Both in the life of a company and the life of a person." He looked down, silent for a long moment. Then in a hushed voice: "That's why I refuse to let this cancer thing rule my life."

The remark came from out of nowhere. I was so surprised, I couldn't respond. We had sat down in my parent's screened-in Florida room to begin another lesson on stocks, and then suddenly this.

"It ruled our lives for too long once before," he added.

When I looked at him he seemed far away. Then he blinked, as if suddenly self-conscious.

"Anyway," he recovered, "I meant to talk about stocks. The companies you invest in should always be progressing, expanding, *growing*. That's generally what makes a stock price rise. Make sense?"

His abrupt change of focus — from hard finance to deepest emotion, back suddenly to hard finance again — left me reeling, feeling like I had just been involved in a hit-and-run. I finally managed a delayed nod to his question, feeling a profound pang that I had somehow missed an opportunity, an opening to discuss something much more important than stocks. But the moment had already passed.

"So you tell me," he continued on, unaware of the internal commotion he had created inside me. "What financial data would we look at to see that a company we are interested in is *growing*, its product line on the move, its revenues rising?"

I shook my head, still trying to get back into the conversation. "I don't have a clue, Dad."

"All right, let me help you." He handed me a *Value Line* report on a company called Analog Devices. "This is a new company I'm interested in. Despite the fact that they're coming out with a micro-chip that will reduce the price of automobile airbags from $500 to $100, for some reason — as far as I can tell, just the fickleness of the marketplace — their price has recently dropped dramatically. In any case, take a look at this report and tell me which set of figures indicates how steadily they've been growing."

I forced myself to clear my head, to forget my missed opportunity. I concentrated all my attention on the report.

The page was no longer such a mystery to me as it once had been. My eyes immediately gravitated to the figures I had become used to scanning: price, three- to five-year projections, book value, etc. But as usual, if my eye went outside this familiar terrain into the jungle of numbers I hadn't learned about yet, all became a blur.

"I'll give you a clue." My father smiled, well knowing my limitations as a detail person. "It's right at the top of the main body of financial figures."

I tried to focus. "Sales-per-share figures?" I asked.

"You got it," he nodded. "Read me the figures for the last three years."

"1988 — $9.37/share. 1989 — $9.52. 1990 — $10.36."

1988	1989	1990	1991	1992	
9.37	9.52	10.36	*11.95*	*13.05*	Sales per sh

"Now read me the projected sales figures for this year and the next. They're in italics so you know they're just estimates," he added.

"Let's see. This year, 1991, is *$11.95* and next year, 1992, is *$13.05*."

"So since 1988, their sales have steadily grown: $9.37, $9.52, $10.36 to a projected *$11.95*, then *$13.05*, right?"

"Right."

"Pretty good sign, wouldn't you agree?"

"Yeah, especially the jump in sales they're projecting for this year: $10.36/share to $12.25."

"You're getting sharp," he smiled.

I blushed. "Well, it's pretty obvious. All the previous years their sales have grown by less then 10 percent. This year it looks like they will almost double that." I looked up at him. "Wow, that's interesting!"

"If I didn't know better," he said as he looked at me out of the corner of his eye, "I'd almost say you were getting to like this stuff."

"Well . . ." I half-smiled. "I'll take the fifth on that."

He nodded. "Okay. But about Analog, let me ask you this. Considering they are projecting such growth in sales this year, what makes that particularly significant?"

"The fact that their stock has dropped?"

"Excellent! See, this stuff really isn't so difficult, is it?"

I shook my head *'no it isn't,'* then nodded *'yes it is,'* then shook it side to side again. We laughed together, my father getting my message. I finally said: "I've got a question."

"Fire."

"I thought you were interested in only stocks that have dropped to 50 percent of their value from the last year or two. This one has dropped only from a high of 12.5 this year to a current low of about 8.5."

"You *are* getting good at this! And you are right. Actually, what I'm going to do is just keep my eye on this stock for a while. I usually only buy a stock after getting familiar with it over a period of months — sometimes as many as 8 to 12. That way, I see if a good deal gets even better — meaning it drops even more. But keep in mind, even I will break my own rules every once in a while if I sense something is 'ripe,' as long as I'm basing that decision on research and not a whim or some hot tip someone has given."

"And you feel that way about this stock?"

"I'll tell you that after a few more months. But meanwhile, the dropped price, the three- to five-year projections, its book value and the assets-to-liability ratios are all adding up to a potential good candidate. Another thing is, if you forget the projected estimates — which can turn out to be totally wrong — and just look at its history — which is *fact* — you will see that the company has experienced steady growth for as long as that *Value Line* report has information recorded. Look at their sales-per-share figures since 1975."

"Looking."

"You see how they haven't had a single year where they've gone backward? Despite that the price of their stock has risen and fallen, every year their sales have been better than the year before."

I nodded. "That's pretty impressive growth."

He nodded too, but suddenly he seemed distant, replying more to himself than to me. "That's what it's all about."

"What's that?" I scrutinized him, unconsciously preparing myself for another hit-and-run.

"Growth. Rising to full potential. Doing the best we can . . ." And then, from that faraway place: ". . . while we can."

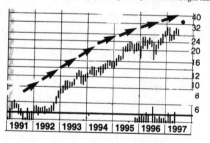

ANALOG PRICE RISE:

8/02/91   **3** (after multiple price splits)
7/25/97   **34**

Chapter 29

*F*acing death gives rise to many emotions, many irrational, many that became all too familiar to me during this time of withholding the 6- to 12-week prognosis from my father. The strongest of my emotions was guilt, not just about not telling my father about the prognosis, but about missing one *cue* after another he was giving me to discuss something deeper than stocks; deeper, yes, than even my holistic views on fighting his illness.

What he wanted most to discuss — what every dying person on some level wants most to discuss, and those in denial most of all — is that which stirs deepest in the human soul, that which the prospect of death brings to the forefront of our mind possibly for the first time in our lifetime: the call of the soul, the existence of it, its place in life and its sunrise in what we call "death."

And my guilt was all the more deeper for knowing that I once intimately understood this soul, once had its essence breathing through my every pore, my every action, my every thought. That the one blessing I had been given in life was this insight that put every other moment of life — the good as well as bad — into perspective.

For years after my sister's death, my only confusion was why had I been given this simple but so profound gift. So many people were scarred by death; why I had been *opened* by it? It had not been me who suffered years of cancer. I hadn't lived the heart attack or car accident trauma leading to a Near Death Experience. For what reason was I so blessed to be given not money, not fame, but rather this simple understanding that made my life one of quiet ecstasy? Though I suffered the loss of a loved one and of innocent childhood growing up with a sister with cancer, my sacrifice seemed little for the eternal reward I was given.

And yet was it eternal after all? For as surely as I grew from a teenager into a man, so too I somehow eventually grew out of that understanding. Yes, I knew it had to do with entering *the real world,* earning money, being absorbed in "making a life." And I know it also had to do with the years I spent overseas, wanting to "come down to earth," to see the world as others saw it, to become part of its "salt" and not to feel all the time "different" — viewing things always from such a distinct perspective from everyone else.

But what I didn't understand then was how my career itself, as noble as it was — fighting disease, fighting *death* — how insidious that, too, had been in propagating my loss of that understanding.

Prior to my father's diagnosis, the main event in my life that let me know I had lost something very special was my difficulty in recovering from another death: that of Avishy, my closest friend from the years I lived in Israel.

As hard as I was hit by Avishy's death, I was hit equally as hard by guilt. Guilt, it seems was the hallmark emotion of my loss of that *understanding* . . . similar to the guilt I was now carrying from not having informed my father of the 6- to 12-week prognosis.

After my sister's death, I had felt guilt, too. When I remembered how in our childhood I fought so vehemently with her over simple things such as wanting to watch *The Man from U.N.C.L.E.* (my choice) as opposed to her choice — *The Carol Burnett Show* — I experienced tremendous remorse, especially knowing how sick she was. But somehow, that *sense of soul* I received at her funeral softened everything, lifted all burdens; for nothing was beyond receiving forgiveness in that light, least of all the irrationalities of a very young boy.

So when, one and a half decades later, I had such difficulty getting over Avishy's death, I understood for the first time just how much I had lost of that precious understanding. The only understanding I had then was the knowledge that "intellectual understanding" held not the slightest power compared to that *light,* for otherwise the deep guilt I was feeling would have been washed away into ethereality, as had been the guilt with my sister.

After I was informed of Avishy's death while serving in Israeli Army reserve duty, I went through a period of shock. I had lived in Israel for close to two years, and most of my time had been spent with him. The idea that he could never again be part of my experience there scarred me in such a way that put a shadow over all the magical memories of my sojourn there.

And I began to be haunted by a recurring dream:

"Michael, the government has assessed me $5,000 in back taxes," Avishy, who was a gem cutter, told me during an overseas telephone call in the dream, his voice unusually urgent. *"If I don't pay within eight weeks, they won't renew my vendor's permit."*

"So pay," I cackled.

"I can't. They've already revoked my permit so I can't sell my jewelry."

"They have?" I saw myself laugh. *"Ha, ha, ha! Don't worry. You'll find the money."*

"I don't know where, Michael," his voice was desperate. *"I just put all my savings down to buy an apartment. And without the vendor's permit, I can't earn any more."*

"Ah, well, isn't that a shame! And here I thought you said Israel was such an easy place to live!"

"When did I say that, Michael?" he pleaded.

"When you visited me here in the States. Don't you remember?" I scorned. *"The car ride with Ze'ev and Sassoon?"*

"What did I say?"

"C'mon, you remember. We were talking about the 70 percent income tax rate in Israel for earnings over $25,000 a year. Ze'ev and Sassoon said they had moved to America to escape the insanity of trying to maintain a business there with tax collectors breathing down their necks every moment. Remember now?"

"I seem to remember something like that, but . . ."

"No buts," I cut him off. *"I had the same problems when I was in practice there. You laughed at all of us. Said we didn't know how to deal with the system. That we could all take a few lessons from you. Well, what lessons do you want to teach us now, havivi?"*

In the dream, I saw my friend solemnly hang up. And in the next scene I was screaming, *"No! No! Don't go there!"* as I watched my friend, Uzi in hand, step in the line of the enemy bullet that would pierce his skull and end his life.

What haunted me most about the dream was that it was largely true. My friend *had* visited the States, *had* laughed at the problems my two Atlanta friends and I had had with income taxes in Israel. Avishy *had* started his own jewelry business and *did* get assessed a $5,000 fine about which he *did* call me. However, I hadn't laughed at him, hadn't scorned him, as I would never do to a hurting friend — even one that perhaps did need a small lesson in humility. But I also made no offer to help him, because I had silently laughed to *myself* when I remembered that car conversation a year before his call. And though Avishy did sound very upset over the phone, he didn't seem to be asking for a loan, which I would have gladly given him even if I had to borrow money myself to give it.

But then, after the numbing call informing me he'd been killed, the guilt set in.

"None of us could have prevented his death, Michael," Sassoon said to me.

I shook my head. "Maybe if he hadn't been in such a state, maybe he wouldn't have walked into that situation. Maybe he would have been more cautious . . ."

"Don't, Michael," Ze'ev said to me. "Don't start plaguing yourself with such questions. Avishy called us all. We all knew about the problems he was having. We all had our little laughs to ourselves. But we all would have gladly given the money in an instant had any of us realized how much the situation was affecting him."

Despite his reassurance, the dream came back. Over and over again. Looking back on it now, I realize that just as my friend's depressed state of mind may have been responsible for keeping his normally fine-edged sixth sense from working, so my overall state at the time of his death might be attributable to the difficulty I had coping with it.

My reaction to his death was symptomatic of the shift that had taken place in my life in becoming more "down to earth." In truth, years before my father's diagnosis, even before Avishy's death, I had been asking myself what had happened to the spirituality that seemed such a part of my existence throughout my teens and early 20s. I had felt that loss almost as much as an actual death.

And now several years after Avishy's passing, in the summer of my early 30s, with the prospect of another death looming — my father's — I felt that spiritual loss more than ever before.

Part 111

THE GIFT OF GIVING

I have a gift for you!
It is the gift of knowing
the secret of giving!
The giving of kind words
of gestures
of smiles
of all that is food
that feeds the greatest hunger.

Such is this mannah
which all brothers and sisters
need to nourish our cells
and nurture our souls.

When in a burst of tears,
an explosion of anger,
or with a telling laugh,
our brother suddenly reveals
a moment when
ego flies away,

The instant when
angels need be poised;
The telling moment when
any day, any hour
with anyone
a life may be changed forever,

When love enters
and Grace finds a home;
In a flash
that is so subtle, so quick
it may easily be passed over,

When the tiny footprint of our words
illuminates a lost path
and sets a soul
back on its way.

The secret I give to you
is the gift you give to others
For the same gift
is shared by who?
None other than
the giver, who
receives Grace, too!

Chapter 30

SUMMER 1992
(One Year Later)

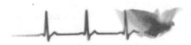

*D*ad entered the summer of his 71st year, then into fall, winter and spring, until he was a full year past the 6- to 12-week prognosis. He still continued to play golf three times a week, still continued his passionate cat-and-mouse game with the stock market, and still continued to look healthier than nearly everyone around him with his enviable mahogany tan.

"I just can't believe it," his doctor would say over and over again. "It just beats everything I know." And my father was honored when the doctor asked if he could make a case study of him.

For me and my mother, there was tremendous relief. Relief from the guilt we had both felt in withholding the prognosis, but most of all, tremendous relief that we still had our loved one with us.

But despite that I felt confident enough to take a brief overseas trip, something still gnawed. My father thankfully had cheated death — so it at least appeared — but I couldn't help feeling left empty by the experience; as if I had cheated life, a chance for growth, because all my conflicts concerning that loss of deep understanding were still unresolved. And my father's reprieve — as short-lived as it would numbingly turn out to be — was my excuse for stopping the search.

And yet the search was bigger than me; it didn't stop. It found me. Like a parent that waits patiently for a wayward son to mature and return home knowing *life* itself is the only cure for his restiveness, so too circumstances were occurring around me that continuously made me look deeper.

"I don't know what's going on," I told Antoine when he came to Atlanta that summer for another seminar. "I suddenly have such serious things happening in my life."

"Like what, Mikey?" he asked, using the affectionate nickname he alone called me.

"Well, first and foremost, there's what happened with my father." I was surprised to feel a constriction in my throat. "You know, dealing with the prospect of death again and everything that's attached to it."

"Yes," he lowered his eyes in quiet acknowledgement. "He's still doing okay?"

I laughed. "Better than either of us, Antoine. Every time I go to my parents' home, he exhausts me on the golf course! Do you know what kind of shape you have to be in to play 18 holes every day in the broiling Florida sun?"

Antoine smiled but then turned serious again. "How long has it been since your sister made the transition, Mikey?"

I swallowed, the constriction suddenly back in my throat. "Sixteen years." How after all these years could I still feel such emotion?

"So many lessons from that time, Mikey," Antoine shook his head. "You learned so much at such a young age. Things many people never learn."

I nodded, my friend's soft French/Vietnamese-accented words touching something in me that hadn't been touched for a long time. That I had once *known*.

We were walking around the lake in Emory University's Lullwater Park. I was silent a long moment as we passed a young father holding his tiny son's hand out to feed bread to a flock of swans. "I feel I've lost a lot of that, Antoine," I finally rasped. "That understanding."

My friend turned to me with a soft smile. "It's not lost, Mikey."

I cleared my throat, trying to absorb the absolute certainty that had been in his voice. *It's not lost . . .*

He gently put his hand on my arm. "What else is happening?"

I forced myself to concentrate on addressing his question. "Well, there's also the situation with my mom. You know, the prospect of what life may be like without a partner after 40 years of marriage."

My friend blinked behind his glasses. "I thought your daddy's doing so well?"

"He is," I reassured. "But what happened with him made my mother look at that possibility for the first time. When I'm alone with her, it still causes her so much emotion."

"Mikey, your mom still isn't . . . *certain?*"

How did Antoine always read so deftly into me, make me voice that which I was keeping silent even to myself?

"No . . . she's not . . ." I whispered. "She's not convinced . . . he's well . . ."

We passed from the cement walkway surrounding half the lake to the dirt trail surrounding the other half. Antoine just nodded, gracefully sensing, as always, the right amount to say . . . and leaving the right amount for me to work out myself.

A jogger flew by us, leaving the air astir. "What else, Mikey?" Antoine asked.

"Strange things, Antoine. Do you remember Mona, the lady who lived with her daughter and husband in the apartment below me when we were in school?"

"Your first patients in student clinic?"

"Yes. They made a barbecue for us when we graduated."

"Of course. How is she?"

"Not well, Antoine. Her daughter called me several weeks ago. I hadn't heard from them for many years."

"What's wrong?" he stopped in his track, his brow furrowed.

"Mona's in a semi-coma, Antoine."

My friend shook his head, pained. "From her diabetes?"

"Yes," I answered. "She refused to modify her diet despite her condition. You remember. Now it's finally caused her to have a stroke." I proceeded to tell him how her daughter, Suzie, had called me. She had been just a child when we knew the family back when we were in chiropractic school. She was a grown teenager now, had tended to her mother alone for two years, the father estranged, gone from their broken home. Mona had another stroke and finally the State of Georgia forced Suzie to put her in the hospital so she could receive intensive care and Suzie could manage some type of life; alone and still in high school, with three ulcers at age 16.

"Poor kid," I told Antoine. "She was trying to make some sense of her life."

"Is that why she called, Mikey?"

"No. In one of Mona's lucid moments, she awoke and asked Suzie to find me. She wanted to see me." I shook my head. "I still don't know why. When I came, it hardly felt like she knew I was there."

"But she did," my friend said knowingly, not asking.

"Yes," I nodded. "She slowly opened her eyes, smiled, then went back into her state. That was it, Antoine."

Antoine slowly nodded. "She's halfway between here and there. She's making the transition." He looked up at me. "How did it feel to you? Being there?"

It took me a moment to answer. "It was strange. She was on a respirator, on I.V., with half a dozen needles and tubes inside her; she had lost probably half her weight, her bones were sticking out, her skin was translucent and her tongue was thickly pasted . . . hardly recognizable to the bouyant, overweight Mona we always knew. But I wasn't shocked, Antoine. I can't describe it. I felt . . . *strong*. I felt I had something to *give*. To both Mona and Suzie."

"You felt within yourself, Mikey," he confirmed.

"Yes. Yes, that's it."

He nodded to himself, and for several moments there was silence between us.

"There's more?" he finally asked, his inner sense unerring.

I picked up a flat rock, rolling it around in my palm as we continued around the lake. "There's more," I nodded.

Antoine shook his head. "Mikey lives so many lives, has so many lessons, in just one lifetime."

I smiled, warmed by his remark which he had made several times in the past. I skimmed the rock across the water, watching it jump, then proceeded to tell him about what was occurring to another close friend.

Vivianne was someone with whom I had had a very close relationship when I lived in Switzerland, someone who embodied for me all the elegance, romance and idiosyncracies of the French culture. Through phone conversations, letters and rare visits, we still shared our lives with each other, each providing for the other deep friendship and the fresh perspective of a different culture and gender. It was one of those wonderful relationships that last a lifetime.

And now Vivianne was going through something with which I had only too much experience. Her father was dying. Of cancer.

For several months, just about every night I would spend five minutes, 25 minutes, perhaps an hour on the phone with her, helping her cope with the difficulties of this time, trying in some way to share whatever strength and comfort I had to offer until her father finally died.

And again, despite my sadness over her situation, there was that feeling: of rightness, of wholeness, of — as Antoine described it — *being in myself*.

"What's happening?" I asked Antoine, stopping suddenly, just staring across the lake.

"What do you mean?" he asked softly, stopping with me.

"All these strange things, Antoine. I thought I foreswore attracting such seriousness in my life years ago."

"Why so strange, Mikey?"

"You know," I said, knowing he knew me better than anyone; also knowing he wasn't asking without reason. "Since I was 24, when I left to go abroad, I was committed to simply having fun, forgetting all my seriousness — yes, even my spirituality. Between the years spent with my sister's illness, then jumping into chiropractic school at such a young age, then the responsibility of having my own practice when I was just 21, I felt like I never had a childhood. For the last seven years, ever since I returned to the States after my three years abroad, I've studiously avoided anything weighty, have tried just to have happy-go-lucky friends, a happy-go-lucky practice and happy-go-lucky times."

"Did you succeed?" he asked, his gentle smile perceptive.

I hesitated. "I don't know." I thought deeply. "More or less."

"And now?"

"Now suddenly everything is changing. First, the situation with my father. And having to deal with my mother's emotions as well. And the situation with Mona; then Vivianne . . . Suddenly all these serious things. Antoine, I thought I left this all in my past. What's happening to me?" I half laughed, unable to hide my bewilderment, my gravity. "I just wish someone could explain this all to me."

"Mikey, didn't you say you were trying to find that *understanding* again?"

"Yes?"

My friend looked at me for a long moment. Then: "You've heard the expression, 'when the student is ready, the master comes'?"

"Yes?" I ruefully smiled. "So where is he?" Smiled, despite that I was hanging on to my friend's words as if for life itself. He replied:

"Sometimes he — or she — comes from the outside. But always, the master helps you find the master that is inside." Antoine looked me softly in the eye. "And always, life is his lessons."

Chapter 31

A master did come. Or more correctly, I unknowingly came to him.

I was in my new practice following seven years of post-graduate study in kinesiology. And the patients I was now seeing weren't easy ones. Severe environmental illnesses, chronic irritable bowel syndromes, depression, debilitating migraines . . . I attacked these cases with zest, glad for the opportunity to apply my slowly acquired skills in the holistic field and on problems other than disc and back-related ones, but apprehensive knowing I was the last resort for these desperate patients who had already tried everything conventional medicine had to offer.

And in that exciting/frightening first season of practice in this new field, a realization came to me. Despite all my additional years of studying physiology, neurology, kinesiology, acupuncture, herbs and homeopathy, there was another level to the problems I was seeing — one I had ignored in the past but could ignore no longer.

The emotional counterpart of these chronic illnesses was glaringly obvious. Not from the standpoint that the illnesses were psychological — one just had to see the way these people's lives had been altered by their physical burdens, by their struggle for some normalcy, which I only understood too well from the experience with my father and sister — but "emotional" from how their lives were affected in this way.

And yet there was some part of me that, without knowing it at first, was beginning to question if that same helplessness, struggle and/or fight was not some expression of a similar dynamic that had existed on a less physical level *prior* to their illnesses.

Many of the patients I was seeing had been sexually abused as youngsters; others had overly protective parents; still others came from extremely religious backgrounds. In short, these people were as diverse as the more healthy segment of the population where "perfect," "normal" and "American Pie" didn't exist, other than as an image from *The Brady Bunch* or *Happy Days.*

I was just beginning to have some sense that in my patients there had been — this was so hard to explain, for I didn't have words for it then — some *magnification* of some *underlying dynamic.* Even my sister — who came from parents as loving as anyone could have ever been — seemed to have had some sensitivity, some fragility which her illness had just highlighted. Or was it her illness that just made me remember her this way, even from the time before she was diagnosed with cancer?

Yet if I looked at myself, I asked the same question. I wondered if the terrible allergies I had suffered in my childhood and early teens hadn't been the result of a different irritation other than to the pollen and molds for which I had received weekly injections. Had there been something already irritated inside me . . . such as the helplessness of watching a sick sister's struggle? Or maybe something deeper than that, something perhaps I couldn't even fathom?

And my father . . . hadn't there been a part of me that *wasn't surprised* by the diagnosis of stomach cancer? Something unmercifully *appropriate* about it given his personality and temperment?

Was illness — in some seed form at least — just an expression of some stuck state of the soul? was the notion that had begun wisping unformulated in my thoughts.

"*You?*" Marty Finkelstein, a chiropractor friend, laughed when I told him my theory. "*You,* of all people, are now interested in *that* sort of thing?"

"Yes," I laughed. "Me."

"I still remember that conversation we had four years ago," Marty said, staring at me over lunch at Rainbow Grocery, an Alanta hangout for holistic practitioners. "Do you remember the conversation I'm talking about?" He had a twinkle as he asked, looking at me out of the corner of his eye.

"I remember," I nodded.

"And what did you say then, Dr. Norwood?"

I blushed. "You're going to make me repeat it?"

"Absolutely."

"No," I grinned. "You tell me."

He nodded. "You were saying that you didn't like to waste clinic time with patients listening to their personal problems. That was after I told you my favorite part of my practice was really getting to know the people who came to me, feeling I could share in their lives, perhaps pointing something out to them they didn't see with whatever problems they were having." He began poking his finger in my shoulder, in my chest. "Do you remember what you said then? Huh, Dr. Norwood? *Huh?*"

I had my hands raised up, laughing as I tried to defend myself from both the verbal and physical assault. "No, why don't you tell me, Finkelstein. Seeing as how you're going to anyway."

"All right, big shot. You said — and I quote from the scar you see it left — 'You keep spending half your day doing that, doc. I'll stick to *healing my* patients.' "

"Hey," I grinned. "I didn't say I like listening to problems any more now. I mean, I still don't see what good it does allowing patients to just wallow in them. I'm just saying I've been getting a feeling lately that the physical problems I've been seeing and the patients' personal problems may have some connection. That maybe there's something deeper there that we're all missing."

My friend nodded at me appraisingly, his tone more serious, matching the change in my tone. "That's a good start, Norwood. But how do you think you're going to find what's going on *beneath* the surface if you don't first find out what's happening *on* the surface?" He paused long enough to let the remark sink in. He then asked: "And what is it in you, Norwood, that's so adverse to talking with patients about their problems in the first place?"

I stared at him, just nodding, the smile that I couldn't keep from slowly fading away not hiding the fact that he had touched something deep.

Chapter 32

I first heard about the upcoming seminar from another kinesiologist. "Yeah, Solihin is unbelieveable. A real hoot," Dr. Eric Weiden was telling me. "You should go, although his system is complex and takes a lot of time to use in practice."

Eric Weiden was like me: He loved physiology and anatomy and would rather see three to four patients an hour and do something "concrete" than spend hours with one person and deal with intangibles. Thus it mystified me that he would recommend this seminar at all.

"Why should I go if I'm not going to apply it?" I asked him.

"Just go for the experience," he said. "It'll be something you'll never forget. Just take my word for it."

I did take his word, several things piquing my curiosity: First, Eric's enthusiasm. Second, the interest I had in finding out more about the emotional end of illness. Third, I could use a small vacation, and this seminar was being given in a bed & breakfast in the North Carolina mountains as opposed to the typical stuffy hotel rooms where most Atlanta seminars took place. And lastly, if I had learned anything from all my years of education, it was that a great teacher — as Eric described this "Solihin" to be — was a rarity, and usually anything they taught was worthwhile to learn.

I drove the five hours up to the mountains of Boone, North Carolina, totally unaware I was spending the last hours of my life in a mode that was about to change forever. I was innocently oblivious to the knowledge that the return on this road five days later would spell a shift so major in me, I would never again look through the same eyes of the young health professional who was earlier just casually enjoying the cool-aired Confederate scenery.

I should have felt some premonition of what was to come when I arrived at the bed & breakfast. A winding, isolated dirt road led to it, and inside, the cozy living room's sliding glass doors opened onto a wooden balcony which overlooked the pure, gentle beauty of the North Carolina Blue Ridge. Whoever this Solihin was, he didn't seem concerned about having space for hundreds of doctors. By his choice of location — so distant from Atlanta, the hub of health practitioners in the Southeast — I sensed that this man liked to give his seminars a special air and, at the same time, make a nice life for himself — at least if every other place he held his seminars was as special as this.

I was in store for another surprise when I walked in.

"Hi," a man in baggy linen pants greeted me after I was directed by the inn owners through the living room to my room downstairs. Without even a split second of hesitation, the man rose from a recliner on which he had been enjoying the view and stepped toward me. "I'm Solihin."

I put down my bag to shake his hand, taken by surprise. His easy informality and lack of formal dress was in complete contrast to the protocol of other seminars I had taken where your first impression of the speaker was an isolated, finely dressed man standing at a podium with a microphone — a god of sorts with the special knowledge you knew he had and you didn't.

"Hi," I replied, and that is all I remember from that initial handshake. The five days to come were so packed with meaning, somehow I can't connect the complete ordinariness of that first encounter with the renowned British osteopath to the absolute extraordinariness of the experience he would lead a few hours after that handshake.

Yet contained within that totally spontaneous greeting might be described the entire essence of what I learned from him that weekend: that dealing with a patient's problems isn't, as I had thought, about establishing doctor/patient relationships, but rather human-to-human contact. That dealing with "problems" has little to do with "psychology" and everything to do with "life." That whatsoever you find in the patient is nothing less than a seed for something you yourself might have resonant inside you. That written within our code, our very chromosomes, is the history of mankind in the form of the thousands of lives of our ancestors who contributed to that code. That in every one of us, and at different times, various aspects of that code may arise, causing us to act in some inexplicable way, causing us to have some unexplainable illness. That by reconnecting back to that code and by simply understanding its origin, there is a tingle of recognition inside ourselves — as if from the very neurons that contain the code — which at once may free us from its binding influence and possibly from whatever physiological form it has taken as an alternative pathway to express itself.

I heard many things that weekend, saw sessions done on people in the seminar that touched something so deep in me, I had to run down to my room two to three times a day for a cold shower to cool off my overloaded circuitry.

Among the things that hit me most was when Solihin talked about how literally every aspect of our lives created our identity, which in turn might be something that was hiding our deeper identity. The seminar was called *Integration of the Vessel,* the idea being that we as human beings are vessels: vessels of our soul, vessels of love, vessels of God and of some unique life song. What gets in the way of the playing of that song is when we over-identify with some aspect of our lives, which starts determining our behavior for us, as opposed to us having the *flexibility to change* from moment to moment as life dictates.

Our culture, our religion, our parents, even the neighborhood we grew up in has the potential to create such binding influences. Simple examples are the tidiness or disorderliness we may inherit from our parents, the fears we take on from an overly zealous religious leader, or the code of "ignoring pain" that might have served us on the football field but not in relationships.

"Even the very wonderful things in our lives contain the potential for placing something on us," Solihin told us. The example that I sensed held true in me was meditation. I had been meditating since the years of turmoil with my sister. The deep silence I had found within was both a refuge and a wellspring of great knowledge and creativity. But now, I suddenly sensed, it had also in some way *put me in a box,* or, as Solihin phrased it, *placed something on me.* Rather than acknowledge anxieties, tensions and inner turmoils, I had learned to wash them away with silence. This, I saw, was at least partially why I didn't like to get patients talking about their problems: I had always felt if they could just *put their problems aside* for a little while, rather than make them a theme of their lives, many of the problems would disappear.

But suddenly here was this very refined British osteopath with a strange name clad in baggy linens demonstrating how the very problems we have — all our conflicts and inner turmoils — were simply paths we had taken away from our true selves, and in re-finding that path we often find the "yellow brick road" back to that inner kingdom of love, of acceptance, of our *selves.*

"The mind should be our tool," Solihin said at one point. "For many of us, though, it has become the center of our universe." He talked about how the mind could lock itself into certain frameworks of thinking, couldn't see outside the framework it thus created, blocked us from *feeling,* from *opening* ourselves to the tiny whispers of Grace that guided our vessel, that connected us to all that was holy.

So rather than engage a person's mind with direct questions, Solihin's work asked questions using specialized *neuromuscular testing* procedures to find what was going on *behind* the mind. Just as a lie detecting test will measure involuntary pulse and blood pressure changes that occur when a person tells a lie, so do muscles temporarily lose their "locking mechanism," giving them the appearance of "going weak" under similar circumstances. This occurs as a result of the involuntary inhibition of certain neurological pathways. However, the difference between standard lie detector tests and how Solihin was using neuromuscular testing was that most patients don't *intend to lie* when they're trying to get to the root of their problems. But *the mind* has already created its own explanations, which are similar to lies. If it truly had the answers, the person wouldn't be in the state he or she is in.

"The mind is our friend," Solihin said, the combination of his profound message, his easy humor and his British accent riveting the 15 people in the seminar. "But it also has the potential of being *a trickster.* It makes us believe certain things that are mere shades of truth, often blocking us from hearing a deeper truth."

I was open-mouthed later as I watched how, by using the muscle testing procedures in conjunction with specialized *hand modes,* Solihin was able to bypass this *trickster* and get right to the essence of a problem. Demonstrating on a classmate lying face-up on a table in front of the group, within minutes Solihin had isolated the first clue to the man's skin problems and marital conflicts. Solihin put the man's fingers in a certain position then tested one of his arm muscles by simply pulling on the wrist of the upraised arm, the muscle previously having been perfectly strong. Somehow, however, with the man's fingers in that strange position, the arm seemed to lose its resistance even though the man was quite large.

"This hand position, or *mode,* as we call it," Solihin explained, "signifies *integrity of the core* — something we need to look at inherent to Bob's core, to who Bob is. So," he asked the class, "who *is* Bob?"

"A *man?*" one of the students suggested.

Solihin nodded, then looked at Bob. "So does this have to do with you being a *man?*" Rather than giving a verbal response, Bob watched along with us as Solihin pulled on his upraised arm, testing the strength of his deltoid muscle. Amazingly, the muscle again went *weak.*

"So the answer is *no,*" Solihin explained. "So what else *is* Bob?"

"A father?" someone suggested who knew him.

Solihin tested again, and again the muscle went weak. "No, it doesn't have to do with that, either," Solihin said. "Any other ideas?"

"Try doctor," someone said.

"Does this have to do with you being a doctor?" Solihin asked, and suddenly the muscle stayed perfectly strong. "Aha," Solihin smiled, his eyebrows raising. "This may be a good demonstration of how our careers, too, often block our true identity. After all, our careers are an area where we use — and potentially *overuse* — our minds probably more than any other. A lot of room for *the trickster* to come into play."

"So," he addressed the man, "what major thing about being a doctor is going on in your life right now?"

The doctor described the increasing conflict he was having maintaining a conventional medical practice while slowly, over the years, having become more and more holistically oriented. "It's like I've got this giant schism inside me," he described, the class silent in respect for the deep emotion he was sharing. "I just can't make the careers match. My colleagues think I'm crazy, and I myself have a difficult time getting my own patients to want anything other than a quick-fix pill or surgical procedure."

I had the strangest sensation as the doctor described his problem concerning this . . . *schism.* It was as if somehow it made me sense *schisms* inside my own self; schisms in maintaining a writing career and a chiropractic career; schisms in my love for those and the part of my mind that now had to additionally deal with learning the stock market, of all things. And strangest of all, schisms between my desire to learn about the connection of emotional problems to physical ailments and my inability/lack of desire to *deal with* patients on this level.

I involuntarily quivered, looking around to see if anyone had noticed. But all eyes were glued to the front of the room.

"And does this create a schism in other areas of your life as well . . . ?" Solihin asked the physician, pausing for effect before adding, ". . . such as . . . between you and your wife?" He touched the man's shoulder as he asked.

The man shook his head. "Not directly."

"Your wife supports you?"

"Yes," the doctor nodded. "*Yes!* Maggie's *wonderful!*"

Solihin looked him gently in the eye. "Then what's wrong?"

I felt my own throat tighten as I watched the man nod for several seconds, words not coming. Finally: "It's me. I . . . I can't seem to find . . . my own self." He exhaled. "In my career . . . nor . . . nor in our relationship."

For a long moment Solihin just leaned over the man, looking him deep in the eye, saying nothing. I sensed some great power at that moment — in the silence, in his simple ability to *be with* someone.

"We identify ourselves as *doctor,* as *teacher,* as *a professional,*" Solihin finally said, turning to the class. "And we shade our view of the world with that screen. *But are you a doctor?*" he asked turning his gaze back to the man.

The physician couldn't speak. He shook his head, not knowing how to answer.

"You are," Solihin said, "but you are not." He again looked deep into the man's eyes. "So what are you?" And when again the man shook his head, he pressed: "First and foremost, at deepest core, *what - are - you?*"

The doctor's voice was hoarse. "A human being."

"Yes," Solihin touched his shoulder a second time. "A human *being* with a divine soul which at times takes on the identity of *doctor,* at other times *husband,* and at other times *baseball coach, father* or *waffle-maker.*" He smiled kindly at him, whispering: "And yes, that doctor may have conflicts, as does the husband and the other identities at times. This is the process of being human.

"But all that time you are still that *being,* still that *soul,* still a vessel of divinity, the deepest part of which has no conflicts. It is only the *mind* — the *trickster* — which locks us into believing we have to be one thing or the other."

That was the beginning of the session. Solihin would later find things that related the doctor's severe eczema to that schism as well. All the while, Solihin continued to use the muscle testing procedures and hand modes to get unexpected answers that at once surprised and obviously deeply touched some hidden truth in the doctor. Solihin resorted to direct verbal responses only after the hand modes pinpointed the areas that needed to be revealed. The most remarkable thing was how *precise* each finding seemed to be. As strange as the procedures themselves were, they somehow seemed to *cut through* to nothing but the most pertinent information.

The hand modes Solihin used could be described — on one level at least — as specific finger positions which stimulated certain acupuncture points which abound on the hands and, when linked together in specific combinations, contained particular meanings.

"On a deeper level," Solihin told us, "the hand modes are a sign language of sorts. A silent dialogue between me and my client to get both our minds out of the way — for I, too, often don't know the meaning of a mode until I look it up." There were hundreds of these modes, each found to have a different significance. One position, for example, might represent a past trauma, another an ancestral issue and another, something to do with cultural influences.

"But most importantly," Solihin continued, "the modes represent a language between a person and him or her self — the deep *inner self* of the soul and the external *outer self* which may have lost touch with that inner one."

What was so fascinating to watch was how the muscles of each person would stay strong or go weak depending on the mode's appropriateness, thus slowly piecing together the person's story as if completely independent from what the person might think that story really was.

"This is the language of our *inner*," Solihin described. "The prince or princess inside all of us that, no matter what wounds our *outer* — our *outer minds*, our *outer bodies*, our *outer selves* — undergoes, always remains pure, untouched, unscathed and servant to the divinity inside each of us."

I might have been able to doubt the English doctor's beautiful words, and did indeed initially doubt the experience of my own muscles responding to the different hand modes when inexperienced classmates worked on me. But what I couldn't doubt was the look in the eye of each person after Solihin finished a session on them. I was captivated by the bewilderment in their eyes, the tears and the radiance of something having been touched — from where, or how, they understood as little as I — but nevertheless, something having been *touched*.

Somehow, after five days I had managed to be the only attendee that Solihin didn't work on in front of the class. Though I didn't say it, I sensed Solihin knew I didn't want this, on whatever silent level he seemed to know so much. And I don't know why now, after all the other difficult parts I have written about in this book — stories that are such a part of me and *touch* such a deep part of me — why now, as I write *this*, tears should come.

"The object of this work," Solihin stated over and over again, "is non-violation. Complete non-violation. Nothing is done without 100 percent consent of the patient. Both outer verbal consent and inner self consent via neuromuscular testing. Anything less than this is violation, the practitioner inserting his or her *will* into the process, making his or her own process — his or her own dynamics — a force that potentially creates a new problem in the client."

The fifth day of the seminar, the final hour, I asked the question that, unbekownst to me, caused the sequence of events that would forever change my life.

It was a completely innocent question, one that had no intention behind it other than to find an answer to something that had been bothering me since the beginning of the seminar; since even before, when Eric Weiden — the doctor who told me about the seminar — had said Solihin's work was very time consuming and complex to apply in practice.

"Your material is wonderful," I addressed Solihin, the class suddenly, as if by premonition, silent. "But where does it fit in when working on the average patient who comes in off the street suffering from some pain or dysfunction?"

"If all you want is to treat pain and dysfunction," the British physician replied in a way that made me feel he had been waiting for me to ask the question, "then perhaps this work isn't for you. However, if you want to provide a medium of growth not only for your patients but for yourself as well, this is what you need to be doing."

He began to turn away at that moment, then slowly, as if moved, turned back toward me. Looking me dead in the eye, he asked: "What's irritating you?"

I choked. *"Huh?"*

"What's irritating you?" he repeated, this time more penetratingly.

"Why, nothing," I laughed, suddenly very self-conscious of the 15 pairs of eyes glued on me.

"What's irritating you?" he said again.

"*Nothing*," I again laughed, feeling incredibly uncomfortable, unable to figure out what I had said to provoke this . . . *attack?*

And he said it again: *"What's irritating you?"*

And for what felt like the next half hour but in truth was probably just a few minutes, the doctor, clad so casually but resonating with all the British righteousness and bulldoggedness of Winston Churchill, persisted.

When I look back on it now, I suddenly sense a similar dynamic as when, so many years earlier, my father called from the funeral home where my sister was lying in state to tell me that he thought *"it would be good for me"* to come. That, after I had plainly told my father earlier that I didn't want to come.

It seems that the same angel who prompted my father to make that call — which subsequently lead to the life-changing revelation I would experience upon seeing my sister's body — must have prompted me to make my remark to Solihin, and Solihin to pursue me, as well.

And just as the British doctor was teaching how the seed to find the true human was contained within every trauma, every issue, every wound we exhibit, I now can see how this probably holds true for every word, every action we also make.

Just as Solihin's entire persona seemed contained within that initial spontaneous greeting to me when I entered the bed & breakfast, and similarly, how his whole essence might be perceived in the fact that he preferred we address him by his first name as opposed to what was the universal protocol in such seminars . . . as *Dr. Thom* . . . so, too, perhaps, my entire seed was contained within the question I had posed to him: all my doubts, all my hesitation and all my discomfort in dealing with seriousness and conflicts in both my own life and that of my patients.

But at that moment, as Solihin — from my viewpoint — pummeled me over and over again, asking, *"What's irritating you, what's irritating you?"* there was no such philosophical or intellectual processing going on in my mind. There was only the bewilderment and skewness of my entire history rising to the surface, nonplussing and totally disorienting me like the sensation I had experienced one daring time when I jumped from a plane into 150-mile-per-hour somersaulting oblivion before my parachute opened.

On one level, I might have perceived Solihin's persistence at that moment as him violating me, violating everything he was teaching. So much so, in fact, that finally, after all his pursuing me with: *"What's irritating you, what's irritating you?"* I responded:

"The only thing irritating me is your thinking something's irritating me!"

But then there was his suddenly gentle response: "Would you be willing to allow me to see if there is something behind this?" And similar to finding myself suddenly dressing to go to the funeral parlor after my father's call, I was surprised at my own choked response of, "OK."

And from that moment on, even though I knew there were 15 pairs of eyes glued on me, it seemed like there was only Solihin and me in that room.

Yet it felt like I had *two selves* there: The self that was verbally responding to his direct questions, and the part of me — seeming almost *apart* of me — that gave him much of the information through the nonverbal neuromuscular tests.

Looking back on it I now understand this is why I hardly remember anyone else being in the room — why I was so captivated without, perhaps, even realizing the degree. The part of me telling my story wasn't conscious . . . wasn't *me* . . . at least not the *me* that had any control over the neuromuscular testing responses I was giving. And yet . . . it *was* me. Some deeper part of me that spoke with an honesty, an innocence and a truthfulness that caused me to tremble.

"This mode is called *Occupying Your Space*," Solihin addressed the class after putting my fingers in a certain position. When he pulled on the wrist of my upraised arm to test how my muscle reacted to the input, much to my amazement, I had little strength to resist him. At first it felt like Solihin was pulling much harder than when the muscle stayed strong. But what confounded me — even after watching this work on everyone else over the last five days — was the knowledge of how strong I could make myself; that when I set my mind to it, no one could budge me. Even though I have a slim build, all the way back in high school, there had been few people who could beat me at handwrestling — even the football players who generally weighed up to 100 pounds more than me. I won a lot of quarters that way.

Yet here was Solihin, someone my approximate size, who would put my fingers in these strange positions and get my arm to weaken as if through no will of my own.

"On one level," Solihin said to the class when he first started working on me, "by the amount of 'fight' he's putting into the muscle test, he's demonstrating that he doesn't really want to talk to us. But on another level, the fact that his nervous system and muscles *are* responding to the proper modes, a deeper part of himself is saying, *'Yes, I do want to talk — please help me.'* "

Now, 20 minutes into the session, Solihin looked down at me with those penetrating, hooded eyes. "So, Michael, what's *occupying your space*?"

I shrugged. Solihin turned to the class. "Anyone have a feeling?"

"His religion?" someone suggested. Solihin tested my muscle after asking: "Is it your religion?" Much to my amazement the muscle again went weak, meaning in this context *no, not your religion.*

"His education?" someone else volunteered. Solihin proposed the question to me, and again I went weak with a *no.*

"Some trauma?" Solihin asked in response to another suggestion.

Slowly acclimating to this new language, I was expecting the muscle to be strong, meaning *yes, a trauma.* I knew if there was anything *occupying my space,* it was the experience that had earlier occupied such a large portion of my life: the trauma of the six years of my sister's illness and, most recently, the repeat experience with my father's diagnosis.

But to my great surprise, the muscle went weak, meaning *'no, it's not a trauma that's occupying your space.*

"Can you test that again?" I whispered. Solihin looked down at me, nodding. Again, the muscle went weak.

"A trauma may be part of it," he gently said, "but it's not the most important piece of information that you — in your deepest self — want us to start with."

I nodded, somehow feeling choked, knowing I indeed did not like — did not now want — to talk about my experience with my sister's death . . . or my father's diagnosis.

"Is it a belief?" another classmate proposed.

Solihin raised his eyebrows to me. "Is it a belief?" This time when he tested my arm, much to my amazement, the muscle stayed perfectly strong, meaning *yes, it is a belief.*

Solihin tested the muscle again, pulling with all his weight, knowing I needed the verification. But I wasn't budging now, the muscle suddenly an iron post that barely even perceived the force being exerted upon it. And yet . . . I couldn't relate to the idea of *a belief . . . occupying my space.*

"Any clue what this belief is?" Solihin asked me directly.

I shook my head.

He looked down at me with thoughtful eyes. "Let's ask if it's appropriate to find this belief. Is it appropriate to find this belief right at this moment?" he questioned, testing the muscle. This time it went weak — meaning *no, it's not appropriate* — boggling me with the sudden change from its iron post state. And yet, on some deeper level that I didn't yet comprehend . . . it felt . . . *right.* This, despite that now, with my curiosity piqued, I really wanted to know which belief was being referred to.

Another classmate suggested, "Ask if it's appropriate to first find where the belief is coming from."

"Good suggestion!" Solihin nodded, then looking at me, asked: "Is it appropriate to find where this belief is coming from?" The muscle was an iron post again, meaning *yes, it's appropriate.*

Again, Solihin took suggestions from the class, asking me, "Is it coming from a person, a group, your upbringing, an authority figure . . . ?" all to which my muscle went weak, meaning *no, it's not.*

Finally, someone said, "Ask if it's coming from a book."

My mind immediately said *no*, knowing that at that point in my life I never read philosophy, religious or self-help books, where I supposed beliefs came from. But to my astonishment, the muscle stayed strong saying *yes, the belief is coming from a book!*

"Uh-hum," Solihin's eyes gleamed. "Any idea, Michael, which book?"

I shook my head, bewildered.

"Is it a book you've recently read?" he asked, and again to my surprise, the muscle gave a strong *yes*.

"What books have you been reading recently?" he asked.

I laughed. "Well, certainly not any deep philosophy books. Just James Herriot's series — *All Creatures Great and Small . . .*"

Solihin was nodding, as if he suddenly understood something; obviously something I didn't understand. Being British, I knew he was familiar with the stories: they had been multimillion-copy bestsellers in both the U.S. and abroad. Written by one of Solihin's countrymen — an English provincial veterinarian — the books told the most wonderful, heartwarming stories of people and of the animals Herriot cared for in the wild mountain dales of northern England. The books formed a series of four, each of which I had read several times, all the while feeling *this is the way life ought to be.*

I told this now to Solihin, responding to his question of what about the books had attracted me so.

"But this is not the way life really *is*," Solihin said to me. "Is it?"

"Why not?" I answered defensively.

"Because life is not all humor and warmth and 'saltiness,'" he replied. "Each of us has our own pains, our own conflicts . . . our own traumas."

"Yeah," I nodded, not feeling I needed to justify my view of life after all I had been through to arrive at it. "But if we go around complaining all the time, wrapped up in our problems, we never get beyond them."

"And what's beyond them?" Solihin asked.

"*Life!*" I practically shouted.

"And what is life?" Solihin asked again, his voice suddenly quiet. "In life — in *your life*, Michael — have you been able to escape all pain and all trauma?"

I bit my lip, feeling furious all of a sudden, not knowing why. And then there was the part of me that was thinking of all that had happened in the last months: with my Swiss friend Vivianne's father dying, with Mona's diabetic coma, with her daughter's struggle to deal with it all. I shook my head, my eyes spitting fire at Solihin as the other part of me continued to think . . . with my sister's death, with my family's trauma . . . with my father's diagnosis . . .

The session continued a long time — I don't know for how long. And during it, it seemed one thing after another led me to slowly tell all these parts — about my sister, my father, my three years overseas to become more "grounded" — revealing these stories with my direct verbal responses and my silent neuromuscular responses. And all the time, Solihin kept asking me a question:

"Is this making sense to you, Michael? Is this making sense?"

And to that question, my constant reply: "Yes, but it's not telling me anything I don't already know. So what's the point?"

Solihin's final remarks came closest to summing up what seemed to me at the time a very jumbled two hours of unrelated, disjointed information.

"From what happened with your sister," he said, "you were given the gift of insight and spirituality at a very young age. Then you needed to get away from it, to become more grounded, so you went overseas for three years and spent the last seven years since your return trying to continue in that down-to-earth mode. But now, Michael, *life* has caught up with you. It is giving you the chance for something very special . . . to have it *all*. To not be one way or the other, but to bring it all into balance. And lastly — without losing yourself in the process — to share the gift you were given with others."

I was silent for the last part of the session, exhausted on some deep level.

Despite myself, I whispered, "What do I do?"

Solihin grasped my shoulder, looked me deep in the eye. "Pray. Open yourself up as a vessel," he said. "Ask for God to help."

I left the seminar feeling rebellious. Though English, Solihin had been brought up for a time in Kuwait. His father, a doctor, worked as Chief Medical Health Officer for the Kuwaiti Oil Company.

"Ma-ah salaam," were my last words to him, the Arabic way of saying goodbye, which I knew from my time in Israel.

I don't know why I chose those words; on some level they were said with a hint of rebelliousness, to show I was still fighting what he told me, to accentuate the difference between him, a Moslem — he having taken on the religion of his boyhood country — and me, a Jew.

Yet on the level of the words, if not my tone, the words said: "Let

God/peace be with you." Exactly what Solihin was saying to me.

When I drove off, I didn't feel like anything that extraordinary had happened. When I think about it now, it reminds me of the only time in my life I got high.

I was at a party with some college roommates who, after years of trying to convince me, finally got me to take a few tokes of marijuana. I did, and nothing happened. No change. I was strong, impervious. I wasn't disappointed.

Then the walk into the other room, where the party was. And the incredible sensation of suddenly realizing I had been transported to another realm . . . to a new understanding.

This is what I experienced the first hour of the dark five-hour ride home from the North Carolina seminar to Atlanta. Transported. *Touched.*

Touched by I knew not what, only that somehow some major shift was then — at that very moment — occurring in my life. There, driving along a dark country road with faceless headlights occasionally piercing the night, some inner vision had been illuminated.

Much later I would realize that when Solihin had been asking me, "Does this make any sense to you?" and I had replied, "Yeah, but you're not telling me anything I don't already know," this was precisely what the Englishman's system did: It told you exactly what you already knew.

However, what I now understand is that we know *so many things,* our lives are filled with *so much,* all the neuromuscular testing procedures do is somehow focus us in on the most important part of ourselves that we need to see *for this moment in time,* to make whatever shift was needed to bring us back to that inner world of truth, peace and of soul.

"Pray. Open yourself up as a vessel. Ask for God to help," had been Solihin's last words to me, words that confounded me. I believed deeply in God . . . ever since my experience at my sister's funeral. But strangely, I had no idea how to pray. To ask for help.

But this I would later learn. It would take me many months until that time, many months to process my experience with Solihin, and many more months until I started fully using his work in my clinic. But whatever was opened in me then went far beyond neuromuscular testing, far beyond hand modes.

So much was brought up during that session, I had no recollection what Solihin had sensed inside me that had been *"irritating me,"* that had been *"occupying my space."* But what happened as a result was beyond those words.

It was as if something long asleep inside had been awakened, given light, given wings. And the ability — the "specialness" which resides in all of us — that had laid dormant in me for so long suddenly had avenue to exercise itself.

But for something I would, to God, have preferred not to have soon thereafter needed it for.

That which began happening with my father.

Part 1V

THE GIFT OF BRAVERY

Where is bravery
in an age when knights are no more?

Bravery is in . . .
Your words, my friend
breaking the news . . .
Or standing by my side
when I received word
of how my earthly journey
would end.

Bravery is in . . .
Your uprightness in battle
when you chose not to leave the field
where I was falling.

Bravery is in . . .
Your gleaming lance
which lead the charge
against the great enemies
of Fear, of Hopelessness, of Doom.

It is in . . .
Your boldness of faith
Your smile of assurance
Your brilliance of garnering all my forces
to never give up hope,
until, together,
we reached the Promised Land.

It was you, dear Knight
who was conquerer
of all that which
blocked the road to freedom
so that I may ascend the throne
to my new Kindgom.

And this now is my gift to you;
You who have already won
The gold heart of immortality
The sunne in splendour.

It is invincibility!
For you have won the greatest war
against the greatest enemy;
So to whom, in your future
shall you fear to speak Truth?

And what man will not fall
in step with you
to share the grace of your gentle leadership?
For who, of value,
won't want to live in your divine land?

My gift to you, dear son, dear daughter
was only to provide the means
for your great bravery
to open hearts,
and rejoice in
what the open heart gleans!

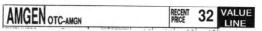

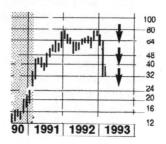

Chapter 33

EVOLUTION
(Insight 8)

The most important factor in making a stock selection . . .

We were sitting in my parents' screened-in Florida room when my father posed the question, "What single factor is the most significant thing to consider when determining which stock you invest in?" This was the first time I had visited in five weeks — a long time compared to the exhausting weekly trips I had made during that frightful period after the doctor informed me of his 6- to 12-week prognosis.

"Gosh, Dad, I don't have a clue," I replied to his question.

"Take your time," he smiled.

I rubbed my forehead, mumbling to myself. After more than a year of lessons, just when I thought I was getting to know this stuff, I didn't have even the slightest notion of what my father looked for when making a stock selection. I took only slight comfort in the fact that he enjoyed being a riddle-maker, liked keeping me sharp that way; and I knew that if he had already told me the answer to the question, he wouldn't be asking. Then again, the riddle assumed I should have figured it out for myself by now.

"I don't know, Dad." I shook my head in frustration.

"Think!"

I puffed out a breath of air, stretched my neck back, as if by looking up at the sky through the screen behind me I could somehow divine an answer.

I abruptly sat up straight. "Growth?"

"Excellent!" my father beamed, and just as I was about to gloat, he added, "Excellent try!"

My shoulders slumped. "That's not it?"

"That's as close as you can get." He smiled encouragingly. "But it's not quite what I'm looking for. Now think . . . what determines growth?"

I rubbed my forehead. "I don't know."

"Yes you do. What drives the price of a stock up . . . or down, for that matter?"

"Earnings?" I gandered.

"Ahhh," he smiled. "That's the ticket."

I nodded as if having known all along, waiting until my father's eyes were averted to wipe a nascent bead of sweat off my forehead.

When he looked back at me, he said, "Just like you've invested years in studying for your profession, and as your practice *evolves,* you begin to see a rise in your earnings, so too a company should see its earnings — and subsequently its stock price — rise, if they've made wise investments in laying the groundwork for their continual evolution."

It was funny he should mention it. I had been thinking quite a lot about that lately. Ever since I came back from the seminar with Solihin, as I slowly tried to incorporate bits and pieces of his system into my practice, I marvelled at how many years it had taken me to reach this point in my career, how long it could take for a life to come together, to evolve into something beautiful.

Throughout my preteens up until age 16, I had only wanted to be a writer. However, after the years of my sister's illness and thinking during that whole time, "There has got to be a different way than medicine," I came upon chiropractic. It was the same year Janie died and I felt compelled to enter this new field.

Yet once I entered practice, I was miserable. Though I helped many people with back problems and occasionally some other disorders, I couldn't handle just working on spines all day. I had the spirit of an artist, and repetition of any kind was anathema to me. I probably would have felt this way even as a surgeon.

Kinesiology opened up an entirely new world for me, both of fascination and of healing. But strangely, after years of studying it and then finally being qualified to practice it full-time on patients with the wide variety of ailments I was seeing, I had discovered even *it* could be repetitive. Not only repetitive, I realized, but limited as well — if I confined myself simply to its more physically based facets, even if that included such subtle energies as those tapped by acupuncture, herbology and homeopathy.

But now, working with Solihin's system, my world had suddenly evolved into something unlimited — I was no longer just working with these refined physical systems, but with the non-physical *soul*, as well.

The realization that I had come full circle was dawning on me.

After so many years of conflict, trying to mold the part of me that only wanted to write with my health career, the two fields were suddenly merging. Using Solihin's system, I was once again writing stories: stories of the human soul. Though my pen was the upraised arm of a patient whose muscle I would test in response to certain hand modes and questions I'd pose, my product was still a story; a story about my patient and how he or she came to have a particular illness, as revealing and thrilling and ever more touching for its living, breathing dimensions than any novel I could write.

And my facility from years of writing gave me that slight advantage during a session in recognizing elements of the story unfold, in tying the components together to make the patient understand — to *touch* them — with its connection to their more physically based ailment.

These were the rewards I was beginning to reap after many years invested in both the scientific and artistic field. The sense of coming to peace with myself, my evolution. And my joy, my earnings.

"Let's look at a company that has made some wise investments in their future," my father was now saying. He handed me a *Value Line* report.

"This company is called Amgen. They're a drug company with two excellent products called Epogen and Neupogen, used in chemotherapy on cancer patients."

My heart skipped a beat. "Don't invest any of my money," I interjected before he could say another word.

"Why not?" He creased his brow.

"*I've* got to tell *you?*" I looked at him. "Dad, you're the one who refused all medical treatment last year. *Why?*"

The question just hung there . . . along with the unspoken memories of my sister's medically prolonged travail.

"And *I'm* the chiropractor," I finally added.

In my practice, I regularly referred patients to medical doctors when I felt a problem could be life-threatening or the slower-working but more permanently effective holistic procedures weren't working quickly enough to keep a patient comfortable. But the idea of giving money to the medical profession after they fought so many years to exclude chiropractors from the health field was unthinkable to me.

"Son, I don't know how to tell you this . . . I'm sorry . . . but I've already put some of your money down on this company."

I felt hot blood rush to my face, tried to control my anger, didn't succeed. "Dammit, Dad!" I spit. "Why didn't you ask me beforehand? You know I would have said no!"

"I said I'm sorry," he replied defensively, his own voice rising. "The stock took a sudden drop. I knew its low price wouldn't last long because it's such an excellent company. I plunked some of your money down along with ours before I could think about how you'd react."

I shook my head from side to side. Not trusting myself with another word, I got up and stormed out of the house.

I went to the beach, walked several miles, swam in the waves. I punched and kicked at them, consciously trying to release my fury at the decision my father had made that he had to have known I would reject; at the control he had always tried to exert on me since I was a kid.

"I would have preferred that you'd have gone to medical school," he had said to me once when we were in the heat of an argument years earlier. It was right before my second trip to Hollywood, when I was talking about taking a quarter off from school to give myself extra time to get some of my television and movie scripts sold during my miniscule three-week summer break. *"With your grades, you could have gotten in anywhere,"* he had shouted. *"But now that you're in chiropractic school, finish it, for crying out loud!"*

I had given in to his pressure, despite that my Hollywood agent and all the other key people I had gotten to know there had beseeched me to stay just a little longer, considering that I had progressed so far in the short time I had spent there. "The only way you can make it in Hollywood is if you are *in* Hollywood," they had said. But I let my father's will override theirs . . . and mine.

His remarks about medical school hurt me on two levels: that he didn't completely support me in my writing, and that his support was only partial for my chiropractic career — a field I felt very dedicated toward. I never even considered entering medicine after all I'd seen with my sister. I believed wholeheartedly in the holistic field, despite my secret agony back then at the thought of eventually having to enter practice if I couldn't succeed as a writer.

Years later — after meeting Kostos, the Greek fisherman — I would understand that my father was only trying to steer me in the direction of greatest security out of deepest love for me. But what I felt then, when he made the remark concerning his previously undisclosed preference that I had entered medical school — similar to what I felt now with his informing me about this offensive stock selection of Amgen — was the weight of his force upon me; of clandestine violation.

I now sat in a shallow tidal pool, tiny waves lapping against my midsection as I stared blankly out across the horizon.

Do you have any idea how much your father loves you? was what Kostos had asked me more than a decade earlier.

An hour later I returned home. My father was still on the porch.

Respect, that's all he asks of you, were the fisherman's words . . . words I was now urgently trying to recall, to again feel the power they had had on me when the Greek angel had initially said them. *Anything* to overcome my feelings of violation, to avoid perpetuating the dreaded clash. I brought the Greek's memory back with difficulty.

I sat down across from my father. "OK, show me the stock," I said to him, trying not to clench my teeth.

He stared at me. "I said I'm sorry."

"It's OK, Dad," I said, my voice rising. "Just please, show - me - *the stock !*"

He looked at me, saw probably a reflection of his own nature, knew better than to push.

"OK," he acquiesced. He pulled out the *Value Line* report; sighed. Then: "You see by the graph line how precipitously Amgen's price has dropped?"

I took it from him. "OK," was all I could trust myself with.

"I was telling you about earnings. Well, Amgen's price dropped so much — from 64 to 32 in just a few days — because their first-quarter earnings were less than what analysts expected."

"Must've been *a lot* less."

"The analysts were expecting the earnings to be 60 cents a share," he replied, not hearing the unintended bite in my remark. "They turned out to be only 55 cents a share — about 8 percent lower than what was predicted."

"And the stock price dropped 50 percent as a result?" I was surprised at my own involuntary display of interest.

My father nodded. "Investors overreact all the time. The interesting thing is that even at that 55-cents-a-share earnings, Amgen's earnings were still 12 cents higher than the earnings for the same comparable quarter one year before when the earnings were 43 cents a share. And their earnings are estimated to continually increase at the rate of 26 percent a year for the next three to five years. See?"

I nodded as he pointed to where the estimate was written on the page.

"The price of a stock generally evolves with the earnings," he continued. "If the earnings increase, so does the stock price — usually at a faster rate than the earnings. And the price has already increased since I bought it for you. You're a couple thousand dollars richer now."

I was about to say something, about how it wasn't a matter of money. That he just plain and simply *shouldn't - have - bought - this - stock - for - me!*

But I caught myself, a word he had used in describing the reason for the irrational price plunge of Amgen sticking in my mind: *Overreaction.*

"Investors *overreact* all the time," was what he had said.

And abruptly, thinking about my intense emotion over his purchase of this medical stock for me, part of me couldn't help wondering: *Was I overreacting as well?*

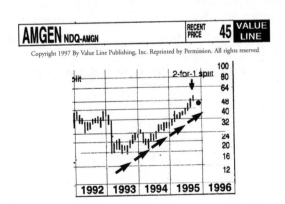

AMGEN PRICE RISE:

4 / 93	16 (after 2-for-1 split)
11 / 95	45

*T*imes of change are often uncomfortable — they make us face areas of our lives where we've gotten stuck. Was I being overly stuck in my opposition to drug companies? Wasn't this lack of flexibility symptomatic of something that needed to be looked at the same way as all the other things Solihin had pulled out of me during that August session?

Here I was, allowing my wrath against the drug companies to place something between me and my father — to place a *schism* there — the last thing in the world I could want, especially now after the all-too-real expectation of tragedy from last year's 6- to 12-week prognosis and the rediscovery of how precious my father was to me.

But the difficult lessons I still had ahead concerned not how medicine had almost come between us, had become an area I needed to look at regarding my inflexibility. The lessons concerned how something much more relevant — much more insidious — in my life was making me less than, in the words of Solihin, *"a vessel of God"* and more a rigid being of preconditioned responses.

What I would need to look closest at was that with which I had finally begun to feel harmony with after so many years.

"Even the very wonderful things in our lives contain the potential for placing something on us," the British doctor had said.

Slowly, as imperceptibly as that which began to inexorably happen to my father — that which would force me to confront something deleterious in my newly found career harmony — I began to see how all my years and all my beliefs in the holistic field might be the most pernicious factor preventing me from aiding my father with all that began to befall him.

Chapter 34

"Michael, someone has to tell your father," my mother's anxious voice whispered over the phone. "He keeps losing weight, Michael. He can't understand why."

It was 18 months after the initial diagnosis. My father had long since passed the grim prognosis his doctor had given. Eight months after that, knowing it would then empower him and not depress him, I told him how the doctor had originally given him only a few months to live.

"You see," my father had triumphantly exclaimed. "I knew those few cells couldn't kill me." He was jubilant. "Boy, am I happy I decided not to have the surgery! If they had removed my stomach, I would have been off the golf course for at least four months, and I never again would have been able to eat a full meal."

"Dad, you truly accepted the diagnosis but defied the verdict," I pumped him up, quoting Norman Cousins. "Not to mention that with surgery, there still would have been no guarantee. There's still a high rate of cancer return."

Despite my confidence that he had won the battle, I continued flying home. Prior to the cancer diagnosis I visited only two or three times a year. After, I began flying to Sunrise Key every third or fourth week, knowing my parents needed all the support I could give them.

"It's really not necessary for you to come so often," my father constantly told me. "I'm doing great. Besides, it's costing you a fortune."

In truth, it was, but to me there could be no higher priority. Besides spending so much money, I was slowly burning myself out, working 14-hour days putting a new practice together and desperately needing the weekends just to do food shopping and recuperate; but I ignored these considerations. It was my parents' time of greatest need and that was that.

"I just look at the airfare like tuition," I told my father. "Tuition for all the lessons you're giving me about the stock market."

"I thought you weren't so interested."

"You've made me interested," I smiled. "Besides, someday I'm sure I'll more than make back my tuition." Though this was an excuse for my real reason, I actually had to acknowledge to myself that I felt this way. Though I never thought much about my own finances, I worried about what life would be like for my mother if anything ever happened to my father, and knew his system was the only thing that would secure her future. And I have to admit, seeing my father consistently earn so much with their savings and mine, it was hard not to be interested in what he was doing.

But there was something else even more important to me. Through all the years of tension between my father and me, there was never any doubt of a constant bond of love; however, we shared literally no common interests. He liked golf, I liked basketball; he lived for the stock market, I lived for creativity and discovering the wonders of the human body and soul.

But now, learning about the stock market provided that missing medium of interaction. Whenever we talked on the phone, whenever I came home, the market was for us what baseball was to other fathers and sons. Instead of quoting home team scores, we groaned or laughed in triumph over the rise and fall of stock prices. DSC, MCI and Compaq Computer were the clubs we rallied behind in our season of communion.

Since his diagnosis I had let golf become another form of interaction with him. My dislike of the game hadn't changed, but there was something else I found at once fascinating and gratifying: My father had become sort of a folk hero at Pelican Bay Golf Club.

It certainly wasn't because of his golf skills, which were nearly as bad as my feelings for walking the course in the intense Florida heat. However, people whom he'd never even spoken to before would come up to him in admiration for his triumph over the dreaded disease they all somehow knew he had been previously diagnosed with.

"Damn, John," they'd say. "How you doing?"

"Doing great," he'd reply, chipper as spring.

They'd pump his hand as if he was a celebrity, scanning him up and down. "You look great, absolutely fantastic!" they'd repeat. In fact, with his slim, muscular build and mahogany tan, my father looked healthier than me! Indoors all day, building my practice, my skin was still white as a baby's.

"I wouldn't have had the guts to do what you did," they'd say, referring to his refusal of surgery. "Jeez, this whole thing hasn't stopped you a bit!" Though my father normally wasn't a very ostentatious man, somehow he loved this attention. It was as if it fortified his resolve.

"When I go," he'd tell them, "I want to go like Huey." He was referring to another man from the club who, despite a crippling lung disease, had been seen on the golf course a day before his death. "That's the way to do it," my father affirmed, nodding his head reverently as his golf cronies followed in unison.

For the last year and a half, each time I'd come to Florida and go to the golf course with him, I'd silently grin at this oft-repeated scene. But then came that September phone call from my mother, affirming what I had been trying to ignore: that my father, however slowly, was losing weight.

At first it was just a pound every few weeks. Then it was a pound a week.

"It could be from anything," I originally tried to explain it away when my mother asked me about it. "Just something his body's processing." But after he lost 15 pounds, it was impossible to overlook how it had affected his previously trim 180-pound frame.

"Someone has got to tell him," my mother anxiously now repeated. "He doesn't understand what's happening. It's the cancer, Michael. *It is.* It's just like the doctor said would happen."

"Yeah, but the doctor said it would be a lot more weight loss in a lot less time," I argued, as if I somehow could save my well-constructed universe — as if words could somehow save my father's life. "He's already lived a year and a half past those predictions," I tried one last time.

But the words sounded flat even to me. And for the first time I saw myself and my father from a different perspective. Despite the nobility of our battle, our raised swords no longer gleamed with the sunlight of inspiration. Continuing on this track, we were no longer King Arthur and the valorous Lancelot. I suddenly saw something more akin to Don Quixote and the hapless Sancho Panza. What was most distressing was, this well-intentioned but incapable pair were not up against imaginary windmills, but rather a true-life monster that would kill one of them . . . and all the more sadly for their ignorance.

And it was with this acknowledgment that I finally knew we had lost.

For the first time I saw my father's image as my mother had so ago-nizingly seen every night of the last year while he changed into pajamas: the once proud 180-pound muscled body of the former aviator and army boxing coach slowly revealing more and more bone and progressively less bulk.

It would seem that, if anything, since my father's diagnosis he should have gained weight. He was indulging his taste buds in a way he hadn't in many years, since he had a heart attack. The period following his first brush with mortality was one of the few times in my parents' marriage where my mother wouldn't be overruled. Health conscious all her life, she put him on a low-fat, low-cholesterol, low-salt diet that essentially elimi-nated all his favorite foods. He reluctantly gave in, eventually telling peo-ple, "If it weren't for my wife, I probably would have been dead a decade ago."

After the cancer diagnosis, however, when it became apparent that his heart was suddenly the least of his problems, my father made up for the years of abstinence with a vengeance. For the last 18 months, bacon, eggs, steak and ice cream were all he ever ate, it seemed. And when he started losing weight, he went at his new regimen with almost religious fervor.

"God, Dad," I'd exclaim. "Don't you think you could occasionally fit in a carrot?"

In answer, he'd theatrically hold a strip of super-fat bacon above his mouth before delectably inhaling it. My mother and I would cringe. But despite our quiet protest, neither of us discouraged him. I would have pre-ferred to put him on a high-nutrition, low-carcinogenic diet, but I knew the *joie de vivre* of eating steak, eggs, bacon and ice cream whenever and in whatever quantities he desired stimulated an animal life force in him that was just as important in beating the cancer as a good diet.

But now, on the phone, as my mother focused me in on the reality I had been trying to ignore for months, I knew she was right.

As if to confirm everything she had whispered, my father got on the line.

"Hey, son!" He sounded robust.

"Hey, Dad. How's the golf game?"

"I'm still driving 30 yards farther with those clubs you bought me. The guys are beginning to think I faked my handicap!"

"Just don't let them in on your secret."

"I won't. Hey, you been following the stocks? We've been doing great! We've doubled on MCI."

"Yeah, I've seen. All I can say is, you're a genius." I cautiously slipped in: "So tell me, Dad, how've you been doing?"

"I'm feeling great!" He hesitated. "But . . ."

"Yeah?"

"Well, I just can't understand it, Michael. I keep losing weight . . ."

Uncertain of myself, I tested the waters. "What do you think it is?"

"I don't know. It's really got me befuddled."

"Well, just keep eating your ice cream," I joked, not sure then just what more to say.

"I am," he sounded disturbed. "But I also feel like I'm losing some of my appetite." As if knowing I didn't know how to respond, he quickly covered. "Hey, have you been watching Ford? It's gone up eight points in the last two weeks!"

"Yeah, and DSC is up another five," I automatically rejoined. We spoke awhile longer, mainly about the stock market. But in the back of my mind the other thoughts wouldn't stop.

When I came to Florida the following weekend, I had my work cut out for me.

I, of all people, should have been able to accept death. After all the lessons I had learned through my sister's slow death, I always considered myself lucky to have confronted and surmounted this greatest fear that people lived with most of their lives.

But why was I now having so much difficulty talking with my father about what was happening to him? It was the weekend after my telephone conversation with my mother. I had arrived at my parent's home in Sunrise Key two nights before and still hadn't gotten the words out.

"Have you spoken to him about it yet?" my mother had asked for the second time the night before.

I bit my lip. "Not yet."

"What are you waiting for?" she anxiously whispered.

"I don't know."

"Michael, if I could talk to him, I would." Tears came unbidden to her eyes. "I just know I'd be too emotional, though."

I put my arm around her, trying not to show how choked up I was myself. "Don't worry. I'll speak to him, Mom."

"You've been so good at it," she encouraged. "He listens to you."

"I know, Mom. I'm just waiting for the right moment." I sighed. "I promise I'll talk to him before I go back to Atlanta tomorrow night."

I saw the burden lifted from her and felt thankful. But I felt a great heaviness in my own heart, trying to figure out how I was going to do it.

My father was dying. No matter how many times I said it to myself, I couldn't objectify it. The the man who was there since my conception, the man who I had fought with and learned from and loved all my life — the man whose seed *was* me — was dying.

It was almost surreal to think about. The slowness of the process had made it easy to ignore. But I could ignore it no longer. Could no longer be in denial. Could no longer take refuge in the inspiring possibilities portrayed in the bestselling books by Chopra, LeShan, Dossey, Cousins and Siegel; possibilities which I had seen become real in my practice but somehow were not working now in my life. In the one situation . . . with the one person I would have given anything to see them work just one last time. As if by clicking my heels . . .

But, no. I was no longer dealing with rainbows. The hard, surgical reality of my father's doctor's words . . . his prognosis . . . were slowly becoming reality to me. Though I knew it didn't always have to be that way — had seen so repeatedly in practice — it *was so* in this circumstance. And though more than a year and a half had passed since the oncologist gave my father only a few months to live, the verdict, however belated, was now coming true.

My father was dying. However much I said it to myself, I still couldn't embrace the idea, couldn't accept it. *My father would soon no longer be there.* Whether in a month or in a year, his time was *limited.* Measurable, ironically, not by a clock, but by a weight scale that was slowly but inexorably ticking down, as if by grains of sand in an hourglass.

It was past midnight when I silently slipped out of my parents' home. They had gone to bed an hour earlier. A cool breeze whipped my skin, a harbinger of the coming fall. Above, night clouds whisked past a full moon, making it change shapes like a fragmenting Rubic's Cube. A half block away I could hear the slapping surf, where I headed.

I stood for a long time on the wooden stairs leading down to the beach, feeling the moist sea tang fill my lungs and wet my skin, beginning to clear my thoughts. The ocean . . . nature . . . has always been a balm for me, a gentle force — even when displaying itself as a gale. It whispers patience, peace and acceptance. *You cannot stop my wind, you cannot halt my tides, you cannot change my ebbs and flows,* it says.

And now it conveyed a new message to me; but one that was somehow old and familiar:

You cannot change what is. The past is past, the future comes. Be here. Be present. Simply allow . . .

Allow? Allow what? Allow my father *to die?*

Life has a beginning and an end. Yet it has no beginning or end. Allow change. Accept. Trust.

These were the silences that filled me when I finally turned and headed home.

My father had refused help from the start; had refused surgery, had refused my advice, had refused all intervention. For whatever reason, he had chosen this course. And now I understood, from what the oncologist had previously told me, that his course would choose his future. There was no turning back, no surgery that could halt the spread of cancer already inside him at this point. And even if there was, I knew he would still refuse it, as I knew he would refuse any holistic intervention I might offer. For whatever reason, he had plotted his path this way.

Though I didn't realize it then, there were two things affecting me. First, I was slowly making the transition myself, from full support of my father's efforts of self-healing to acceptance that this strategy wasn't working. Encouraging him on the self-healing path had been relatively easy; it was in essence what I did every day as a holistic health professional. I had entered chiropractic school when I was 18, and slowly, over the years that followed, the body of knowledge and clinical experience I accumulated made me believe there was indeed a holistic answer to nearly every ailment . . . if we just knew which of the thousands of remedies and procedures to use. By harnessing the life force inside ourselves — either directly via a mind/body technique or through the aid of some quantum stimulus, such as a homeopathic or herbal remedy — answers existed to almost every problem!

But it was this very universe — filled with thousands of hours of postgraduate courses in kinesiology, acupuncture, neurology, herbology and nutrition, as well as reading hundreds of awe-inspiring books such as Dossey's *Space, Time & Medicine,* Chopra's *Perfect Health,* LeShan's *You Can Fight for Your Life* and Siegel's *Love, Medicine and Miracles* — that I now had to break free from.

Cutting through these years of deeply ingrained, beautiful but now paradoxically limiting beliefs, what I was left with was the solidity of faith I had gained through my sister's illness.

Over the next months I would fortify the foundations of this new but familiar universe with books such as Raymond Moody's *Life after Life* and Betty Eadie's *Embraced by the Light*. Whereas my years in health had focused me on the potential of not just the human body, but the human *being*, now I had to expand my universe even further to include my original understanding of the human *soul*.

But I didn't have the luxury of time at the moment. I had to speak to my father. *Now.*

Unfortunately, all the reading in the world couldn't help objectify the second part of what was affecting me: That this was not someone else I was reading about; this was *my father.* No matter how great one's faith, how do you tell someone with whom you've been through so much — someone who, despite everything, you love so much — that he is dying?

How?

Even after my midnight walk, I couldn't sleep. I hadn't slept much, in fact, for the last week since my mother had said *someone* needed to tell my father why he was losing weight, not knowing how that *someone* — me — was going to do it. Even if my mother had been able, I felt it my responsibility. Once my father had shown his adamance about the surgery, I was the one who had encouraged him on his path of the righteous self-healer.

Yes, I had taken the responsibility then and I would take it now.

But suddenly the universe I was operating in had changed, and the rules with it. The absolute certainty I had developed in the body's ability to heal after so many years of study and reading, which I tried to convey to patients with such statements as "There is no disease that doesn't have *some* documented cases of spontaneous remission," and "*Any* condition can potentially respond to the body's wondrous self-healing capabilities," now no longer applied. Forthrightness and boldness of words had to be replaced with subdued patience and surrender. This much I knew — an instinct left from the final months with my sister — when there was no hope, just this sense of other-worldliness, of God.

"I'm just waiting for the right moment," I had said to my mother, and indeed I was. This was one of the rules of this new but somehow familiar universe.

Move when moved.

Patience.

Prayer.
Surrender.
And as I knew somewhere deep in my heart it would, the moment I was waiting for did indeed arrive.

Chapter 35

*I*t had been many years since I had gone fishing with my dad. Once he had started golfing, the peace of fishing became a forgotten experience. Anyway, neither of us was any better at this sport than my father was at golf. This, along with my distaste for killing any living creature, put an end to the occasional times when my father and I had trudged off to the beach, only to return empty-handed. We often wished we had saved the shrimp bait to eat ourselves, rather than feed it to the wily blues and whitings that were obviously more adept at this sport than we were.

But something moved me that September morning to ask him if he'd like to go, and he consented. Thus we assembled our aging rods, tackle box and catch pail, and, looking like we knew what we were doing, headed off to the beach.

"Have the skillet ready, honey!" my father optimistically told my mother as we walked down the driveway.

"Try to get some flounder," she instructed, even though we all knew it would be a lucky day if my father and I caught *anything*, never mind being able to *pick* what we caught.

"One for each of us!" I called back, playing along.

I felt a special tranquility as we made our way the half-block to the ocean and crossed over the two-lane A1A highway. Despite how long it was since our last fishing expedition, it brought back fond memories of our frequent trips those first months in Sunrise Key, when living a half-block from the ocean was still a novelty. Shortly after that, my sister had a relapse, and for the two years following until her death we would not share this joyful — if not fruitful — venture for a long time.

But this September morning was perfect in almost every way. It was just 7:00 a.m. as we entered the gravel walkway to the beach. The sun was muted in soothing pastels behind wisps of clouds, water almost dripping from its ascension from the sea. Every few hundred yards along the beach, dark silhouetted figures of fishermen were casting lines. Early risers walked along the beach, thankful for the secret knowledge that most visitors — intent on experiencing the neighboring town's wild night life — never realized. That this hour of morning was the hour of bewitching.

As we walked, both my father and I were silent, both feeling the magic. Over the years Dad had sacrificed this quiet ethereality for his love of golf; I, by moving to the city. But every time I came to Sunrise Key, it was what I craved — the one thing all the life and activities available to me in Atlanta had never replaced. In the city, after work, I would go to a sterile health club to walk a Stair Master or ride an exercycle. Here I would run through the waves, gauging the length of my workout by the rising or setting sun, not by a computerized timer.

Off in the distance, pelicans planed along gentle ocean swells, occasionally rising up, then rocketing down beneath the surface to catch unwary fish in their expandable bills. And scattered for miles along the beach were hundreds of seagulls, fretting about, poking tiny beaks into the sand for a frenzied breakfast of coquina and sand crabs.

I've got bread, I silently whispered, in the right frame of mind to have something special happen. And almost instantly, it did.

The first seagull that came soaring from the distance flew with a fixity of eye that let me know he had heard. We weren't even down the steps when, from every direction, birds were homing in on us.

"How did they know?" my father asked, both bewildered and thrilled at the flap-happy gathering.

"I told them." I smiled, opening the tackle box and removing the bag of stale bread my mother had given me, then ducking a low-flying sweep one gull made near my head in anticipation of the goodies.

"Well, I guess I've got to believe you," my father laughed, waving his arm at three birds that were hovering just two feet above his head. "I certainly know they couldn't have smelled it from half a mile away when the bread was still in a bag in the tackle box."

I held the first morsel aloft. A quick-reflexed seagull immediately dived and plucked it from my hand without ever touching my fingers.

"I silently said to them, *I've got bread,* and they came," I told my father, with my eye on the next bird that came swooping in for my second offering.

"Hmm." My father shook his head. He walked to the water, setting the catch pail down to assemble his pole.

As the birds continued their skillful dive-bomb assaults on my proffered treats, I felt good, knew that Dad felt good. He hadn't even scoffed at what I told him about silently calling the birds. Small as it seemed, my comfortableness with these strange miracles well described the difference between us. I lived in such a world, felt perfectly comfortable with its galaxies of subtleties — whether it had to do with balancing the fine energies of a patient's acupuncture system, harnessing the power of the tenuous but very real mind/body connection, or plucking trinkets of artistic expression from intangible consciousness via writing.

My father preferred the world of facts and numbers. Though he, too, had a creative side, it was expressed through things you could readily touch and see — such as the graph of a stock market cycle or the hard reality of a financial statement. "I'm from St. Louis," was his favorite expression. "Show me."

But this particular morning held a certain spell, and even Dad was not immune to it. Calling the seagulls started it.

The first time I ever did this was by accident. I was walking to the beach on a cold winter day, a bag of bread in my hand to feed the birds. My mind was wandering, but when I got to the access way I remember looking far off in the distance at a flock of gulls scanning the cold waters for food. As soon as I thought to myself what a treat I had in store for them, it was as if my thought was projected out via microwave radio transmission. Instantly, from close to a mile away, the flock changed direction and headed straight toward me. I stood in disbelief as the birds zeroed in then encircled me, waiting impatiently for me to open my plastic bag of bread.

Since then I have duplicated this experience numerous times. It doesn't always work — only when my thoughts are subdued, when I'm in a state of surrender, and when, in a certain sense, I'm not attached to whether or not the birds will come.

When I *try* too hard, say *C'mon, birds, I've got something for you, dammit!,* it invariably won't work — which of course is always when I'm with a friend, making it into a *trick,* trying to show that it does indeed work. However, when I'm quiet and accepting and not in judgment of myself, the phenomenon invariably occurs.

One of my favorite lines has always been something I heard regarding Jesus: *". . . And he did not do many mighty works there because of their unbelief."*

This was why it is sometimes so hard to get people in our technological "show-me" society to see the wonders that lay just within reach — the tiny miracles that make this a beautiful world. Science has provided us with a life of incomparable comfort, but it has made many of us lose patience for all but the most readily available gratification and stimulation.

The type of magic I have described, however, has no instant on/off switch. The singular passport to this kingdom of subtlety is acceptance and patient expectation. Acceptance that this may not be the right moment, and the patience to wait until it is.

And this day, this perfect weather, and the *coincidences* that would yet manifest on the beach as if orchestrated just for my father's benefit, were now my reward for this patience.

It didn't take long after we cast our lines for the magic to begin. The ocean resembled a lake with just the subtlest swells. Our baited hooks hit the water with a definitive *plunk*. On most any other day there would have been no sound, the weighted tackle quickly submerged beneath foaming surf.

"Take a deep breath," my father told me, breathing gustily in himself. "You don't get this type of air in Atlanta."

I followed suit, enjoying the feel of sea tang in my lungs. "You don't want to take your shirt off, Dad?" I asked, slightly intoxicated. "The air will feel great on your body."

"I'll decline." His eyes temporarily clouded as he stared out at the horizon.

Damn, I thought to myself, immediately regretting having asked. I had forgotten how self-conscious he was about his weight loss. But it was only a tiny mar on what I gauged to be a perfect morning for somehow talking to him about . . . about what was happening to him.

But *how? How was I to bring it up?* Despite the magic, I felt a lump in my throat, the words not coming. *Wait. Just wait,* a reassuring whisper told me.

And then it happened.

"Look at that," my father gaped.

Three dark circles perfectly round and perfectly spaced apart had appeared in the water, just 25 yards up the shoreline from where we stood.

"My God," I replied, in absolute awe of whatever it was we were seeing.

People walking along the beach stopped to look as well. "Do you know what that is?" a sunburned older tourist asked us, his eyes wide.

"Never seen such a thing," my father replied, unable to take his eyes from the sight.

Slowly, almost imperceptibly, the circles moved toward us. My father and I stayed in the water, sensing no danger. As the three 10-foot circumferences moved closer, we could see the surface water in their interiors dancing with activity.

"Why, they're schools of mullet!" my father exclaimed. "Thousands and thousands of tiny mullet!" Seventeen years living near the beach, neither my father nor I ever had witnessed such a phenomenon.

"Will you look at that?" The tourist shook his head. "It's a wonder they don't move from their respective circles."

"Who knows why," my father stared, just as bewildered as the man. During our years living by the beach we had often seen large schools of fish. They usually came sweeping in like a misdirected wave, big blues chasing tiny mullet, tickling our skin as they glided through our submerged legs in their race to wherever. This time, however, there was not one school but *three,* all in perfect formation, all moving in perfect unison, not a single fish breaking rank.

"There's not one of them in a hurry," my father said with strange tranquility. "No predators and no prey today."

Indeed, a heavenly harmony seemed to rule, making it a day of the extraordinary not only for us, but for the mullet as well.

Besides the perfect squadron formations, what was so unusual was how the three circles stayed before us for the next half-hour, ever so slowly moving up the coast, coming within just five feet of where we stood for an extended time.

"Gosh, they're so tightly packed," I told my father at one point, "we could probably catch the entire school with a single cast." We usually took a circular mullet net with us to collect bait. With sharp eyes, quick hands and a little luck, on a good day you could sometimes rein in a few dozen of these fingerlings per cast. Today, however, a single cast would certainly have netted more bait than we could have used in a lifetime . . . if we'd had the physical strength to even rein the catch in.

This thought was far from our minds, the beauty of what we were witnessing too profound to upset with fishermens' zeal. But the life and death struggle was not far away at all at that moment. Our lines still cast 40 yards beyond the schools, my father said to me, "This must be the most relaxing day those fish have had in their lifetime. I doubt there's a moment they can normally drop their guard."

"Do, and they're some other fish's dinner," I grinned.

My father didn't notice my humor, profoundly thoughtful. "This is the cycle of nature. Of life and death. Of all living things."

And in a quiet instant, I knew there it was. The moment I had been waiting for.

"Dad, what are your thoughts about death?" I asked with no hesitation, the question feeling so inexplicably natural . . . despite that it had taken me months to arrive at this moment.

My father's gaze seemed misty, as far away as the horizon he was unseeingly looking out toward. He shifted the end of the 8-foot rod to a more comfortable position on his waist and said: "It's as natural as life. All creatures are born and someday they must die."

"Are you afraid of death?" I asked him, the corner of my eye as fixed on him as his eyes were on the horizon.

An almost imperceptible smile came to his lips. He was silent a long moment. "It's as I told you and your mother once before. I expected to die 50 years ago in the war. That's 50 more years I've had that I never bargained for. Actually, over 50 . . . it's already 18 months since I said that . . . and 15 months longer than the doctor gave me to live."

My eyes felt misty but my voice remained strong, my next question the real one that had been so long in coming. "Dad, do you know why you're losing weight?"

In slow motion, he turned to me. He nodded. "I know, son."

I hadn't expected that to be his answer. For months he had so oft repeated that he didn't know why, he didn't understand. He had been eating endless bowls of ice cream, thinking that would reverse the process. And now . . . he said he knew.

This was the time. No more games. I had to be sure. "You know it's from the cancer?" I asked softly, my gaze steady, my trembling unseen to him.

"I know, son."

I put my arm around his shoulders — an unusual gesture for me, our love usually unexpressed physically. "Mom and I were worried you didn't know what was happening. You acted as if you didn't."

He slowly nodded. "I know I did. I guess I was just afraid to let your mom know it. She gets so emotional." There was a long silence. "And I guess I didn't want to admit it myself."

A small breeze blew. "Does it feel OK?" I asked.

"Feels fine," he smiled. "It's easier getting it out."

"It's easier for me, too." I sighed. "I've been encouraging you so long . . . about beating this . . . this thing . . . it's hard switching directions."

He clasped my shoulder. "You're a good son, Michael."

"And you're the best dad." I wanted to hug him, but my look said it all.

His gaze turned to the sea again. "I just want to live however long I've got left, just like I'm doing. I want to be able to play golf until the end. I just don't want to be an invalid or a burden on anyone."

My stomach knotted. Something told me now wasn't the moment to tell him everything else his doctor had said . . . about the pain he would endure, about the degree of weight he'd lose, about how much his life would yet be compromised. No, not yet.

"You're still in amazing shape, Dad," I said. "Your doctors can't believe it. You've still got a lot of golf games ahead of you yet."

"I just want to play until the end," he repeated.

The last of the three circles passed us. I swallowed, searching for that place of peace in myself. *Gentle honesty.*

Words came to my lips: "Just accept it all as it comes."

He nodded, somehow having heard.

There was a sudden tug on my line. "Woah!" I yelled, the rod almost yanked from my hands. Reflexively, I arched backward, yanking the pole upward.

And almost simultaneously, I saw my father do the same. "They're hitting!" he yelled, his rod arched to what looked like breaking.

In the corner of my left eye I saw a rapid shadow sweep in, traverse my line of vision. In an instant, the three perfect circles that had so slowly crossed to our right were scattered, pandemonium loose. The water broiled beneath our knees, the school of blues that had arrived bumping into our legs in their mad dash for the breakfast mullet.

"Keep your line up!" my father yelled, reeling in furiously. I followed suit.

Over the next 20 minutes we managed to reel in three fish apiece. They weren't flounder, as my mother had requested, but five were well-sized for eating. The only one that wasn't, my father released back to the ocean.

"Boy, will Mom be surprised." I jovially clicked my heels together as we walked triumphantly home an hour later. "It's been years since we've had a catch like this!"

My father nodded. "This should be enough for a couple of good meals, at least."

"Five out of six good-sized fish," I gloated. "What a lucky day!"

"Not for the fish," he grinned, then added, "Well, maybe for the sixth one. I imagine he's back with his buddies now saying, 'Boy, do I have a tale to tell you guys!' "

We continued laughing, our first true laughter in a long time.

Part V

THE GIFT OF SOON-TO-BE ANGELS

I have a gift for you!
It is the same gift
unfolding for me
As my rebellion turns to acceptance
and my pain distills
all suffering into purity
As my body's chaff
separates from my soul's grain,
a gold-hued hand
reaches down
And I find I have wings.

And you, dear loved one
You who have steered my flight
through stormy skies, until
the light shined through
You, dear loved one
Now have wings too!

This is the gift of soon-to-be angels
And the gift from you to me
The gift of death,
My gift to you
Wings of eternity!

Chapter 36

Six weeks later . . .

When I picked up my father at the Delta gate, I had to force myself to hide my shock. I had just seen him two weeks earlier in Sunrise Key, and even though he had lost just another two or three pounds since then, somehow seeing him outside the familiar environment of my parents' hometown, he now appeared to be a different man.

The halting, almost imperceptible slowing of his gait over the last few months suddenly seemed exaggerated. His jacket appeared to hang on his now stooped shoulders, rather than being filled with the hidden power and intensity he once always radiated. And for the first time in my life, the man who had once loomed larger than life to a young boy's eyes seemed . . . *fragile.*

Perhaps it was the enormity of Atlanta's International Airport — the world's busiest air hub with an underground train to shuffle passengers along its mile-long length to its six giant concourses, each with dozens of gates — but my father seemed swallowed by it. I hesitated as I watched his eyes anxiously search the crowd for me, giving myself a moment to adjust to the new vision.

But when I finally mustered myself and greeted him, embracing him, the bony frame confirmed that the vision I had seen was no illusion. I closed my eyes for the moment my arms were around him, silently asking to be cleaned of the vision so that my behavior with him wouldn't be shaded by it.

When we arrived at my apartment, he asked for a little time to rest before we went out for lunch. "I'm not as young as I use to be," he smiled at me.

"Well, you're still out playing golf in heat that would knock most young men out," I encouraged.

What neither of us mentioned was that he had cut down from 18 holes to 9, and from five times a week to twice a week. And that he could no longer walk the course . . . that even riding in a cart for a few hours of play so exhausted him now, it would take him two or three days until he was capable of playing again.

Since our talk on the beach, an ease had entered our relationship. There was no longer the subversive tension of two people holding a secret of which both were in denial. It hadn't been necessary to talk much more on the subject. I knew he still didn't want to let the disease dominate his life, but that was OK now — now that all was out in the open.

But on a deep, sad, silent level, not allowing it to dominate his thoughts wasn't stopping it from slowly, inexorably dominating his body.

"All right," he had said, agreeing to let me fly him up to Atlanta. "Let me see that practice of yours one last time." A stab of chill hollowness went through me at his acknowledgement of what we both knew — that this would be his final trip . . . *ever* . . . to Atlanta. How do you reply to something so unbelievable, so horrifying, stated so matter-of-factly and so acceptingly? The immediate impulse is denial, but because I wouldn't give into falsehood, all that was left for me was silence.

I had arranged this trip as a celebration, wanting to give my father one last view of the world outside Sunrise Key, to pack the three-day weekend with as much life and love as he could handle.

I had hoped to get tickets to the World Series game the following night, but it was long ago sold out when it became apparent that this was going to be a banner season for the Atlanta Braves. But I had several other things carefully planned — all spaced out as my mother had cautioned me to do to allow for plenty of rest, yet somehow still have maximum interaction between us, father and son.

First I took him to my office. It consisted of just three rooms: a reception area, an enclosed space for the secretary and a treatment room — a speck compared to the lavish 15th-floor, 1,500-square-foot clinic I had sold to another doctor in downtown Atlanta several years earlier.

"I don't know about this kinesiology thing you're getting into," my father had said when I first opened this new practice. "You've been so successful with just chiropractic, why change?"

I had tried not to argue with him. "It's not even a choice," I had said. "I'm in my 30s and going into my fourth practice. I've left every other practice out of dissatisfaction. I'm starting this one to make a life, not an empire."

Now, a year after opening, I was barely paying my expenses, spending 30 to 90 minutes with each patient for just about the same fee I previously received for a 5- to 10-minute visit. But my father couldn't ignore the absolute joy I radiated from my work. As he shuffled around the office, he smiled at the simple cash-based ledger accounting book on the front desk, comparing it, I knew, to the computerized, multi-secretaried insurance processing machine that had been my downtown office.

"It ain't Beverly Hills," I smiled to him. "But it's home."

He nodded, proceeding into the treatment room. There were no fancy $8,000 electric tables, but rather a flat, wooden patient bed. The hundreds of mineral, vitamin, homeopathic and herbal remedies filed neatly along shelves above the table — along with acupuncture tabs, essential oils and Bach Flower Remedies — held his fascination, appearing to him, I knew, more like a pharmacopia in some exotic foreign marketplace than the office of a modern Western physician. My father scanned my bookshelves — standard medical *Gray's Anatomy*, *Guyton's Physiology* and *Physician Desk References* intermingled with hundreds of manuals with such exotic names as *Electromagnetic Acupuncture Balancing*, *Homeopathic Energetics* and Solihin's ethereal references of *Essence, Integration of the Vessel* and *Signals*.

I was proud of the office, every unusual item in it a tiny monument to some subtle understanding of esoteric yet wondrous microcosmic laws I had mastered after nearly a decade of postgraduate study. And though my own father — of all the people I wanted to help with that universe of subtleties that comprised my world — refused my treatment, he couldn't help but be touched by the many stories I'd told him of patients I had helped.

As he finished his inspection, he turned to me nodding and said, "You *have* built an empire, son. A different kind of empire, granted," he smiled. "But an empire, nevertheless."

He didn't say it in words this time, but his eyes told it all. He was proud of me.

It couldn't have been a more perfect day. It was early November and

Atlanta looked like a Chinese New Year celebration with its explosions of autumn reds, purples and yellows. I opened the car windows slightly, allowing my father to be bathed by the refreshing breezes as we sailed north along Interstate 75. I glanced sideways to assure myself he wasn't chilled, his body so lacking in fat now. But his chin was up, eyes half-closed, as he tilted his head to the incoming wind stream, exulting in the tiny pleasure in a way only children or pets can . . . or someone who knows their time is limited.

We were silent for a long time. Then he turned to me and said: "So you don't think you could do just a little insurance billing? Even just a *little*?"

I laughed. "I know that's where the money is, Dad. But as soon as you start dealing with the insurance companies instead of collecting directly from patients and letting them deal with the insurance companies, you start putting your mind on business rather than on patients. And I just don't have it in me any longer."

"But you could get *five times* the money you're now getting if people didn't have to pay out of pocket."

"I know, Dad," and left it at that.

After a few moments, he said, "So, any interesting patient stories this week?"

I smiled. Despite his business mind, despite his bull-headedness of accepting any treatment for himself, he loved hearing the many stories I had to tell. It was as if they touched something inside him.

"Did I tell you about the young mother who came to me unable to breast-feed?"

He shook his head. "I haven't heard that one yet."

I proceeded to tell him the story of a woman who came to my clinic because of difficulties lactating, having a slow, decreased flow. Her baby, only a few months old, had been born 12 weeks premature.

"The very first thing we found," I related to my father, "was an imbalance of the jaw, or what's called the *TMJ* or *Temporo-Mandibular Joint.*"

His brow creased. "What does the jaw have to do with a breast-feeding problem?"

I shifted the car into the far left lane to make better time. "Well," I explained, "you know how people sometimes clench their jaw when they're under stress?"

"Yes?"

"That's because the TMJ contains many nerves that connect it to our hormonal system. Clenching actually causes the brain's pituitary gland to release hormones that turn on the body's fight-or-flight mechanism — which is how our body responds to stress."

"So how does that relate to breast-feeding?"

"It relates because the pituitary also gives off something called *oxytocin* — a hormone that triggers milk production in the mammary glands. So if a stressful incident has caused a reflex problem in the TMJ, it can potentially create a problem in the pituitary and with milk production as well."

"Hmm, that makes sense," my father nodded. "So what problem did you find in — how do you call it? Her *TMJ*?"

"Right. Testing one of her shoulder muscles by pulling on her wrist when her arm was upraised — you've seen me do it — the muscle would go weak when I'd have her clench her teeth."

"Why is that?"

"Well, it's somewhat complex to explain, but because there was a problem in her TMJ, *any* muscle I'd have tested in her body would have then gone weak. It's a reflex phenomenon of the nervous system that temporarily *turns the power off* to the muscles when something is done to insult the body. This is the whole basis of kinesiology."

My father is a very skeptical person, but he had watched in the past as I worked on my mother and had let me demonstrate several times how it worked on him. He had been absolutely fascinated by the undeniable weakening of his own muscles. It's a phenomenon that, after more than a decade of working with this system testing hundreds of muscles every day, even I still never grow weary of.

"So what was causing the muscle to go weak?"

"Ahh," I smiled as I shifted the car back into the right lane, allowing a truck to pass. "The weakness was coming from a fiber problem in one of her tiny TMJ muscles. Here's the interesting thing, though. When I began doing a procedure to relax the overly contracted fibers — which involved just manually stretching the muscle — I suddenly sensed something wrong."

"Something wrong?" my father squinted. "What do you mean?"

"I don't know. I just sensed something. Not something physical. Rather some emotion. As if it had suddenly risen to the surface." It was hard for me to explain, for I didn't quite understand where this sense came from.

My father, meanwhile, had turned strangely quiet. When I glanced over at him, he was staring straight ahead. I felt something inside me tingle. Dismissing the feeling, I continued on with my story: "So I asked the patient, 'Are you OK?' In response, her eyes suddenly filled and she began to cry."

My father remained very silent. The tingling inside me returned. And that moment I sensed something very odd — a similar emotion in my father. As if by relating the story, a chord of some hidden memory of his own had been struck.

"Yes?" my father whispered when I was silent for some time.

"Anyway," I recovered, "I stopped what I was doing and took hold of the patient's hand. 'It looks like we've triggered some emotion that's been harboring in your jaw muscles,' I explained to her as gently as I could. 'Do you have any idea what that emotion is?'

" 'As soon as you began pressing there, I started having flashbacks of all the trauma from my son's premature birth,' she said, trying to blink away her tears. 'It was almost like watching a video.'

"Would you like to see if we can find if there's anything preventing you from releasing that trauma?' I asked her, to which she nodded."

I stole a glance at my father again. Almost imperceptibly, he was nodding, too.

"Anyway," I continued, forcing myself to concentrate on my story, "I proceeded to the *Inner Natures Integration* work I've described to you before. Remember? The system I learned up in North Carolina last summer with the English doctor?" He nodded. "Out of the thousands of categories contained within that system," I continued, "each describing a certain sphere of possibility of the human state, the neuromuscular testing procedures isolated a very specific subcategory called *Creating Illusions*.

"Dad, are you listening?" I gently asked.

His head jerked. "Oh . . . yes, son . . . I'm sorry . . . it's just that, well . . ." He hesitated, then seemed to recover. "Your story's fascinating. Tell me more."

"Well, now we had to find out what *Creating Illusions* meant. When I asked the patient directly, she didn't have a clue. So I proceeded to ask her indirectly by checking the response of her shoulder muscle as I questioned, 'Does this situation concerning *Creating Illusions* have to do with your baby?' There was no change of strength in her muscle, meaning the response was *yes*.

" 'Does it involve your relationship with your baby?' I asked. This time the muscle lost all of its strength, meaning *no*.

" 'Does it involve your husband's relationship with the baby?' I proposed. There was no change now, thus *yes*.

"I finally asked her directly, 'Do you have any idea what this is about?' She scrunched her brow and shook her head."

"Meaning she didn't know what it was about?" my father asked.

"Right."

" 'Does it involve your perception of how your husband *views* your baby?' I asked her, retesting her muscle at the same time. It stayed strong now, meaning *yes.*"

"Meaning, *yes, it did have to do with the father*?" Dad asked.

"Right."

"Where did you get that idea from?"

I hesitated. "I'm not sure. It's as if you're in the middle of a mystery, and you keep getting clues which get you closer and closer to intuiting the final answer to the puzzle."

"Hmm."

"Anyway, I looked the patient in the eye and as gently as I could, asked her directly this time: 'Do you in some way — on some level — feel that because your baby was born prematurely and had to be put in an incubation unit, that perhaps your husband *rejects* the baby?' And suddenly she was crying again, giving us both the confirmation we needed."

"Meaning she *did feel* her husband was rejecting the baby?" my father asked, open-mouthed.

"On some level, yes — on a level probably not even previously acknowledged by her. To clarify whether the emotion was based in reality, I asked, 'Does the deepest part of you *really* think, in *any way*, that your husband actually feels this way?' The muscle went weak now, meaning *no.*"

When I looked at my father, his gaze was again out the car window; through, it seemed, *time.* And just as the young mother I was describing originally had no idea what had been locked inside her — had no idea there was *anything* locked inside herself, at all — I now sensed something similar inside my father, arising, paradoxically, just by hearing about this dynamic in someone else. I moved this revelation to the back of my thoughts to finish telling my patient's story.

" 'So is this rejection of your baby by your husband just something that has been created in your own mind?' I asked. And when the muscle stayed strong — meaning, *yes, it is!* — the patient did something beautiful, Dad."

He snapped out of his reverie. "What's that?"

"She laughed. It was just like in that movie, *Steel Magnolias.*"

He looked at me, bewildered. "What do you mean? I didn't see the movie."

"There's a line in that movie that's wonderful — it describes the essence of this *Inner Natures* work. The line comes at the end of the movie when a mother finally breaks through her depression to laugh for the first time after her daughter's death. Her friend exclaims: '*Tears turned to laughter. That's my favorite emotion!* '"

My father just nodded, suddenly off in that distant place again.

"*Tears . . .*" he whispered.

*I*t was three o'clock when we arrived at Kennesaw National Battlefield Park. I skirted by Kennesaw Mountain, where a famed Civil War battle had been fought, choosing instead a more level, less visited area of the park where I knew it would be easier for my father to walk.

Once on the forest trail, the silent beauty of the whispering magnolias and beech trees enveloped us. We moved slowly along the rocky path. I never strayed beyond arm's reach of my father. His gait was so unsteady, I frequently had to shoot an arm out to lightly touch his shoulder when he swayed too much as if he was going to fall. I tried to make my move seem almost accidental, as if I was just brushing up against him. He was a proud man, and I knew losing weight and his faculties — more than the prospect of death itself — was tearing him up inside.

"Old soldiers never die. They just fade away," he had smiled after I learned he had lost another five pounds when I went to Sunrise Key last time. "That's what's happening to me."

But out here, in the intoxicating splendor of the tie-dyed autumn forest, beauty rather than humor was his salve.

After a brief rest, I helped him up off the log he had sat on. As we moved deeper into the grove's cloak, he said, "I wish I could have had this type of experience with my father."

Had we not been walking, I'm sure I wouldn't have been able to hide my dismay. I was in my 30s and had never once heard him talk about his father. My grandfather had died before I was born and I knew little about him.

"My father was Hungarian," Dad continued. "Straight out of the old school. I guess that with six children, his only concern was making sure we had enough food on the table." He was silent for a long time. "I don't think I ever had a conversation with him . . . not the type we've been having these last months."

This simple revelation caught me by surprise. Thankfully, my quiet seemed natural in the forest. I finally said, "You were drafted into the army when you were so young. Then when you came out, six years later, you moved to California, right? Maybe you would have gotten to know him better if you had stayed in New York."

"I don't know," he shook his head sadly. "I don't know."

Though we hadn't gotten farther than half a mile, we'd already been in the forest 40 minutes. Sensing my father's fatigue, after another rest I headed back along the way we came.

And in that silent walk, like some giant yet invisible boa constrictor watching us, gauging our step, I sensed more and more what I had felt in the car — *something* was there, coiled and ready to make its presence known; something long hidden, something so powerful . . .

With a hunter's instincts — cultivated from years of dismantling boobytraps on the dusky path of my sister's death and most recently honed by the gift of Solihin's work — almost unconsciously I plotted the course of my father's emotions, navigating with some internal compass along invisible magnetic lines that were now pulling him to reveal the presence of the serpent, that long-held skeletal secret.

I didn't have the advantage of the technology of muscle testing to track the hidden emotion I used on my patient with the lactation difficulties. To do so would have been to shine a direct light . . . and shadows disappear when lights are too high; they disappear also when the light is too low. Thus, as gently as I was steering my father from tripping over the many roots and rocks on the forest path, so I instinctively steered the conversation as well.

"Tell me more about your experiences in the army, Dad," I said, not knowing why I chose this subject, somehow just *feeling* it was right.

"Well, I've probably told you most of my pilot-training stories when you were a kid. I don't know if I ever told you why though, after all that training, I ended up in command of a land division."

I shook my head, suddenly realizing that in my boyhood fascination with his stories, I had never thought to ask.

He nodded. "I got a bad cold shortly before I was due to get my pilot's wings, so they cut me from the program. It devastated me at the time, but it turned out to be the luckiest event of my life."

"Why's that?" I asked.

"Right after the class graduated without me, all the guys I was with were sent over to North Africa for what became known as the Battle of the Kasserine Pass." My father's eyes clouded. When he spoke again, his voice was subdued. "Every one of the guys I had trained with . . ."

"Yes, Dad?"

"Every one of them was killed."

We walked the rest of the way out of the forest in silence.

*I*t was coming. I could feel the anaconda, or whatever it was inside my father, moving forward, along some dusky path, begging for light, begging to be released, like some aborted fetus that his body no longer could handle.

I had no idea what that dead weight was; I knew only that the experiences he had just revealed concerning his father, then the death of his pilot classmates — however deep an impression they had left on him — were not the full measure of miasmic clouding I was sensing.

Slowly, with all the patience and deftness that I often lacked in so many other areas of my life, I waited. Waited with the attentiveness of the native hunter, strangely quiet inside myself. I understood that I was somehow now — after so many years re-finding that lost capacity from my childhood with my sister — sufficiently *present* to respond as prompted, to find the beast's spore, to nudge its black mass to slowly reveal itself and to allow it its own pace lest I violate the sanctity that had led up to its long coming.

I'll never forget the moment. We were nearly back to my apartment after our forest walk, exiting off the highway onto Piedmont and Cheshire Bridge Road. The air still hung heavy with my father's stories. Something then prompted me to say, "Dad, I don't know if I ever told you this. But all those years leading up to Janie's death?"

He jerked, as if the car had suddenly braked. But we were still moving. I continued: "Those years, Dad . . . as terrible as they were . . . they were the most important years of my life in forming me into who I am."

He was looking blankly out the window now. I no longer knew why I was saying what I was saying, had only some feeling of rightness, some inner guidance that told me my compass was set to true north.

"Remember how I didn't want to go to the funeral, Dad?" I said. "Remember how you called and told me, for whatever reason, that you thought it was important for me to go?"

He didn't respond. But he was hearing.

"That moment of seeing her body . . . it was the most important moment of my life. At that moment I knew there was such a thing as a soul. That hers . . . Janie's . . . had simply left and gone on to some other level."

His head was nodding ever so slightly. But not in rhythm to my words; more, it seemed, to some deep, deep discordant song, long ago locked away.

"Her death . . . instead of scarring me," I said, ". . . somehow made me stronger . . . gave me a spirituality and a strength I don't think I could have gotten otherwise."

He was way off now. Inexorably, I continued on. "I don't know how to say this, Dad . . . I don't know why it's so important for me to say it now . . . but I sometimes feel . . . I sometimes feel her life . . . from some deep level of the soul we don't understand . . . was a gift for me."

His breath was in pants now. If that wasn't signal enough for me to stop, my throat then tightened up on me.

I waited, my heart pounding, not knowing if I — or whatever had moved me — had gone too far.

Then suddenly he was speaking, his voice somehow disconnected, hoarse, but strangely calm.

"And I don't know if you ever knew about this, son. About what happened . . . that last day . . . when your Mom and I took over from you at the hospital . . . right before your sister died."

It was my turn for speechlessness. I could just nod for him to continue. He did, not seeing me.

"Janie had been in a coma for two months . . . two months since she had said her last words . . . a month since they hooked up the artificial life support . . ."

Suddenly I wanted to stop him. I didn't know what he had to tell, but suddenly something felt so heavy, so wrong.

"NO!" I wanted to shout, "NO!" But whatever had impelled me to lead him on to this moment suddenly paralyzed me, paralyzed my throat, leaving me helpless to watch as my father revealed the serpent, the aborted fetus, the knife that for all these years had been pressing up against his heart.

His voice was no longer detached. The next words were choked, his eyes blinded. "She woke up, Michael. That last day . . . from out of nowhere . . . she woke up. She whispered, 'Hold me, Daddy.' I took her in my arms. 'I'm here, sweetheart. Don't you worry about anything. You're going to a beautiful place.' And then . . . then . . ." The damn burst. "Then she died in my arms . . ."

We were stopped at a light now. I shook my head, feeling helpless, bereft, holding onto his shoulder with one hand, staring on unbelievably as wave after wave of sobs came out of him. I was almost as paralyzed by the sight of him crying as I was by the revelation. I hadn't seen such emotion from him since so many years ago at my sister's funeral.

The light turned green. With a line of cars behind me, not knowing what else to do, I unseeingly pulled ahead.

My father's tears were still coming. He wiped his eyes, helplessly trying to stem the flooding. "I don't know where this came from," he choked. "I had forgotten about it. I didn't remember it had even happened."

"I know," I whispered, his sobs in full force again. I let them come, a strange calmness suddenly entering through my emotion, surprising me.

"Why now?" he asked in bewilderment after he regained a small amount of control. "Why now of all times did it come back?"

"It's probably not important to know why, Dad. Only that it was there all these years — locked inside, begging to be released — and somehow, today . . . found the key."

Chapter 37

"I'm tired," my father said simply when we arrived back to my apartment. I led him to the bedroom where he had his luggage. I left him curled up under the covers, asleep before I had the door closed.

He slept for hours. I woke him only because a friend of mine, Uri, was coming shortly to take us to an Atlanta Hawks game. "I know you couldn't get tickets to the Braves game," Uri had called to tell me earlier in the week, "but I've bought tickets for all of us to go to the basketball game instead. Do you think your dad will like that?"

"He'll love it," I smiled, thankful for the wonderful friends I had in Atlanta who were so supportive of me during this time.

And just as I predicted, my father had a great time. "YES!" he yelled hoarsely as high-flying Dominique Wilkins zoomed in for a dunk. "NOOO!" he groaned when the ball was stolen from another Hawks player, lost in the emotion and frenzied high of the packed arena. Everything that had occurred earlier that afternoon was now forgotten — the events somehow cleansed him, leaving him fully free to enjoy the moment.

The whole evening seemed orchestrated just for his behalf. The Hawks came from behind at the last possible moment to edge out their opponents by a single point, leaving us and 10,000 other fans bedazzled in the flush of the exultant conclusion.

Trying to exit the packed parking area, we were hemmed in by traffic. "Boy, this is a mess," my father declared, shaking his head, his customary impatience arising.

From the back seat, I watched as Uri — an irrepressible Israeli — turned to my father. "Hold on, Mr. Norwood," he smiled.

With that he pushed the accelerator to the floor, tires burning rubber beneath us. I saw my father's eyes pop as our car shot out of the lane of traffic. Uri then hit the brakes, pulled the wheel hard left, then right, pistoned the accelerator again and off we went, weaving through spaces I would have deemed impossible, into lanes that were totally illegal, and around and through dozens of immobilized cars filled with passengers too dismayed by the maniacal Israeli to shout obsenities.

Within minutes we were on the highway, screaming along at 85 miles per hour. "There ya go, Mr. Norwood," Uri smiled to him, my friend's habitually insane driving somehow even crazier tonight, as if he sensed some appropriateness to it, despite that he seemed totally oblivious to my father's absolutely whitened features and stiffened limbs.

"Careful of the traffic. OF THAT CAR!" my father croaked, his throat so tight it came out high-pitched.

Uri laughed. "What traffic?"

My friend dropped us off in my apartment complex parking lot. With a wave and a last screech of rubber, he was gone.

As I escorted my father through the darkened lot, I turned to him and asked, "Well, how did you enjoy the evening, Dad?"

The color was just beginning to return to his face. He was silent for a moment before stiffly replying, "Your friend's a real cowboy."

I smiled to myself. Despite my father's conservativeness, despite his rigidness at times — despite all that had happened that afternoon — he had had a great time.

Chapter 38

Look out your window," I said the next day as we zoomed along the freeway. "It's coming up on your right."

"What's that?" he asked.

I never had to answer. The next moment, the awesome sight materialized through the grove of roadside trees, quickly dominating the skyline as our car banked a turn.

"Wow," my father involuntarily sucked in his breath.

"Thar she is," I smiled triumphantly. "Stone Mountain. The single-largest naturally occuring granite formation in the world." The sight of it never failed to amaze me, even after living nearly a decade in Atlanta. One moment you're cruising along the highway, the terrain somewhat rolling but for the most part flat. And suddenly, out of nowhere, is this massive granite edifice, 800 feet high, five miles around at the base, rising up from the earth like some orphan moon.

My father and I were not the only ones so impressed with it. The mountain, along with the park surrounding it with 400 acres of lakes, was one of the reasons the Olympic Committee chose Atlanta for the 1996 Olympics, nudging out England, Australia, Canada, Yugoslavia and even Greece for the 100th anniversary of this grandest of sporting events.

Dad stared in awe at the shear-faced palisade as we entered the park. An under-rated Southern version of Mount Rushmore, giant bas-reliefs of Civil War heroes Jackson, Lee and Davis were carved out of the face of the precipice, a gargantuan effort by three separate men spanning over a half-century.

"The best is yet to come," I told him as I guided him to the ticket office of the Stone Mountain gondola ride. And indeed, I wasn't exaggerating.

As we climbed out of the gondola after a dizzying ascent up the mountain, a gust of refreshing air swept us, the temperature 5 to 10 degrees cooler than at the base of the mountain. "Here, Dad, I've brought a jacket for you," I said, helping him into the windbreaker I had folded up in a small backpack.

Putting his arms into the sleeves, he almost lost his balance, so taken was he by the landscape. "It looks like the moon up here," he intoned.

"Wait, Dad, you haven't even seen the view yet." I guided him from the cement walkway out onto the grand plateau of the mountain top, its thousands of craters still glistening with tiny amounts of water from a rainstorm several days ago. With the terrain so rough and his balance so compromised, it was impossible to use just a ghost of a hand to steady him as I did during our forest walk at Kennesaw; I had no choice but to hold his arm firmly now. But the fresh air and the spectacular 360-degree view were so mesmerizing, pride was the farthest thing from his mind. I don't think he even noticed my hand.

"Why, that's downtown Atlanta, isn't it?" My father pointed a finger in wonder at some distant specks of skyscrapers.

"Yep," I nodded. "That tubular shaped building is the Peachtree Hotel. It's so clear, you wouldn't know we are probably 20 miles away."

"And what's that mountain there?" my father asked, pointing well north of the city.

"That's where we went yesterday — Kennesaw mountain — probably a good 30 miles from here."

Ever so carefully I guided my father around the circumference of the aerial plateau as we silently — omnisciently — took in the entire forested city spread in quiet splendor before us. From this elevation, one could still hear the beep of a horn from an impatient driver or the siren of a racing emergency vehicle. But the sound was muted, the events detached, we benevolent witnesses. Life was taking place down there, people were going places, the city was growing. What is it about high places that touch us so?

And suddenly, almost without realizing, words of a distant song my soul had once sung filled me:

High above the valley, bordered by an expanse of

magnificent forest, and rising into a broad-faced moun-
tain with a snow-capped zenith, the spirit hovered . . .

Then I knew . . . what had moved me to take my father here. What vacuum this place was filling, capable like no basketball game, golf course or Wall Street ticker tape to fill a soul with the grandness of its own immortality . . .

Like rays of the sun covering everything, yet each beam
focusing on a particular point, the spirit observed the
entire paradise with all of its being . . .

I wanted my father to imbue himself with the memory of this place, with the silent beauty of a high altar, with the holiness of a spirit's eye.

The valley was composed of a large lake whose crystal
clearness reflected the verdant forest into which it bla-
tantly cut. At the sight of such pristine beauty, the spirit
dropped a single tear into the glassy water spreading con-
centric circles to each end of the lake which rebounded
back to the bosom of its formation.

"Thank you," my father whispered as we stared out over the lake that surrounded the mountain, past the miles of forested carpeting, beyond the downtown skyline, into the seamless horizon. "Thank you for taking me here," he repeated.

I never had to say a word, never had to say that I wanted him to remember this sense of what a spirit's world perhaps was like, beyond the world of man's machinations, his creations, his technology, his worship of statistics, numbers and money.

I would later give him a copy of the essay I had written many years earlier, a few months after Janie's death . . . that he might see what had been stirred in his son's soul . . . that perhaps he may now have stirred inside himself.

Stirred, now that he had arrived at the final dire months of his own soul's earthly journey.

Chapter 39

The memories my father took with him from Atlanta were some of his last of earthly joy. I had meticulously planned for this joy, sensing on some deep level the trial that lay just ahead for him.

That final night in Atlanta I invited a number of close friends to my apartment to watch the fourth game of the World Series. The Atlanta Braves would win, making another perfect evening for my father's visit.

My friends gathered there were people from all over the world who I knew in Atlanta — Narsi from India, Osnat and Uri from Israel, Quing from China, Antonio from Italy, Cynthia and George from America, Kim from Korea, Cecelia from Mexico . . .

"Why, it was like a meeting of the U.N.!" my father would later exclaim to my mother and to golfing buddies who'd visit him. "My son can challenge Ted Turner with the international network he has!"

My friends came that evening with intention. They knew what was going on with my father, knew why he was in Atlanta, why I had been flying so frequently to Florida for 18 months now. They knew how much their coming meant to me, how much the evening was designed to touch my father. And they knew I wanted it to be a celebration.

"We fight the angel of death with life," I recently heard a clergyman say on a televised sermon to his Oklahoma City congregation after the Federal Court House bombing there. And that's what I tried to do that night. To have a celebration of honor, of laughter and of triumph. But most of all, a

celebration of life.

Chapter 40

*A*s I sit here and write, for the first time I am empty of words. It is two-and-a-half years since I began this book, nine months since I began a concerted effort to finish. And suddenly the next page doesn't come.

And so perhaps it was with the real story. The part that I — and all who have been through a similar experience — *wish* did not happen, the part I *wish* did not have to be told. Until now it has been natural for me to fill the lines with the beauty and spirituality that I was blessed at the time to recapture from my youth. But those final six months . . .

How can I maintain this narrative without forsaking the pain and awesome terror of a disease gone haywire? How do I avoid denigrating the terrible trial my father — my family — went through, at the same time conveying how like in the eye of a hurricane, another reality was always present? How do I tell of this ultimate duality . . . of immense suffering and ethereal revelation?

I sit in silence, not knowing.

And then it comes to me. What I've known all along. The answer is in how I've chosen to tell this story from the start.

On one hand, the events of this narrative live in the realm of ultimate materialism — on the level of the stock market where the singular goal is the acquisition of *MONEY* . . . motivator, mover and *God* of so many of us — perhaps even the attraction of some readers to buy this book. Yet all along, as I learned about this world, there was an entirely different level always present: the love that motivated my father to teach it to me, the love that made me ignore my distaste for this world so that I would allow my father his legacy; and most significant of all, the spiritual blossoming in having to confront death again while all this was going on.

For this is life at essence — a fight, a struggle, a daily existence in the heart of living, where whispers of something deeper constantly challenge us to open our eyes and ears to hear the deeper rhythm, but somehow to do so without losing the louder beat of life — the stock market one of its many drums.

So I tell of the final lesson of my father's legacy.

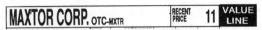

| MAXTOR CORP. OTC-MXTR | RECENT PRICE | 11 | VALUE LINE |

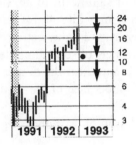

Chapter 41

BODY & SOUL

Form vs. Content
(Insight 9)

P/E (Price/Earnings) ratio.
Interesting if particularly low for its industury group. Low p/e may be appealing but not always revealing because there may be other factors more important.

"*I* think . . . I've found . . . possibly the next . . . DSC Commu. . . Communications."

"You have?" I said, hoping I was able to affect enough enthusiasm to cover the hollowness I was feeling seeing my father in this state, listening to his broken whispers.

"This stock, Michael . . . contains . . ." He had to pause to find the strength. ". . . the . . . potential . . . for being a . . . ten-bagger."

It was a month after my father's trip to Atlanta. He had lost another seven pounds. The dull, intermittent pain that started in his abdomen four months ago had slowly increased in frequency and intensity. Now it was almost constant and of such high intensity, at times it took his breath away. Golf — one of his few joys — was no longer possible for him. It took tremendous energy for him just to talk.

"A *ten-bagger?*" I exclaimed. "Wow!"

He started to say something, grimaced, then as if knowing he didn't have the breath to finish the sentence, leaned forward on the Florida room couch, holding the armrest, trying to gather strength. He could barely keep his head up, his chest heaving now from the effort of speaking.

I clasped my hand over his. "Dad, why don't you rest awhile, then you can finish telling me about this a little later."

He nodded, leaning back on the seat, face etched in pain as he closed his eyes. I quietly stood and took the *Value Line* report he had given me into the other room. In truth, I had no stomach for thinking of finances, didn't know how my father could still be doing so. But I also knew it was the only pleasure left for him in life, the one thing he could still do, rising above the debilities of his illness to yet make several more pointed stock selections — all of which would later turn out to be, in his lingo, *double-* or *triple-baggers.*

This stock — Maxtor Corporation — that he was now so excited about would prove to be the one exception. But in a far different way than he expected.

I forced myself to shake off what I was feeling. My mother had warned me about these episodes of pain and exhaustion Dad was now undergoing. Most of the time he could still talk fairly normally, still had a reasonable amount of energy to shuffle in his faltering gait around the house or the yard. He had even *driven* last night *by himself* the 15 minutes to the airport to pick me up. Despite my mother's protests, he was not a person to be overruled, even at this stage.

It was only a few weeks since I had last seen him. And despite how well I hid it, every time we re-enacted the scene of him picking me up at the airport, I couldn't help but feel deep shock. Each trip he weighed progressively less and less, his cheeks more and more hollowed, his gait ever more faltering. Somehow, after being with him a few hours, it wasn't so upsetting. But that initial shock . . . rather than diminish, increased from visit to visit.

Looking back now, I realize that part of the reason I never acclimated to it was because the image of him that was so ingrained in my mind was not that of sickness, but of a trim and muscular former boxing coach. It's the same phenomenon I experience with people who haven't seen me for a long time.

"Michael, have you lost weight?" almost everyone always asks me. In truth, I weigh the same as I did in high school. My weight hardly ever fluctuates. But because I am slim and carry myself with an air of high vibrancy, people probably store in their minds the memory of vibrancy, not slimness. Thus it's always a surprise when they first see me.

So it was with my father. And even though he was indeed progressively losing weight and his faculties, my mind never incrementally compared it to the last time I saw him, but rather to the quantum fall from the image I had of him in full health.

I forced myself to shake free from the comparisons, from my sadness. Though learning about stocks never fulfilled me, it did distract me. So I observed the *Value Line* report my father had handed me on Maxtor Corporation.

Dad had highlighted the p/e, or price/earnings ratio, in yellow marker. Of all the concepts my father had been teaching me to grasp, this was the most difficult.

"The price/earnings ratio is often an indicator of how good a deal a stock is," he had told me earlier.

"Better than a dropped stock price?" I asked.

"Not better, just another factor to consider. The price/earnings ratio illustrates the relationship between a stock's price and what the company is earning — whether it's over, under or fairly priced compared to other companies in a similar industry and compared to its own growth rate. For example, if a company is earning a lot of money but its stock price is at a relative low, you know the stock is a better deal than if its stock price is at a high and it's comparatively not earning a lot of money, right?"

"Makes sense," I nodded.

"Another way to look at it," he said, "is it's the difference between the company's outer *form* or *perceived* value, versus its deeper *content*, its *true* value. A stock's price — its *form* — changes moment to moment. But a stock's earnings — its *content* — is much stabler, much more indicative of what a stock is truly worth."

Body versus soul, I thought to myself. *The body always changing, the soul always constant, always true.*

"So if a stock drops in price," my father continued, "that will affect the price/earnings ratio. Can you see how that would work?"

"I think so," I replied hesitantly, fascinated by the spiritual metaphor I had perceived, but my head swimming trying to visualize my father's mathematical figuring.

"Well let me give you another example. We bought MCI Communications at $24 per share. Its last four quarters' earnings at that point totalled close to $3 per share. So to figure out the price-to-earning ratio, you divide the price by the last four quarters' earnings — or $24 by

$3. So what does that make their p/e ratio?"

"Um . . . 8?" I queried, easily doing the division, but my mind scrambling in the process of making sense of it all.

"Right," he smiled. "So their price/earnings ratio was 8, whereas the rest of the telecommunications industry had an average p/e of 13 — meaning the stock prices of these similar companies were higher and their earnings were lower, relative to MCI. So which was the better deal? MCI or one of the other companies?"

"Well, since I know we've doubled our money with MCI, I'm sure it's MCI, right?"

My father nodded. "Precisely. The price began increasing when investors got over their fears of the dropped price and realized it was a great deal."

He had gone on to explain how most investors think short-term — 3 to 6 months ahead — and thus it took a while until the price started rising, because everyone wanted to first see that the price was moving up. Because my father always invested with long-term prospects in mind — 1 to 5 years — he was able to buy the stock at its lowest point when few other investors wanted it.

This was his rationale for buying Maxtor Corporation, the stock he was currently showing me. He bought his first shares when the stock had fallen from its high of 19 a few months earlier to the then-low of 9. Total earnings for the last four quarters then was approximately $3 per share, giving it the phenomenally low p/e of *3*.

"That's almost unheard of," my father whispered to me later that afternoon, after he had rested awhile and got his breath back. "The computer hard-disk drive industry . . . which Maxtor is part of . . . currently has an average p/e of 7 . . . more than twice that of Maxtor. And the average p/e of the entire stock market is . . . is currently *14.*"

"So is that why you said this stock has the potential to be another DSC Communications?"

"Yes," my father smiled, his excitement causing his respiration to begin shortening again. "Maxtor's price can more than double, and . . ." He paused momentarily to get his next breath. ". . . and only then will its p/e . . . match that of its . . . competitors. But the entire disk drive industry is currently . . . is currently slow . . . so once it gets over this . . . cycle . . . Maxtor will . . . boom."

*I*t was one of the few stock selections my father made that turned out to be wrong. He would later invest more in the stock when it fell to 7 and even more when it hit 6. I'm sure that, as sharp as my father was, he would have soon thereafter pulled all his money out, accepting his losses when it became obvious the hard-disk drive industry had a lot of hard times yet ahead before turning around. (At this writing, two-and-a-half years later, it hasn't recovered yet.)

However, lacking the time, the experience and the hair-trigger feel my father had for gauging stock conditions, once I took over managing the stocks, I would continue to invest in Maxtor all the way until it hit 4.5. I would later pull out of it when it was at 2.4, finally doing the research to realize the company's health had fallen along with its stock price, thus making it a company my father would have long ago left.

Distraught over how much money I lost — my own and particularly my mother's — I would later take comfort in the fact that the year we recorded that loss, our portfolios had still substantially risen based on the profits from many other excellent investments my father had made and I had maintained.

Meanwhile I had learned an invaluable lesson. Not just about stocks but about life, as well. Yes, both stocks and life have their ups and downs. Like companies, as a person goes through life, their *earnings* — their knowledge, their experience, their *content* — generally increases, even though at times they may have low points. But following such low points, just as long as these life earnings are still high, they will rise again.

However, sometimes, as was the case with Maxtor — up to the time of this writing, at least — companies *don't recover.* Whether we are talking about a country, a stock or a person's life, nothing — other than a soul — lasts forever. Countries fall, corporations go bust, and people die.

This was the difficult lesson I would learn not only with Maxtor, but with my father as well.

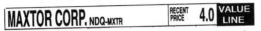

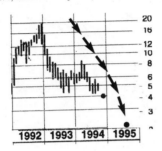

MAXTOR PRICE FALL:

| 12 / 92 | 20 |
| 08 / 95 | 2.4 |

Chapter 42

Stomach cancer is one of the most painful of all diseases. Yet despite the excruciating shock waves that so frequently ripped through his body, my father refused all medication.

"Why are you so stubborn, John?" my mother would beseech him. He'd just wave her away.

"Dad," I'd try to convince him, "you know how much I'm against unnecessary medicine. But this is *necessary*. Why not allow yourself the relief?"

But he'd remain stubbornly silent, his quiet agony the very shield that prevented me from pushing him further on the issue.

Then, finally, one day when the pain wasn't so bad and his mood was higher, he admitted to me, "I'm afraid to take the medication, son. The one distraction I have left is the stock market. I don't want any medication to scramble my faculties." He paused for a long moment, then gave the deeper reason. "And the one thing I want to leave this earth knowing is that I've left your mother secure."

In the few years since he began investing, he had multiplied their savings at an astonishing rate. That was after paying all their bills and taxes with their stock earnings. "Just a little more time," he said to me, "and I'll know your mother won't have any worries." He paused. "But it'll be your job, son, to take her to the finish line."

So he bore the pain through the ensuing weeks and months without remediation of any kind, as I began flying to Sunrise Key every week, staying at first just Saturdays and Sundays, then Fridays, then Mondays as well, never knowing when it would be my last visit with my father, my fledgling practice slipping away as a result of my constant absence. But this was hardly a consideration; I could build it back later. After . . .

With the last of his strength, I watched my father invest in Artisoft and Filenet, two software companies that would, within a year, triple and quadruple in value. Nine to 18 months later, selling these multi-bagger winners, my only regret was that I hadn't added substantially more shares to our positions when I initially took over from my father. We would have just a small fraction invested in them, compared to the immense investment I kept adding to the ever-falling Maxtor.

One of my most deeply ingrained memories from the ensuing period was how my father struggled to not give up following the stock market. With golf long gone and his being in so much pain, it was the one earthly joy he still had. His consuming desire to leave my mother secure fueled that passion. Even when he started seeing double, my father continued his daily vigil, struggling through *The Wall Street Journal* and watching the *Financial News Network* for hours every day.

The double vision was the cruelest of cancer's tricks. It mocked my father's ability to monitor the stock market and stay, in some small degree, in the heart of life. Bereft at how he yet still fought against the ever-advancing disease, I gently asked him, "Would you like me to take over at this point, Dad?"

He was silent for a long moment. "I don't mind this double vision," he finally said, summoning some strange mixture of bravery and humor. He pointed down at his portfolio outline. "It makes it look like I've got twice as much stock!"

But then finally, a few weeks later, came the one memory my mother and I will never forget. My father was in the living room, barely able to sit upright any longer, the pain so intense. And as he did every day, he reached for the phone, struggled to focus on the numbers, trying to dial *Fidelity Investment's Touchtone Trader* hotline where, through the phone, he received automated updates on the rise and fall of every stock in our portfolios.

Yet, this time, something was different. Despite his immense concentration, he couldn't get his fingers to hit the right numbers. Over and over he tried, unaware of my mother and I, who, sensing something wrong, had simultaneously entered and stood speechless at opposite ends of the room. For five . . . ten . . . fifteen minutes he continued to try, squinting his eyes, poking helplessly at what must have been just a blur before him.

He finally put the phone back in the cradle, it rattling until he got it to settle properly. Then he flopped back exhausted. His eyes turned to me, as if he'd known all along I had been there. And in a gesture that to this day sears me, he whispered, "Time for you to take over, son."

After that, he gave in to taking the medication, as well.

Chapter 43

During the last four months of flying to Sunrise Key every week, I kept telling myself *I would know* when I should no longer fly back to Atlanta. *Something would tell me* when my father's time was near, that I should no longer leave.

How I knew that I would know, I cannot say. *Intuition, the whisper of an angel* . . . that I don't know either. I just *knew that I would know. Would know* when I could no longer leave my father even for just a few days. *Would know* when I could no longer leave my mother — earthly angel, exhausted being — so close to physically and emotionally collapsing, originally after the six years of my sister's illness, now from two years of my father's.

But above all, *knew that I would know* when any reason I might have for leaving — to maintain my practice, to maintain some degree of mental health — would no longer exist; when there was no place I was supposed to be other than at my father's and mother's side.

Henri, the Hospice nurse, had already begun her weekly visits more than a month ago. "She's *wonderful*! " my mother had told me on the phone. "Your father loves her."

"Your Mom's right." My father's voice had come through the receiver, hoarse, but stronger and with more *force de vivre* in it than I had heard in a long time. "She doesn't try to hide anything. It's very comforting having someone who's so straightforward."

I had not met her yet; had no premonition of the circumstances under which that first meeting would take place.

Then it happened. That night after so many months of being unsure whether it would be my father's last night. The night when, after so many hours of excruciating pain — even with the medication — my father fell into his deep, troubled slumber. When I would awake to find him fumbling with the bottle of tranquilizers, not knowing how many he had taken to escape the misery which 99 percent of the time is relieved by the powerful pain medications Hospice provides. Medications that were only partially effective with my father; some journey, some lesson of his soul overpowering the earthly force in a severe purification process my father was destined to endure before leaving this plane.

The night when I would listen to the so-difficult-to-hear words of my father telling me he was proud of me, proud of how I had grasped his stock system, that I was now the care-taker of my mother. The night when, sometime in the wee hours I would leave my father's room, not knowing if I had just heard his last words. To seek comfort in a book from his generation, *The Caine Mutiny,* and awaken a few hours later to a silence that made me scramble to his room. To find his still body, to be stunned thinking he had finally passed, then suddenly, amazingly, hear a gasp of breath from him 45 seconds later. Then, two hours after, to watch him awaken when the Hospice nurse entered the room and hear her say to him those brave, awesome, acknowledging words: *"You almost went last night, didn't you?"*

To see the tears — my father's, the nurse's and those of my mother standing stricken beside me — then to see the tears turned to smiles, and the smiles amazingly to laughter, as the angel-guided nurse helped an old warrior learn of Grace and Surrender. Tears that were yet locked in me, even when portraying that scene in writing three months after its occurence but which since have begun to flow freely . . . through the process of two to three years' writing . . . of asking every day during that time that my own vessel be opened so as to avail to even just one reader the ethereal gift that death had somehow availed to me.

And so I write, trying to transcribe some distillation of pain and suffering, of beauty and divinity which I sense is the wine I have cultivated; the fruit of the years growing up in the shadow of death somehow the seed for these passages; the pain of yesterday's fomentation and crushing, the liqueur of my life's celebration today.

And this, more than anything, is what I have hoped to convey. That through life's most feared event — death — life can again be found, brighter, livelier and more sweet and succulent than ever before.

"*Where's Kevorkian when you need him?*" the Hospice nurse had smiled at my father, lightening the awesome acknowledgement of his near death.

"*Give him my regards,*" my father had, through a flow of tears, smiled back, exhausted but comforted, displaying an amazing resilience of spirit.

Death is indeed the ultimate lesson to live life in the moment . . . as reverently and as fully as God has intended us to do. For the best of the grape is found only after passing the extremes of pressing . . .

Chapter 44

"Michael, is your father well enough for us to see him?" The question was hesitantly asked of me over the phone by Mani, a very close Indian friend from Atlanta, a week after that first night of my father's near death.

Even though Mani — a professor of industrial engineering at Georgia Tech — was a little squeamish about such things as hugging, had he been there with me when he posed the question, I would have crushed him in my embrace.

How can I ever repay these friends, whose earthiness and humor were what I craved most at that dire time? They showed me their love not through words, but in the most beautiful way possible — offering this wonderful gift of themselves to me and my family.

"Let me ask him, Mani," I had replied. "I'll call you back."

Through a haze of pain and drugs and exhaustion, the mention of my friends' names caused a phenomenal reaction in my father. "Do I want to see them?" his eyes popped open. "Are you kidding? Of course I want to see them! When are they coming?"

I blinked, amazed at the physical transition simply hearing the offer induced in him. "They want to come next week."

"Absolutely!" he emphasized. "Let them know I'd *love* to see them." Then, more serenely, he stated, "Just let them know I may not have the energy to spend much time with them."

"They'll understand, Dad."

A week later my friends Narsi, Mani, Mani's wife, Heju, and a Korean friend, Kim, arrived after an eight-hour drive from Atlanta. The moment they entered my parent's house, I could tell everything would be OK.

"Hello, Mani . . . Narsi . . ." My mother greeted each of them with such happiness, as excited as I to have my friends' auras of lightness and laughter penetrate the quiet somberness that had become our world. "Hello, Heju, . . . hello, Kim, . . ." she continued, receiving warm hugs from the girls and shy kisses on the cheek from the guys.

Narsi, a colleague of Mani's at Georgia Tech, was the first of these dear friends I met when I moved back to Atlanta from overseas. Narsi's humor was beguiling to me, as flavorful and enigmatic as the multitude of spices from his native land. It reflected all that quixotic transcendality I associated with India, as well as a Pandora-like wiliness. A professor of information systems at age 26 with an IQ that defied gravity, it was treacherous for anyone who might try to match wits with him.

One day we were discussing types of foods from his homeland. "You don't have much seafood in India, do you?" I stated, more than asked.

"Michael, you couldn't be more wrong," he woefully shook his head, always enjoying his role as benefactor of my enlightenment. "In India we have many fishes . . . *so* many fishes!"

"Fishes?" I grinned delightedly, thrilled to find myself suddenly one up on him. "Did you say *fishes?*"

"Yes," he creased his brow. "Fishes. Is something wrong with that?"

"*FISHES?*" I guffawed, even more surprised he didn't recognize his gaffe. "C'mon, Narsi. You're a professor. *FISHES?*"

"So?"

"*So?*" I dug it in. "Narsi, *fishes* is not a word! The plural of fish is *FISH!*"

Whatever I expected his reaction to be, it wasn't what I received.

"Michael, Michael, Michael," my unflappable friend smiled sagaciously, shaking his head in pity. "This is what you Americans have done to the Queen's English."

"C'mon, Narsi," I said. "You're not going to get out of this one. Especially making claims to speak *the Queen's English* with your accent!" I glowed from the added jab. With his rolled *r's* and his Indian lilt, Windsor Castle was the last place I'd expect to find him teaching fine points of the language.

"First off, Michael," my friend stared me unnervingly in the eye, "considering there are 900 million Indians compared to only 200 million Americans, I'd say it's *you* who's the one with the accent." The unabashedness of his remark caused my jaw to drop. "And second," he continued unrelentlessly, "you are wrong. *Fishes* is a proper usage."

His doggedness floored me. A week later I would come home to find an unmarked package on my doorstep. Mystified who could have put it there and what it contained, I popped it in my VCR before even changing clothes. A beautiful underwater panorama filled the screen as a diver swam with eerie tranquility amidst a sea of coral, sea anenome and immense schools of Clown Triggers and Rainbow Wrasses.

My palms unaccountably began to sweat, part of the queasy premonition I was beginning to have. I shifted uncomfortably in my seat as the narrator's voice filled the air to the background popping of underwater bubbles:

"... and it is only off the coast of this small atoll, amidst the vast expanse of the entire Pacific, that such huge numbers of the enigmatic Purple Reef Wrasse can be found. Solitary for the rest of the year, the resilient denizen travels the South Seas as a lonely voyager for all but a few days of the year, where finally in one huge Mardi Gras-like gathering, this colorful sea parader joins it's kin and massive schools of other **fishes** for this annual celebration of beauty and pageantry. Such **fishes** live for this event ..."

I clicked the video off, sitting for a while in bemused silence. But my friend wasn't done with me yet. I then noticed a piece of paper that must have fallen from the package to the floor. It turned out to be a photocopy of a page from Webster's Dictionary. The following was marked in yellow on it:

fish (fish), n., pl. (esp. collectively) fish, (esp. for kinds or species) fishes ...

Yes, it would be a while before I'd argue with Narsi again.

*K*im was the newest member of our tiny clan, having just moved to Atlanta from Korea a year earlier. Though her English was hesitant, her warmth and sweet nature made us accept her immediately into our extended family fold. My parents were crazy about her.

"Do you like her?" they had asked repeatedly, first when they met her, later when my friends came to Florida on an earlier visit to see my father.

"Like her?" I asked. "I *love* her!"

"Then why don't you do something about it?" my father had encouraged.

I frowned. *Why not, indeed?* "I'm too close to her," I said. "She's like a sister to me. You just can't start a relationship with someone like that."

"Don't hurt her," my mother warned, showing the exact extent of her feelings for the young girl, this type of protectiveness usually reserved for me. "She likes you too much."

That I knew. One of the things that so charmed me about Kim was her complete lack of guile and the ease with which I could make her laugh and show her feelings. Because of this I loved to tease her, to catch her off guard.

As we were walking around the lake at Emory University's Lullwater Park one day, I suddenly stopped in my tracks. My mischevious smile didn't belie my honest curiosity when I shot: "Kim, why do you like me so much?"

She whirled on me, her reply just as lightening-like. "Why do I have to know?" she enchantingly stomped in display of her shock that I should need to ask.

The honesty, humor and simplicity of that answer sticks in my mind to this day, having stunned me at the time. And when I think about it, it is those qualities — spontaneity, unexpectedness and caring — found in all four of my friends that made their visit to my father so special.

Mani and his new bride, Heju, each had their own unique charms. But like Kim's and Narsi's humor, each had a similar unexpected quality.

When they were married, Mani had arranged a traditional Indian wedding in which there would be no clergyman officiating. Because of this, a few days prior to the main wedding, the young couple first had to have a small civil ceremony in the downtown Atlanta Federal Courthouse to make their union recognized under U.S. law. Just one other couple and I attended the somewhat mundane affair, held by a judge who, just a few weeks earlier in the same courtroom had arraigned Walter Leroy Moody, the notorious bomber who had been sending exploding packages to other Federal judges. Compared to the incredibly memorable ceremony Mani and Heju would have later with hundreds of out-of-town guests, exotic Indian rituals using pungent incense, goblets of fire and costumes of the

finest Far Eastern silks, the whole governmental affair had an air of, well
. . . a bureaucratic act of state.

Despite this, Mani had been so nervous getting ready for it, I had to
help him put his tie on and button his shirt straight. After the ceremony,
as our tiny group drove out for a small celebratory dinner, Mani's relief was
palpable. When I asked him what was going through his mind as the judge
made the couple say their vows, he replied, "All I could think was: Please
God, don't let me forget my name!"

As the chauffeur, I observed Heju in my rearview mirror, looking daz-
zling in the regalia Mani had purchased for her. Her expression, though,
was as inscrutable as a tiny jade Buddha. I asked: "And what was on your
mind during the ceremony, Heju?"

"I kept telling myself," she replied, " 'Don't yawn!' "

*A*s my international friends greeted my mother in my parent's foyer, I
sensed that their visit to my father was going to be very special. My mother was extremely nervous about Dad becoming overly exhausted. He was
in a medicated daze most of the time now, his moments awake times of
extreme pain for him, while we anxiously waited to see if the medication
would work that day. We were constantly having to ask the daily-visiting
Hospice nurses to get his doctor to increase the dosages.

However, when I walked into his room to gently inform him of my
friends' arrival — similar to a week earlier when I originally told him they
wanted to come visit him — another amazing metamorphosis occurred.
He immediately pressed the button that raised the trunk portion of the
bed, sat up straight and shook his head back and forth several times, trying to shake off the stupor of the powerful medications. Focusing on me,
he asked that I hand him the comb on the nurse's stand.

As I watched him straighten his hair, I worried how my friends would
react to the sight of him. He had lost 40 pounds since they last saw him.

"You all didn't have to take the time off work to drive so far down here
to see me," my father grimaced with a painful, deeply touched smile.

I froze, sensing my friends' undisplayed shock at his emaciation and
the metal-barred hospital bed. But they never missed a beat.

"We're always looking for an excuse to take a vacation," Narsi laughed,
going up and shaking my father's hand.

"Driving eight hours for an overnight stay is hardly a vacation," my father said.

"Well," Mani quickly rejoined, "nothing any of us had to do was more important than coming to see you."

I felt my heart fill as my father took each of their hands, his eyes gleaming with such appreciation . . . that they had gone so far out of the way for him.

"You're all such busy professionals," he persisted, his voice slightly louder than a whisper, but stronger than it had been for many weeks. "You've got more to do than to waste your time visiting a sick old man."

"Oh, you're going to be OK," Heju smiled, leaning over the bars of the hospital bed and giving him a hug.

I froze, but my father took the denial of reality in easy stride. "Well, I don't know, sweetheart," he smiled at the young Chinese girl, acknowledging how difficult accepting the fate of someone you care about can be — especially acknowledging it directly to them. "I think this old soldier may be on his last legs."

"You can never say," Mani shook his head, the exaggerated puckering of his lips one of the many expressions that made even ordinary things he said so outrageously humorous. "In India, my family had a close friend who was dying of cancer. We all went to say our goodbyes to him . . . the doctor told us we should say our goodbyes to him . . . his Buddhist priest came to say the earthly gods were saying goodbye to him . . ." Mani stopped, just standing there, nodding his head in reverent memory. All six of us — my father, me, my mother, Narsi, Kim and Heju — waited with bated breath for him to finish the story. But the storyteller remained still, off in his own world.

"And . . . ?" Narsi finally broke the silence.

"Huh?" Mani blinked.

"And . . . your family's friend died?"

"Oh! . . . Yes . . . sorry! *No* . . . I mean, he did die . . . but not of cancer."

"Then . . . from *what*?" I asked, expressing the bewilderment of all of us.

Mani shook his head with regret. "It was a few days later, when the man got a bill from the doctor . . . then when he received a bill from *the priest*! . . . *then* he died! But not of cancer . . . of a *heart attack*!"

Dad laughed so hard with the rest of us, he ended up clutching his abdomen in pain. My mother had cautioned my friends that my father probably wouldn't be able to spend more than a few minutes with them. But so the next hour-and-a-half went, my father waving aside all my and my mother's anxious inquiries if he wasn't exhausting himself, he exhibiting one last show of strength and vitality that we thought long ago had left him.

"Tell my father the 'Mani comes to America' story," I prodded, once I saw Dad had no intention of letting the group leave just yet.

"Yeah!" Narsi joined in. "Tell it."

"Do you want to hear it?" Mani asked my father.

"Absolutely!" he exclaimed.

"Kim, do you mind hearing it again?" Mani addressed her.

Though having remained shyly quiet since entering the room, she enthusiastically shook her head. "Oh, yes! Please . . . tell it!"

"You don't mind, Heju? You're sure you don't either, Michael?" We both shook our heads, each of us having heard Mani recount the tale numerous times before. It was always we who, as now, prodded him to retell the story whenever new people were present.

The way Mani told of his first moments arriving off the plane from India, lost in the confusion of Kennedy Airport, struggling with four loaded suitcases, bringing one at a time up . . . then down . . . the escalators there, accidentally breaking up a car robbery in progress, enchanting New York's finest cab drivers and seemingly half the city with his natural friendliness and off-the-boat innocence, grew more hilarious — and more outrageous — with each telling of the story.

By the end of it, we were all gasping for breath, the room transformed from a home hospital room into something akin to a comedy club.

When our laughter finally began to subside, Dad said, "And now I have something I want to do for all of you. Can you wait for me in the family room?"

Mystified, my friends enthusiastically agreed, leaving me to help my father out of bed to get his robe on, then lead him on legs that could barely support him any longer down the hallway to where our visitors were waiting for us.

Just as we reached the doorway to the family room, my father paused a moment. Like a distinguished performer gathering himself to make one final grand showing on stage, my father straightened his posture, pushed aside the walker Hospice had provided, then with my hand supporting him, made his entrance into the room.

My friends gave him a delighted round of applause, not expecting this type of display. I myself didn't know what Dad had in mind.

He glided — at least it seemed that way, compared to the faltering stoop with which he barely managed to limp to the bathroom in the last months — over to the piano bench, lowering himself with my help and positioning himself on it, the unintended sweep of his robe appearing like a cape. It took him a moment to balance himself on the bench, then he leaned forward and began to hesitantly flip through a notebook of hand-written pages on the piano.

My friends were breathless as they watched him squint, trying to over-come his affected vision to find the piece he had in mind. He finally stopped at a certain page, peered very close at the scrawled notes for a pro-longed period, then, with difficulty, turned in stages on the bench to my friends. "I can't thank you all enough for coming down and visiting me."

My friends began to protest his heartfelt appreciation, but my father held up his hand. "When you think of me in the future," he said, "I'd like you to remember me with this song."

He began to play. And even though he was no master, always proud that he was self-taught, the original tune and the hoarse words of his crack-ing, untrained whispering voice resounded to us on a wavelength that held each of us captivated.

> *From a place on high*
> *Beyond the twilight sky*
> *With vision ne'er so clear*
> *Your voices ever so dear*

I felt myself bite my lip, looked at my friends, saw their hypnotized looks.

> *You'll wake one day, with a start*
> *Feel yourself, within my heart*
> *A hand to your breast, you will hold*
> *My autumn season, now spring gold*

I was thankful my mother had left our company earlier, too nervous to stay as my father expended every last drop of joy in his pores.

> *I'll always be gazing, where you are*
> *You'll see my wink, in nearby stars*
> *And in the breath, of newborn lambs*
> *You'll yet know, that I still am*

There was just the briefest pause of playing, the briefest silence, right before my father came to the final words:

> *Your name upon my lips*
> *My soul with you yet sits*
> *Until that tomorrow day does come*
> *And we're reunited, all and one*
> *A song forever sung!*
> *A song forever sung!*

The silence remained long after the last note had dissipated into the air. The smiles, then finally the applause my friends and I gave my father, couldn't hide the deep emotion, the deep chord he had touched in each of us.

It was the last time my father ever played the piano.

Chapter 45

*O*nly someone experiencing a similar situation can understand the significance of the gesture my friends made in coming to visit my father. It is this type of outpouring of love and caring that gives meaning to the tragedies people suffer from. If there is a divine purpose to the tremendous ordeals some people must endure — and after spending eight years in the shadow of sickness and death of two of the dearest people in the world to me, I can say I believe more than ever that there is — it is to experience this unconditional love of friends, family and, sometimes, strangers. And for those special people who find the strength and courage within to rise above their fears and the natural desire to spend one's time in the heart of life, they in turn receive a momentary taste of immortality.

In the few years since my friends' visit to my father, Mani and Heju moved to Oregon, Kim became engaged and Narsi teaches at Princeton University, flying back to Atlanta every few weeks to manage his new consulting firm. Despite the occasional gliches that arise in every relationship when people are so close, to this day I will never forget nor be able to thank these friends enough for the love they displayed, taking the time from work and out of their lives to see my father. They gave him the humor my mother and I — so close to the situation — no longer had left in us.

They gave him his last moments of earthly joy.

Chapter 46

"Michael, please come home, oh, please come home," my mother cried over the phone. "Your father's out of control."

"I'll be there in just a few minutes, Mom," I said, my hair suddenly on end. "Just hold on." My heart was tearing, my mother too upset to explain any further. But I needed no explanation.

I had just brought my father's car into a Midas Muffler shop. I had called to let my mother know I was running late. Now, with my car up on the rack, I felt helpless. I rapidly explained the situation to the wife of the shop owner, begged her to have one of her employees drive me home. She took me herself, sharing, as we raced in the car, that she had lost a sister to cancer five years earlier. She understood.

I arrived home to a situation that, of everything I have written about so far, is the most difficult to relate; one which took me several months to even talk about.

My father, in a medicated daze, would one moment be sitting on the family room couch. Then the next moment, with a strength that seemed to have left him long ago, he'd pull himself up and limp around out of control. Any attempt to stop him would result in his incoherently wrenching out of my grasp, as if in some malevolent drunken stupor.

I don't know how I finally settled him down. Perhaps I have just forgotten, or perhaps I have partially blocked out that which was so painful to see: a noble, dignified man of the highest intelligence . . . my father

. . . in a state like this.

And perhaps even more distressful to me is the memory of my mother's helplessness . . . her tears, her shame, her sorrow . . . at seeing what had become of her life partner.

I do remember later taking my rage out on Henri, the Hospice nurse, using that awesome animal force I know is latent in me to make her assign us round-the-clock nurses. Perversely, that force is the same one I dreaded most in my father when I was a teenager, and the same one — through the haze of drugs and illness — that was now preventing him from peaceful surrender.

I would later deeply apologize to Henri, whom I reduced to tears with undeserved guilt. Hers was an overworked staff and as the overseer of my father, there was no science for her to know when full-time nurses needed to be assigned. But even once we had trained nurses around the clock, it was I, over the next weeks, who would be awakened in the middle of the night by my father's semi-coma awakenings, his crawling over the bars of the hospital bed like some skeletal phantom, the nurses unable to stay these out-of-control rages of the 95-pound former boxing coach.

I have chosen not to go into further detail on these difficult memories. Such overreactions to cancer and pain medication is almost unheard of, and I wish not to burden with unnecessary worries those who are reading this for comfort during the sickness of their own loved ones. Every Hospice nurse I have since spoken to has been amazed that the medication wasn't more effective with my father. I've learned that in almost every single case, pain, suffering and anxiety can be controlled to make dying patients very comfortable both physically and emotionally. But with my father, apparently, some remnant force no longer befitting his noble soul had to be exorcised before he could proceed on his journey.

During this most difficult time, I recalled a story Antoine once told me. While we were students, he worked all night at a mental health institution to make his way through school, somehow surviving on only a few hours sleep. Despite his short stature, there was something about him that would compel the nurses to call him whenever a patient went out of control. One night, one of the patients — a Mr. Little — who suffered from psychotic bursts of anger, suddenly jumped on my friend, pinning him to the floor.

At first stunned, Antoine caught his breath, collected himself, then serenely smiled up at the powerful man whose knees were in his chest. "Mr. Little, I never knew you were so strong!"

The man's deranged eyes suddenly focused, bearing their full intensity into those of the young Asian he was straddling. And from out of nowhere, the ill man's distorted features softened as he burst out in a peal of self-seeing laughter. With an embarassed smile, he rose off my friend, helped him to his feet, dusted him off, then walked back to his room.

I don't remember how I handled my father, where I found the ability or the inner strength. What I now understand, though, is how every moment of our lives is preparation for some bigger, more important moment, some greater test we will one day have to face. Part of my preparation had been my special friendship with Antoine; and that which preceded my father's death was my ultimate test.

Chapter 47

By the time C.J. arrived, we had already gone through six different Hospice nurses. As soon as C.J. walked through the door, however, we knew immediately there was something different about her.

How we knew this I can only describe through Solihin's work, where a person's innermost content gets unconsiously projected to his or her physiology as exhibited by the strong and weak "*yes*" and "*no*" neuromuscular responses the person gives to various verbal and nonverbal questions. So, too, I have come to realize, our entire history is encoded in our cells, creating an actual *field* that we project. Con men may get away with lies, manipulators with stepping on anyone who get in their way, the bad may become rich, and a phony may receive the highest accolades. But every gesture we make, every word we utter, every step we take makes a footprint on our souls. In the whispers of our hearts, we always know our own truths and the truths of those we meet; and in those same stirrings, those we meet always know ours.

And so it is with angels. Carried within their field is all the love they have unconditionally given, all the forgiveness they have risen up to bestow, all the goodness that has been received by those who have been so blessed in their path. Their reward is not money, but timelessness. Radiance rather than riches. Sweetness rather than addiction. And the bank from which their paycheck is drawn forever pays dividends, for with every act of giving, so they are receiving — tied not by obsessiveness to whom they can get the most, but bound by silent love to those to whom they can most give.

Perhaps it was the combination of C.J.'s years of experience as a Hospice nurse, or her natural competence, or her inborn empathy, but when this woman arrived at our home, my mother and I sensed something instantly. Two things we knew for sure: this was a soul that had found her deepest calling, and there was no way we were going to let her go.

We begged Henri to not have C.J. rotated out of our household, as had happened with the prior nurses, who were either moved by Hospice headquarters to new cases or who we requested be changed for various reasons. Knowing the extremeness of my father's condition . . . and of our desperation . . . somehow Henri managed to arrange for C.J. to remain with us.

C.J. was the first nurse who could control my father's ghostly rages, the first whose presence started his process of surrender. The first with whom I would finally be able to sleep a night through, her visits during the day setting up a cycle that somehow carried into more peaceful nights as a result of her intuitive knowledge of the precise amounts of medication, love and strength my father needed.

When Patty was assigned to us as night nurse, our long months of desperation finally eased as much as it possibly could, given the circumstances. Patty had the same attributes as C.J. Having two such presences within our midst, along with Henri overseeing, amounted at that time to the greatest gifts from God.

On a *20/20* special recently aired on television concerning the deadly psycho-physiological disease of anorexia, a young teenager brought back from the brink of self-starvation by a most gifted and beautiful health worker is asked by the interviewer, "What have you learned by this experience?"

The young girl very simply replies, "That there are some wonderful people in this world."

My mother and I learned this very same thing. And in perhaps one of the very last lessons he was meant to learn, so did my father.

Chapter 48

"Michael, quick!" My mother burst into the Florida room where I was sitting, staring into nothingness during the eighth week of my father's comatose state. "There's someone calling you from England!"

Solihin! I whispered to myself as I jumped up from my listlessness. I ran into the kitchen and clicked on the portable phone.

"Hi!" I tried to control my excitement. After the last two months in my parents' home, the periods of intense drama were now being replaced by days of quiet desperation as we waited and waited in the company of those special nurses for my father — now in a full coma — to finally pass. The occasional phone calls I'd receive from friends were like cool droplets of water to an exhausted desert traveller. I drank in these little tidbits of life and laughter. The eerie quiet, the whispered voices (lest that phantom being in my father awakened again) and the spiritual solitude of each person present in the household was life-changing in its effect, but a constant, oppressive weight.

It had taken days and numerous phone calls to track down Solihin in England. The day before, I had finally left the message that would get through to him.

"How you doing, mate?" Solihin's gentle accent came through the phone.

"Hey, fine!" I said reflexively, the humor and liveliness that he embodied transporting me, making me momentarily forget how I was feeling.

"Well, maybe not so fine," I said, coming back down to earth. I proceeded to summarize all that had happened, telling him how the nurses couldn't understand how my father could still be hanging on, how every indication — from his long cessations of breathing, to his extremely low pulse and blood pressure, to the lack of any nutritional intake for almost two months now — should have spelled death a long time ago.

"Michael," Solihin quietly requested once I was finished, "can you go into the room where your father is?"

"OK," I unconsciously nodded. I was speaking to him from the Florida room, where bird-song serenades from the fresh-air loveliness gave the small home its great non-monetary wealth. Portable phone in hand, I walked into the living room, down the hallway, to the bedroom I grew up in — now berth of my father's last days. A few seconds' journey, it nevertheless was one that went from the best of family life to a transitional plane of suspended motion.

C.J. was sitting near my father's side, quietly reading. In the hospital bed, my father's gaunt face stared closed-eyed up at the ceiling, the rest of his emaciated body hidden beneath the immaculate sheets C.J. regularly changed. I signalled for her to come out in the hallway.

"It's Solihin," I whispered. "Can you leave me a few moments to be with my father?

The special lady needed no explanation. Over the last weeks I had gotten to know her well, and she me. I had shared with her my experiences with the English doctor's work, and she had listened, fascinated. Despite that she and Patty were in the heart of the medical profession, they both had an undoctrinated wonder for all I told them. Normally, only people who had been in the holistic field for years displayed such interest, but possibly because these nurses lived such unusual lives, constantly in the presence of transitional spirits, they were already well familiar with planes and energies that needed no mathematics, statistics or scientific reports to be validated.

C.J. smiled, knowing how much I had anticipated this contact with the British physician, closing the door behind her as she left me alone in the room with my father.

"I'm here," I whispered into the phone to Solihin.

"Good, then," he said. "Now, let's take a moment of quiet to open ourselves up, to open up our vessels . . . to open a space for The Almighty."

I put the phone down. I looked at my father, leaned over the iron railings, and gave the unstirring body a gentle kiss on the forehead. Then, composing myself, I closed my eyes and relaxed my body. I felt my palms turn outward and immediately felt the sensation I usually experience when beginning every *Inner Natures* session. It's something difficult to describe, for it is so subtle. But the closest I come to putting it into words is a feeling in my chest like petals of a morning flower, ever so slightly opening at the first hint of a rising sun.

Solihin's gentle voice came through the phone perhaps 30 seconds later. "OK, mate?"

"OK," I whispered.

"So, I've received we need to look at something in "Awakenings" directory. You said you have the *RTP* books there with you?"

"Yes," I replied.

"Good," he said. "At the moment, I don't have mine." *RTP* stood for *Restoring the Potential*. I had taken these three huge volumes of Solihin's work down from Georgia with me. Each book contained thousands of spheres of possibilities that can manifest inside a person — the bulwark of human existence — each item a *clue* that wove a picture of the state a person was in. These clues had poetic names such as *Inner Seeing, Ancestral Tree, Violation, Myth* and *Forbidden Fruit*. Normally, muscle testing and hand modes were used for silently getting the person to *script* this story. How Solihin could do it over the phone, I don't entirely know. I do, however, understand it has to do with some extraordinary inner sensitivity he possesses that transcends far beyond anything intuitive. The process of surrender he taught us to begin each session with, and which is the state with which we aim — in some quantum degree — to grace our clients, was the same green vineyard of peace he tapped into to receive his gifted insight.

"So I want you to go now to the 31st file of *Awakenings*," he said.

"He's *dying*," I said to Solihin.

"Yes," the teacher whispered back. "But at the same time, he is *awakening*. To *something*. Why don't we find out what it is?" He gave me a moment to flip the pages. "What does it say there?" he asked.

A lump formed in my throat when I saw the listing. *"Belief in God."*

"Umm," I heard Solihin sigh. "A biggie."

Indeed it was. Whereas my sister's death had made everything in my life some reflection of the *belief in God* that had blossomed in me as a result, the same circumstance had ravaged whatever belief my father had possessed.

"You still with me?" Solihin gently asked.

"Still here," I acknowledged.

He was quiet a moment, then told me: "I want you now to proceed to the 23rd sub-file and read to me what it says."

I went down the page with my finger. When I arrived at the indicated entry, a tingle went up my spine. My whisper was hoarse: "It says, '*Inability to Surrender.*'"

"Ahh," he sighed. "So, what is being *awakened* in your father is a *belief in God*. But first he must learn to *surrender* . . . this is his final lesson before he can make his transition."

My voice was choked. "So what must we do?"

"You must re-learn the lesson yourself," were the teacher's words. "You must open yourself up and, from this state, simply pray by your father's side . . . with him . . . in his field . . . for he hasn't yet been able to do it for himself."

My mother, C.J., Patty and I had all discussed this before, knew that on some level my father wasn't *surrendering,* wasn't *letting go*. But somehow, Solihin's sequence of findings, out of the tens of thousands of possibilities in his volumes, so precisely reflected what we knew, which Solihin — never having met my father — had no way of knowing, it gave it new meaning, some sovereign resonance.

However, my father didn't *let go* overnight; he would hang on another five, seven, ten days. But *I* let go as a result of Solihin's finding. Let go of my urgency to see my father's suffering over; let go — to a much greater degree, at least — of my guiltless desire that the process should quicken so that my mother would also no longer have to bear such an extraordinary burden.

In my father's final weeks it was *I* who surrendered, surrendered to his journey, to the knowledge that there was some greater guidance directing these last days. Surrendered the process to God.

All during this time, my mother would go to where my father lay, forcing back tears, whispering close to his ear, "Michael is taking care of everything now, honey . . . you've trained him so well . . . you have nothing to worry about. You can let go, honey . . . you can let go."

It broke my heart to see the difficulty with which she had to look upon the silent face of her once proud partner of over 40 years. Broke my heart to know how — after so many months — it took all her will to go in and acknowledge what was left of this noble soul, her husband. And broke my heart to see the uncontrollable tears of exhaustion and futility when she finally left his side.

But this, too, I had to let go, to surrender. For this was part of her process as well. And what I was going through . . . part of mine.

Chapter 49

*N*ine days after Solihin's call I gathered our small family together: C.J. and Patty, who were changing shifts, my mother and me. I had come to a most difficult decision.

"I think," I said to these three angelic women, ". . . I think it's time to do something different." The feeling had been rising up in me for weeks, and now as I spoke, I had only a small degree of uncertainty left. "I think we need to allow my father to find his peace." I looked at their begging, inquiring eyes. "I think we need to *help him* surrender."

"How?" Patty whispered.

"I think, at this point, it is *we* who are unknowingly keeping him attached to the thread he is hanging onto. Every time we whisper into his ear, we know he *hears* us. We know he *understands.*" Despite the eerie stillness that marked his coma now, there would be just the ever-so-faint twitch of a closed eyelid when he heard our voices, a palpable tightening of his still strong fingers on ours when we took his hand and asked if he could hear us. Like Morse code flashes from some missing ship, these distant signals let us know his vessel was yet charting its journey before slipping through its final straits.

"I believe it is *us* — our *voices* — " I continued, "that he is holding onto." I gently grasped C.J.'s shoulder, looking the beautiful lady gently in the eye. "I think we should no longer tell him the day or the hour." She had been whispering this to my father every morning, her experience leading her to know that such pieces of earthly news were a comfort to some patients in a transitional state, markers to their flagging ships. "I believe," I said, "such time references are a boundary for him now."

I looked at my mother, whose beseeching eyes once more left me with a now-familiar pit in my stomach. I addressed her and Patty. "And I think we should no longer tell Dad he should *let go*. That it's OK he does so." I allowed myself a small laugh. "Can't you imagine him, Mom, saying: 'For crying out loud, I know I'm suppose to let go! Your reminders are no longer *helping*. Thanks, but *enough* already!' "

My mother's wet-eyed laughter along with that of the nurses warmed me, giving me my first indication that I was on track. I gathered myself. What I had to say next was the most difficult part. Though I intuitively sensed I was right, my own plan made me feel like I was *abandoning* my father, blindly cutting the last tenacious threads of his trusted anchor.

"I think, too," I hesitantly proceeded, "we should no longer speak to Dad. Not aloud, at least. Occasionally kiss him, hold his hand, yes . . . even lightly hug him and let him know we are there. But to no longer bind him with our words." I was silent for a long moment. "I think these — our words — are what he is holding on to."

I suddenly was very uncertain of myself, of my plan — of its extremeness — having no idea how they were receiving it. The quiet nods I finally received after a long moment of hesitation heartened me. But I was, nevertheless, saddened. Deeply, so deeply, saddened.

Chapter 50

*T*hirty-six hours later, my father finally died.

My mother and I had told Patty earlier that night to awaken us if she sensed his last moments were near. When we went to sleep, my father seemed *closer* then ever before, but after so many months of false alarms, we still didn't know.

For some reason, Patty was moved to awaken us only after he had died. Why she chose this, I cannot say. But in keeping with that period, we were all conducting ourselves according to signals we received in the moment, like instruments finely attuned to the slightest breath of a great flautist or the most minute strum of a master harpist. And somehow this was how life played itself out through the young nurse.

Neither my mother nor I ever questioned her about this, for, in truth, there was nothing to question. There was only acceptance. Trust. Surrender. For when one is in the shadow of death — in the shadow of all the mystery contained within the event — when one has been in its cradle for so long, *words* and *rules* and *right ways* begin to blur into ethereality much the same way as the soul, at the center of such happening, has chosen to transition from this reality to the next.

Epilogue

THE GIFT OF FLIGHT

I have a gift for you!
You who have been tethered to the ground
Standing by my burdensome side
linked to me
in my immobility
by threads of gold.

You who have risen with me
beyond all physicality
lifted on love's wings
from quarter and eighth note living
to a soul's soaring
full symphony.

You who have mastered
the silent flight
of man's daring voyage
through heavy gravity
borne aloft
on pacific wings.

And in accompanying me
until an ascending current
bid us adieu,

You now truly know
as only those who have linked themselves
to other souls
by threads of gold,

What it means
to truly be
to truly see
on pacific wings
to be set free!

Chapter 51

*I*t is another day to say goodbye. I am up early, at 5:30 in the morning, to give my last farewell to this friend I may never see again. For 22 years, this stretch of beach has been my faithful companion, my teacher, my balm. Through the difficulties of my teenage years, through the death of several of the closest people in my life, through my maturation from boyhood to manhood, the ocean has accompanied me, whispering its soft, persistent messages of faith and of eternity.

Though the condominiums now dotting its shoreline scar its native beauty, with my back to them I see only waves, horizon and a breaking sun, the latter beckoning me with the golden pathway it casts upon the water. I respond, a compliant lover, swimming out into the warm, jewelled embrace.

It took over a year for my mother to recover from my father's death, another five months until she put the house up for sale, four more to find a buyer. And now, a week past the two-year anniversary of my father's death, I have taken time off from my practice in Atlanta to come to Sunrise Key one last time and help move my mother away.

"You're going to miss your house," people say to her. "Twenty-two years is a long time."

She doesn't argue with them. I, alone, know the desperation with which she wishes to leave this nest of memories of which few people can conceive. "I lost my daughter, my mother and now my husband while living here," she confides to me. "What will I regret leaving?"

Yesterday, when the Allied Van Lines movers came, she broke down crying. Mostly, I believe, from the accumulated tension of the last years by herself in a home that was meant for a family, too large and difficult for a recovering widow to take care of.

"Ah, don't worry, sweetheart," Dick, one of the movers who has come to pack her belongings, says as he pats her back. "Everything will be OK." He is short, extremely muscular and wonderfully compassionate. He is also 75 years old, we are shocked to find.

"We've got 60 years of experience between us," says Mickey, his partner, a younger but equally reassuring man. I sense much of my mother's anxiety wisp away in their presence.

"After all the years of doing this, you never had any back problems?" I ask Dick a little later, my mother overhearing the exchange.

"Nope," he replies, expertly wrapping a piece of delicate china my father purchased decades ago on a business trip to the Orient.

"Do you credit it to good technique or a strong back?" I ask, my professional interest piqued.

Deep, hearty laughter accentuates his wonderful congeniality. "Weak mind!" he replies.

Angels come in many different packages, I contemplate when our laughter subsides. How many types of vessels God has made! Some people were designed just for goodness, their simplicity accentuating the quality.

While Dick and Mickey slowly pack our home away, I look for a way to distract my mother. With nothing left for us to do, she has again become tense. I begin to play a video she recorded a few weeks ago of the television airing of Barbra Streisand's first concert in 15 years, *Barbra: The Concert*. My mother had been anxious for me to see it since my arrival, but as busy as we were, there was no time.

Now, however, as the singer's incredible voice fills our living room, captivating and transporting us entirely as our house comes down around us, I feel a sense of grace, borne both in the star's voice and in the thought that things have worked out to where we only now — at a moment of such emotion for my mother — finally have the chance to watch the awesome performance.

I remember as a child listening with my mother to this extraordinary singer's records. Even then, before any of my experiences with death, I remember being filled with a sense of celestiality, a sense that I was listening to a human who, through song, was being used as a perfect vessel for something divine. During a recent interview, I heard Barbra describe her voice as *"the voice,"* as if it had nothing to do with her, as if it was something separate from her.

Yet the singer very candidly admits to incredible pain and trials in her personal life. During the concert, she quips in a Yiddish accent to the audience, "Have you ever been in therapy before? *Have I ever been in therapy before?"* And listening to her music, I cannot help but feel that these tremendous emotions she describes having experienced are the very filters — like those a photographer uses to create special effects — through which divinity is passed to create one of God's special gifts to the world.

Working with many accomplished performers in my practice, from ballet dancers to Olympic athletes, from Broadway playwrights to well-known novelists, I have come to understand that when a person has an extraordinary talent, it sometimes makes every other area in his or her life pale in significance. Like cocaine addicts, these people are only happy when exercising that gift, for it is only then that they feel themselves as true vessels.

Yet as they get older, many begin to realize that the real sustainable peace and joy they must find is not on a stage or in a sports arena, but rather in finding how to open themselves up as vessels in other areas of their lives as well — ones that don't require an audience of thousands. Areas that are similar to the everyday interactions — the momentary blessings — my mother and I experienced through the kindness of our movers.

> *Change can come on tiptoes*
> *Love is where it starts*
> *It resides, often hides*
> *Deep within our heart*

Ms. Streisand is suddenly singing a song that absolutely captivates me . . . more so than even her more well-known ones.

> *Ordinary miracles*
> *happen all around*
> *Just by giving and receiving*
> *Comes belonging and believing . . .*

Through my sister's illness, re-learned through my father's, I have slowly come to understand how these *ordinary miracles* are possible at the most dire times; as if our pain and tribulation are the doorways through which we can open portions of our deepest natures, our vessels, for the purity of giving and receiving, of experiencing the grace of others, of ourselves and of God . . .

> *And we can all be quiet heroes*
> *Living quiet days*
> *Walking through the world*
> *Changing it in quiet ways . . .*

Through the gift of Solihin's work and the blessing of having a new system birthed through me which creates the possibility of more easily finding grace in ordinary situations, I have come to see how all our interactions with people contain the potential sapphire of holiness. And therein, in our everyday lives, lies the deepest key to peace and happiness.

As Ms. Streisand touches every receptor in my soul with the final words of her song, I understand that she has slowly come to this understanding as well:

> *Ordinary miracles*
> *One for every star*
> *No lightening bolt or clap of thunder*
> *Only joy and quiet wonder . . .*

> *. . . Every . . . blessed . . . day!*

May such grace, dear reader, always fill our hearts.

About the Author

Dr. Michael Norwood is a chiropractor and kinesiologist who has done extensive post-graduate studies in neurology and holistic medicine. He works with hospice patients and their families, and speaks to groups around the country about the life-changing experiences he relates in *Taking Stock*. Per the book's theme, Michael teaches how understanding death can open us up to the most beautiful transformations of life.

Taking Stock is a true story. Because it encompassed a period of almost 30 years, some details may have been inadvertently altered. Several other details were changed to protect privacy regarding the extremely sensitive subjects portrayed.

AUTOGRAPHED *TAKING STOCK*

No extra charge for autographed copies of the book. Tell the operator the names of the person you are giving the books to if you want personalized autographs.

Quantity discounts for 2 books or more:

Copies:

1	$12.95
2	$11.95 each
3 -4	$10.95 "
5-10	$9.95 "

Call for higher quantity discounts.

5 FREE PROLOGUES

To share *Taking Stock* with people you'll feel will benefit from its message, please call to receive 5 free prologues bound in the book cover as sample selections for friends and loved ones. Higher quantities available upon request.

To order, call:
1-800-276-7779

SIGNED SYMPATHY CARD
& *TAKING STOCK*

Book with a signed card/note from Michael as a gift to friends & family who have experienced a loss. No extra charge for the signed card from Michael which will read as follows:

---

*D*ear   <u>**(Name of Bereaved)**</u> :

During the many years writing *Taking Stock*, I would awaken early every morning and begin my writing sessions with the prayer: Dear God, may I be provided with the words to touch just even one reader . . .

It is now my blessing to share this book with you as a result of the kindness of <u>**(Your Name)**</u>, who asked we send you a copy. Beyond the trauma, may a small taste of the grace I experienced through the loss of my loved ones now touch your heart as well.

God bless.

Michael

Dr. Michael R. Norwood

To order, call
1-800-276-7779

COVER POSTER: *"ELECTRIC MAN"*

This is an unretouched photo called *"Electric Man"* taken by Michael in Switzerland. He had only seconds to shoot the picture before the effect disappeared. He returned the next day at sunset with the idea to shoot it again in case he didn't capture the stranger's beautiful aura the first time. To Michael's amazement, the light created no such effect on other climbers that following day nor the days after.

To order a frameable 22" x 34" beautifully reproduced copy, call:

1-800-276-7779

ACKNOWLEDGEMENTS

*Grateful acknowledgement to the following people for reading
all or parts of* Taking Stock *and giving invaluable feedback
on it during the four to five years it took to complete.*

Colleen Goidel who did the final editing with the combined touch of a brain surgeon and master pianist. Linda Downs, former Senior Editor of *House Beautiful,* for her great skills with everything regarding the English language. Claudia Gill, Glenda Coker, Delores Devores and Carey Lynn Page for being the driving force behind *Taking Stock's* first appearance in Atlanta. Anita Sharpe with *The Wall Street Journal,* for her view from the business world and for writing about *Taking Stock* before it was on its feet. Fran Holt-Underwood, formerly with *New Leaf Distribution,* and Candace Apple, owner of *Phoenix & Dragon* bookstore, for their enthusiasm and vast knowledge of the New-Age book market. Neil Shulman, M.D., author of the book-turned-hit-movie, *Doc Hollywood,* for all his warmth and wisdom. Joyce Winslow of *Modern Maturity* for her enthusiastic support and writer's-eye suggestions. Mary Walters and Deborah Drago-Leaf from *Chapter 11,* for the bookstore perspective. Ann Kempner-Fisher for early advise and editing. Bruce Parrish and Carol Gross, sharp-eyed readers and great patients. Jeanie Zibrida, Martigne Musson, Betty Shores, Laurie Morris and Anik Kueller, for their assistance in the past. Grace Hance, Rene Searles and Patricia Tynes of *Peachtree Hospice* for giving me the work that keeps all the beauty of life ... and death ... still alive in me. Cindy Stark-Reid and Sharon Scott, for their perspectives as dedicated *Hospice* workers. Carol Sheron with *Unity Church* and Laura Davis for their excellent contacts. Bob Cohen, for the financial corrections and for recommending IMAX. Paul Bonesteel – film producer of a fantastic father/son documentary. Angustias Caballero Checa, wonderful friend whose own illness has opened her heart. Jean Carpenter for her kind view from the health field. Ed & Pat Kuzela of *Compassionate Friends* for their compassionate suggestions and support. Colin Tipping for his perspective as a cancer-support leader. Gerard Sisnette and Audrey Galex of CNN, and Marta Chacon, Cynthia Zauner, Mark Banov, M.D., Kathy Slough, Joy Gordman, Alla Leydman, Cary Vaughn and Shoshana Rosenthal for their smiles and tears, letting me know I was hitting home. Liz Pelligrin, for her enthusiasm and arranging previous seminars. Alan Vandekamp and Ellen Wickersham of *Whole Life Expo,* for their generous help and fine contacts. Victor Guerra, for his encouragement and contact with Alan. Garry Guan of *Asian American Language Services* for his friendship and technical assistance. Virginia Gellelund, Dr. Marty Finkelstein and Dr. Louis Leonardi – for keeping me on track. Chad Foster, for setting things straight regarding publishing. And particularly to Sara Flanigan, one of my favorite authors, who made me reach deep down.